Hippolyta's View

Hippolyta's View

SOME CHRISTIAN ASPECTS
OF SHAKESPEARE'S PLAYS

J. A. Bryant, Jr.

UNIVERSITY OF KENTUCKY PRESS

Copyright © 1961 by the University of Kentucky Press
Printed in the United States of America by the
Division of Printing, University of Kentucky
Library of Congress Catalog Card No.
61-6555

To my parents

Preface

*M*Y PURPOSE in writing this book is reflected in the title I have given to it. I wanted, first, to say something about Shakespeare's view and practice of poetry, which I believe derived from a catholic and Christian view of life, and, second, to demonstrate the effect of that view of poetry in a representative selection of his plays. This is the view of poetry that I have called "Hippolyta's view" in the first chapter and have either demonstrated or assumed in all the analyses of plays that follow. There are probably some who will find the view uncongenial and others who will question the relevance of it to the study of Shakespeare. If such readers remain unconvinced after thirteen chapters, I may still hope perhaps to convince them in other essays at another time. To readers, however, who object to my calling the view Christian I can say only that I have not wished to speak for anyone who does not wish to be spoken for. If in ages of widespread conformity serious Christians have managed to disagree widely about the essentials of their faith, it is certainly unwise to hope that in our time any one collection of assertions about Christianity, least of all mine, may satisfy everybody who calls himself Christian. The most I hope for is that Christians of the communions which may be broadly termed "catholic" will find my assertions reasonably satisfactory and that the rest will recognize most of them as assertions which Shakespeare's conforming contemporaries might have made without public embarrassment or private misgivings.

I have incurred many obligations during the writing of this book, the greatest of which is the one to my wife and children, who alternately helped and endured during the whole process.

I owe slightly smaller debts to many students, colleagues, and other friends, who from time to time have encouraged, criticized, contradicted, and listened to my views on Shakespeare; and of these I am especially grateful to Neil Bennett of Vanderbilt and Charles Harrison of the University of the South, both of whom have contributed more than they know to this study. Professor Roy W. Battenhouse of Indiana University has read the manuscript through, and his suggestions, corrections, and friendly warnings have saved me from many blunders; but I have stubbornly retained several others, and for all these I take responsibility. My debts to the *Sewanee Review* and its editor, Monroe K. Spears, are as numerous as they are large. I am grateful first for encouragement and support of my first efforts in this kind of criticism and for permission to reprint with revisions essays that appear here as Chapters II, IV, XIII, and a part of Chapter I. I am especially grateful for a *Sewanee Review* Fellowship which enabled me to spend six months writing additional chapters and putting the manuscript into final form. In this connection, I wish also to thank the University of the South for granting me leave to accept the fellowship and for supporting my work during the summers of 1957 and 1958.

The Houghton Mifflin Company has very generously allowed me to take all my quotations from Shakespeare from their New Cambridge Edition, edited by William Allan Neilson and Charles Jarvis Hill. Francis Fergusson kindly gave me permission to quote from his essay on *Macbeth* as it appeared in *The Human Image in Dramatic Literature* published by Doubleday & Company, Inc. I wish to thank also two publishers for granting me permission to use the following copyrighted material: Benziger Brothers, Inc., for several passages from *The "Summa Theologica" of St. Thomas Aquinas*, translated by the Fathers of the English Dominican Province; and Clarendon Press, for a passage from William Walrond Jackson's translation of Dante's *Convivio*.

For assistance in countless ways I am profoundly grateful to the staffs of the Joint University Libraries in Nashville, the library of the University of the South, the Biblioteca CREFAL of Patzcuaro, Michoacan, Mexico, and the Folger Shakespeare Library.

Durham, North Carolina   J. A. B., Jr.
28 August 1960

Contents

One

HIPPOLYTA'S VIEW

THERE ARE many legitimate reasons for calling Shakespeare's work Christian. Some critics have done so because his plays contain numerous Christian allusions, some because they deal occasionally with demonstrably Christian subject matter, and others because here and there they seem to lean upon Christian dogma. Yet none of these reasons—nor, for that matter, any combination of them—can justify one's saying that Shakespeare's work is fundamentally Christian poetry. Numerous as his references to Christian topics are, Shakespeare obviously had a great deal more to say about such things as history, politics, and human conduct—topics which concern everybody, not Christians only. Moreover, when one considers also that Shakespeare wrote his plays for the commercial and profane theater of Elizabethan England and that he wrote primarily to amuse and divert rather than to instruct, one almost automatically rules out the possibility of finding many religious implications in them. Thus he remains for most readers a writer whose concern with religious matters folowed pretty closely the demands of the stories that he used.

This book contains no attempt to prove that Shakespeare was anything other than a secular writer, nor does it contain any speculations about his private faith or public professions. It does suggest, however, that his work is Christian in a way no critic can ignore. The difficulty we have in seeing this is partly the result of our passion for making nice distinctions. We like, for example, to distinguish clearly between what is religious and what is not; and unfortunately, where Shakespeare's poetry is concerned, the tendency to make such a distinction can do a great deal more harm than good. For that tendency is usually accompanied by a special attitude toward poetry generally. People who have it are sometimes given to citing, as reasonably authoritative Shakespeare, Theseus' remarks about poetry at the beginning of the last act of A *Midsummer Night's Dream*:

> The poet's eye, in a fine frenzy rolling,
> Doth glance from heaven to earth, from
> > earth to heaven;
> And as imagination bodies forth
> The forms of things unknown, the poet's pen
> Turns them to shapes and gives to airy nothing
> A local habitation and a name.

(V.i.12-17)

This is a fine passage indeed—provided, of course, one strips it from its context, in which the vision of poetry is reduced to an antique fable and equated with the fruitless visions of madmen and lovers. Taken in isolation, it compares favorably with half a dozen other Elizabethan commonplaces in which the philosopher's "infallible grounds of wisdom" are "illuminated or figured forth by the speaking picture of poesy." To take it seriously, however, would be to risk reducing all poetry to the status of a mechanical kind of allegory. Fortunately Shakespeare does not ask us to take it seriously. Theseus, who is obviously well versed in Elizabethan critical formulations, is saying that he rejects the lovers' strange story of their night in the wood as something no more believable than the tall tale of a madman or a poet. It is not he but Hippolyta who advances the basis for accepting the story, and her remarks are almost never cited:[1]

> But all the story of the night told over,
> And all their minds transfigured so together,
> More witnesseth than fancy's images,
> And grows to something of great constancy;
> But, howsoever, strange and admirable.

(V.i.23-27)

The thing to notice here is that Hippolyta accepts the story not because the lovers' reports agree but because the whole story, told over as one, has the individual vitality to assume a life of its own, grow to something of great constancy however marvellous, and command belief in a way that the things Theseus calls poetry never could. In her humble and uncritical way Hippolyta has redefined poetry for Theseus and his kind, giving to the story of a midsummer night at least as much credence and value as she would give to events of the night itself. For her the transfigured story is the dream that is real, vital, and efficacious; and that dream, whatever else one may care to call it, is poetry.

This study, dealing as it does with the Christian interpretation of Shakespeare, begins with the assumption that poetry is what Hippolyta suggests it is and that her view, if not exclusively Christian, is at least consistent with distinctively Christian teaching. This is not to say that Christianity has ignored Theseus' kind of poetry. According to his definition, the poet apprehends directly something that most mortals cannot readily apprehend and proceeds to translate his vision into concrete terms for popular edification. The poem thus made would be a collection of what Edwyn Bevan has usefully described as symbols behind which we can see.[2] That is, they would be symbols that help the reader on to some superior kind of knowledge, as an anchor in an emblem points in a general way to an understanding of one aspect of hope. Hippolyta's kind of poetry, however, corresponds to what Bevan has called "symbols behind which we cannot see." For her, as for Bevan, this kind of symbol is our nearest approach to reality, and is much to be preferred to any philosophic formulation of the truth it mysteriously embodies. Thus in Hippolyta's view the poet begins, not with an abstract formulation, but with things as they seem to be in their concreteness; and, whereas Theseus' poet accommodates or translates into concrete terms something that is otherwise unperceived, hers transforms what is readily perceived into something that can be known. Theseus' poet orders the data of experience in a dream that we expect to reject as soon as we have grasped the reality to which it points. Hippolyta's poet recreates the data of experience in a dream that is truth itself, or all we shall likely get of truth this side of paradise.

For Christians of Hippolyta's persuasion the supreme exemplar of poet and poem would be Jesus of Nazareth, incarnate creator of the world. There are important differences, of course. In the beginning, it is said, Christ created out of nothing; and his creation, bright and revealing as it is, is not so bright or so revealing as Christ himself, to whom Christians look for as much truth as they with their mortal limitation can perceive. The human poet is not a Christ, and he cannot make something out of nothing, as Christ did; but his making is a species of creation nevertheless. One might call it an act in continuation of that impulse by which the world was made, an act performed in emulation of the original creator, or the human and partial redemption of experience from scattered data and the transformation of that experience into something strange, admirable, and of great constancy. In short, the poet is not God, but he does God's work in God's way.

The two views of poetry represented in this brief exchange between Theseus and Hippolyta are, of course, much older than Shakespeare. Dante made a similar distinction when he set forth the difference between the "allegory of the poets" and the "allegory of the theologians." Unfortunately for some who have tried to relate Dante's formulations to Shakespeare, Dante described both kinds of allegory in terms of the convenient four-level system that had been evolved over the centuries for the interpretation of Scripture; and for both kinds he mentioned literal, allegorical, moral, and anagogical senses. The allegory of the poets as Dante describes it in the *Convito* (Tractate II.i) is simply a collection of symbols (including fable) behind which one can see a number of other, more important, meanings. Poetry looked at in this way is pretty much what Theseus thinks it is—a collection of habitations and names applied to unbodied values and concepts. We might call it parabolic or emblematic poetry, for the reader of it is always expected to take the "literal" tale mainly for diversion and to derive from the allegory the more valuable moral and spiritual insight that lies hidden behind it. In the *Convito* Dante says of the first and second senses:

The first is called literal, and this is that sense which does not go beyond the strict limits of the letter; the second is called allegorical, and this is disguised under the cloak of such stories, and is a truth hidden under a beautiful fiction. Thus Ovid says that Orpheus with his lyre made beasts tame, and trees and stones move towards himself; that is to say that the wise man by the instrument of his voice makes cruel hearts grow mild and humble, and those who have not the life of Science and of Art move to his will, while they who have no rational life are as it were like stones. And wherefore this disguise was invented by the wise will be shown in the last Tractate but one. Theologians indeed do not apprehend this sense in the same fashion as poets; but, inasmuch as my intention is to follow here the custom of poets, I will take the allegorical sense after the manner which poets use.[3]

The allegory of the theologians differs from this in two important ways, one of which has to do with the nature of the literal sense and the other with the nature of the allegorical. First, the term "allegory of the theologians" refers to the traditional application of the fourfold system to Scriptural exegesis and thus carries with it the suggestion that the literal (or primary) sense is historical and factual as opposed to something fabulous or contrived. There will always be a few readers who will insist that Dante, regardless of what he may have written

in his *Epistle to Can Grande,* cannot have meant to apply
"allegory of the theologians" to his *Commedia,* which, strictly
speaking, is at least as fabulous in the literal sense as Virgil's
Aeneid. Recently in answering one such reader, Charles S.
Singleton pointed out that the distinction between the two kinds
of allegory is fundamentally a distinction between two focuses
for reading.[4] If the reader, in the act of reading, regards the
literal sense as "imaginary" and justifiable mainly according to
the "truth" it conveys, he is reading according to the focus of
the allegory of poets. If, however, in the act of reading he can
take the literal sense to be real (as we take any piece of natural-
istic fiction to be real while we read it) and at the same time
find it revelatory of the shape of other events which are also
real, then he is reading according to the focus of the allegory
of the theologians. "How is it," asks Singleton, "that we read
the *Comedy* with essentially the same sense of reality as we get
in reading *War and Peace* and yet get also, in the poem, as an
inseparable part of its illusion, the double vision which is
allegory as Dante constructed it?"[5] His answer is that Dante's
poem is actually a double imitation: first, of the created universe
of God, which is itself a book of symbols of divine things; and
second, of Holy Scripture, which is God's use of history to reveal
his way for mankind.

This is where the second important difference between the
allegory of the poets and that of the theologians comes in. With
the poets the second sense, or "allegory," is a segment of general
truth clothed in the literal fable (as Orpheus tamed wild beasts,
so the wise man tames cruel hearts); with the theologians,
however, the second sense refers to some aspect of the Incarnation, which is the fullest manifestation of God's way with man
and the subject of everything in the Bible. Dante makes this
clear in his *Epistle to Can Grande:*

The first is called *literal,* but the second *allegorical* or *mystical.* That
this method of expounding may be more clearly set forth, we can
consider it in these lines: "When Israel went out of Egypt, the house

of Jacob from a people of strange language, Judah was his sanctuary and Israel his dominion." For if we consider the *letter* alone the departure of the children of Israel from Egypt in the time of Moses is signified; if the *allegory*, our redemption accomplished in Christ is signified.[6]

At this point Dante goes on to define the third and fourth senses, trope and anagoge; but apparently he believes that theologians and poets look upon these two senses in much the same way. Clearly the crux of the matter with him, as it had been with St. Thomas Aquinas before him, is in the relation between the first two senses, which with the poets had consisted simply of a contrived fable referring to some generally applicable truth but with the theologians had consisted of a credible fable, usually a Scriptural one, participating by analogy in the action of the incarnate Christ.

The magnitude of the difference between poets and theologians on this point can be seen by turning briefly to Aquinas' beautifully precise exposition of the fourfold method as he understood it.[7] The literal sense, Aquinas explains, is not the text of Scripture but the concrete object, "that which is figured" by the text. (Drama, one might observe, is the only literary form that avoids the difficulty of an intervening text, since the text of drama, unlike that of narrative, is itself an aspect of the concrete object.) "When Scripture speaks of God's arm, the literal sense is not that God has such a member, but only what is signified by this member, namely, operative power." Thus upon what is signified, upon what is figured, pointed to, depend whatever spiritual meanings the passage may have. If we like, we may say that the literal meaning is that which exists in time or which *is* time—in short, history itself. At the other end of the scale, there is the anagogical sense, which, though it includes time, is not bound by time. This is the Logos that transcends time—being simultaneously (to use the timebound adverb) Alpha and Omega. Mediating between these two is allegory, which is both in time and out of it and is at once the means whereby the anagoge manifests itself in time and the means whereby time becomes significant. Allegory, as Aquinas defines it, refers to the meeting place of the temporal and the eternal, the intelligible center, the Word made flesh. Thus through that allegory we know all that we can ever know of anagoge, or God in the person of the Father; and without that allegory even history would be meaningless for us. Without it, indeed, history would not exist at all.

Allegory in this sense is also the point from which Scripture derives its trope or moral sense. To go back to Aquinas' explanation: "so far as the things done in Christ, or so far as the things which signify Christ, are types of what we ought to do, there is the moral sense." We are not bound by the letter of the old law, for that law was fulfilled in Christ. We are bound instead by the allegory of the law, which is the type of what we under grace ought to do. This is simply another way of saying that Christians live by Christ and reject utterly the attempt to live either directly by ultimate truth or by any other symbol of it. Allegory is the center for all we know or can ever know as human beings—the meaning of history, the pattern of right action, and the reflection of truth, which even as yet we see but as in the dark surface of an ancient mirror.

The danger in using the fourfold system, or any similar system, for interpretation (whether of Scripture or of genuinely Christian poetry) is that we may forget the centrality of the "allegory which is Christ." For that reason we should be cautious, unless we happen to be talking about certain kinds of mysticism, in using the common phrase "four levels" to refer to the four senses. What Aquinas has in mind is nothing like a stairway. A better analogy would be that of a single wheel rotating upon an axle. We might think of the axle as Scripture, or history, pointing to the hub and existing solely for the sake of the wheel. The hub can be said to be Christ or allegory, which reproduces the shape of the axle and bears upon it. Radiating from that hub are spokes, the multifarious ramifications of trope, deriving their force and meaning from the hub and leading to the rim, or anagoge, which encompasses the whole. Such an analogy is imperfect, certainly, but it is better than the customary one of four levels; and it has the advantage of putting the Incarnation at the intelligible center, the point of turning, where it belongs.

There is nothing essentially Christian about the various systems of *multiplex intelligentia,* as systems.[8] Such things came into being long before Christianity and were early acommodated to the Neoplatonic schema of successive emanations of truth. As some of the earlier Christian writers used them, they served as mystical ladders, whereby one could rise through progressively bright stages of understanding to the divine gloom of full illumination.[9] Even among later writers there was sometimes the tendency—but always a tendency to be resisted—to let the allegory become merely a second *level,* one step on the road to something else.[10] But in Dante and in Aquinas, as in Augustine and in numerous others, we find a complete accommodation of the schema to the central Christian doctrine of the Incarnation. The literal "level" of a piece of writing, whether Scripture or nonscriptural fiction, is always the letter of knowledge to which the "spirit *giveth* life." That is, the Incarnation is the fulfillment, the redemption of history rather than the replacement of it. And it is the idea of incarnation that is important, not the critical vehicle that makes it articulate. Sir John Harington's recourse to a system of *mutiplex intelligentia* to defend his translation of *Orlando Furioso* (1591) is notoriously rigid and sterile, but it is no more rigid and sterile than Dante's exposition of four levels in the *Convito.* Dante, fortunately for us, came to see that it was sterile.

The history of the Christian doctrine of Incarnation is an interesting one, complex and variously told, but it has little bearing on this study. Miss Ruth Wallerstein in the second chapter of her book on seventeenth-century poetic placed Donne and some of the other metaphysicals at the end of a long literary tradition of style which she called "Augustinian."[11] One might quibble with her calling the tradition a literary one, or even question her use of the word *tradition;* but she unques-

tionably put her finger on something that is common to
Augustine, Bonaventure, Hugh of St. Victor, and John Donne,
and central to all of them. The notion that the "world is a
fair field, fresh with the odor of Christ's name," as Augustine
once put it,[12] is bound to appear whenever and wherever
Christianity is vital. Dante had the notion; the author of the
Second Shepherds' Play, whoever he may have been, had it; it
appeared in the Chester Plays, and in *Piers Plowman*. It appeared in the work of Spenser and Bunyan, to mention two
whose "allegory" is commonly taken by academics for something
it is not, at least not exclusively. It peeps through occasionally
in Wyatt, and it appears in most of the poems of John Donne.
In our own time it has appeared notably in the work of T. S.
Eliot.[13] In some periods it appears only as an eccentric manifestation, and then rarely; in other periods it seems to be everywhere, common as bread.

One of the periods when it was common was Shakespeare's,
and this in spite of the fact that many of the theologians of
Shakespeare's day had rejected the systems of *multiplex intelligentia* as old fashioned or "popish" or both. Arnold Williams
in his valuable study *The Common Expositor* points out that
even those Catholic expositors who continued to make some
use of the old "mystic" interpretations treated such things more
as plausible applications than as true interpretations.[14] The
important thing to notice, however, is what stood clear and firm
after much of the old exegetical structure had been abandoned,
and what did stand clear was what had all along been the distinctively Christian part of the systems: the principle of typology,
the view that the figure of Jesus Christ is the subject not of the
New Testament merely, but of every history, prophecy, psalm,
and proverb in the Old.[15] Erich Auerbach was perhaps right
in saying that the conception of history implicit in this principle
"was completely alien to the mentality of classical antiquity."[16]
He was also at least essentially right when he went on to say
that "it annihilated that mentality down to the very structure
of its language, which—with all its ingenious and nicely shaded

conjunctions, its wealth of devices for syntactic arrangement, its carefully elaborated system of tenses—became wholly superfluous as soon as earthly relations of place, time, and cause had ceased to matter, as soon as a vertical connection, ascending from all that happens, converging in God, alone became significant." Auerbach's central argument here is certainly not likely to be questioned: the resulting "Western" conception of history was indeed a compromise between history deriving its significance from causal or horizontal connections between separate events and history deriving its significance from events linked vertically to a common source of meaning. Needless to say, this compromise never succeeded in producing a rash of typological interpretations in formal historiography during the Elizabethan period, nor for that matter during any other. Historiography during Elizabeth's time, when it was not dominated by humanists, was frequently "providential"; but historians generally did not go about finding figures of Christ in their pages. They did not even spend a great deal of space in presenting applications of the "lessons" of history, though they invariably in their prefaces invited others to draw them. The emphasis upon typology appeared where one would expect it to appear, in devotional tracts, in exegetical works, and in sermons; and in the sermon, typology had an opportunity to influence the thinking of practically all Elizabethans, whether literate or illiterate.

Almost everybody heard sermons in those days, and almost everybody who heard sermons heard typological interpretations of Scripture. One is not surprised, of course, to find such things in the work of an orthodox Anglican like Bartholomew Chamberlaine, who announced in a sermon on the Passion, preached April 25, 1580:

For, Christ, is the Lambe slayne from the beginning of the world. Slaine in figure, in the purpose of God, in the vertue of his passion from the beginning of the world. Then is Christ slain to euery one, when he beleeueth him slaine. Iesus Christ yesterday, and to day

the same for euer. From the beginning of the world to his ascension,
that is yesterday, from his ascension to the common resurrection,
that is to day, from the common resurrection for euer he is one.
Therefore one faith, one religion, one kind of Sacraments in substance, one way to heauen from the beginning, one spirituall meate
and drinke. Our fathers did all eate the same spirituall meate which
wee eate, and dranke the same spirituall drinke which we drinke.
They dranke of the Rocke which followed them, & the rock was
Christ.[17]

The reformer John Foxe, however, could do almost as well. In
a sermon preached on the christening of a Jew and published
at London in 1578, he said:

their owne Prophets did long before pronounce, that the Messhias
should be persecuted with none so sauage and unmerciful enemies,
as the people of his owne linage: and did also under most manifest
oracles and apparent veiles of shadowish signes prognosticate that he
should be slaine through the treacherous treason of his owne people.
After the same sort was the blood of Abel spilt by the embrued
hand of his bloodie brother Cain: Joseph entrapped and solde by
the sinister practice and procurement of his brother Judah: the
lambe of the passeouer slaine and deuoured peecemeale in the houses
of them, which were deliuered by the blood of the same: so was
Moyses oftentimes contemptuously entreated, and disdainefully railed
upon amongst his owne kinfolkes: king David cruelly assaulted not
of Saul onely, but (which is more horrible) of the folks of his owne
familie, of his neighbours, citizens and subiects.[18]

Henry Smith, Puritan, reader at St. Clement Danes, was even
more fond of typology, if his published works be any criterion,
and equally convinced that Christ is the one subject of the
entire Bible. At the beginning of a sermon on Romans xiii.14
("Put ye on the Lord Jesus Christ") he declared:

I have chosen a text which is the sum of the Bible. For all Scripture
runneth upon Christ, like the title of a book, because he is Alpha
and Omega, Rev. i. 8, the beginning and the end of man's salvation;
therefore he is figured in the law, foretold in the prophets, and

fulfilled in the gospel. Some places point to his divinity, some to his humanity, some to his kingdom, some to his priesthood, some to his prophecy, some to his conception, some to his birth, some to his life, some to his miracles, some to his passion, some to his resurrection, some to his ascension, some to his glorification; all point to the Saviour, like John Baptist, when he said, "This is the Lamb of God, which taketh away the sins of the world," John i. 29. Therefore learn Christ and learn all.[19]

Even Henry Ainsworth, Brownist and leader of the separatist congregation at Amsterdam, could write upon the first page of a preface to a set of annotations upon the Pentateuch:

In the propounding of these things, Moses hath a veil drawn over his bright and glorious face: for in the histories are implied Allegories, & in the lawes are types and shadowes of good things that were to come; the body whereof, is of Christ. In *Genesis*, (which historie endeth with the going down of Israel into Egypt,) we have the Image of a natural man, fallen from God into the bondage of syn. In *Exodus*, is the type of our regeneration, and state renewed by Iesus Christ. In *Leviticus*, the shadow of our mortification whiles we are made sacrifices unto God. In *Numbers*, the figure of our spirituall warfare wher unto we are mustered and armed to fight the good fight of faith. In *Deuteronomie*, the doctrine of our santification, and preparation to enter into our heavenly Canaan, (after Moses death) by the conduct of Iesus the son of God.[20]

Almost everybody could agree with observations like these because almost everybody accepted the principle behind them.

The interesting thing about the Elizabethan emphasis upon typology is that in most cases it was genuinely sacramental; that is, it insisted upon the sign as something participating *in* Christ, not merely standing for him. The literal sense of Scripture, conceived of as event rather than as rhetoric, was all important. In fact, one of the best theologians of the time, William Whitaker, followed Aquinas closely in setting forth this "orthodox" attitude toward Holy Writ, as a few passages from his *A Disputation on Holy Scripture* (1588) will make clear:

As to those three spiritual senses, it is surely foolish to say that there are as many senses of Scripture as the words themselves may be transferred and accommodated to bear. For although the words may be applied and accommodated tropologically, allegorically, anagogically, or any other way; yet there are not therefore various senses, various interpretations and explications of scripture, but there is but one sense, and that the literal, which may be variously accommodated, and from which various things may be collected.[21]

. . . . .

When we proceed from the sign to the thing signified, we bring no new sense, but only bring out into light what was before concealed in the sign. When we speak of the sign by itself, we express only part of the meaning and so also when we mention only the thing signified: but when the mutual relation between the sign and the thing signified is brought out, then the whole complete sense, which is founded upon this similitude and agreement, is set forth. . . . [God] hath set before us the punishment of the Jews pourtrayed as it were in a picture, that we may constantly have it before our eyes. They had indeed many things of a typical nature, the cloud, the passage through the sea, the water from the rock, the manna; which all were symbols to the pious of heavenly things. As the water flowing from the rock refreshed the weary people, and the manna fed them, so Christ cheers and preserves us. As they were enveloped in the cloud, and set in the midst of the waves of the great deep, so all the godly are washed by the blood of Christ. These were all sacraments to them, and so the pious understood them. When, therefore, these are expounded literally of the things themselves, spiritually of celestial graces, we do not make two diverse senses; but, by expounding a similitude, we compare the sign with the thing signified, and so bring out the true and entire sense of the words.[22]

From the conviction, here expounded, that the events of Scripture are sacramental it is only a short step to the conviction of St. Augustine that the whole world is fresh with the odor of Christ's name. Donne, who liked a typological interpretation as well as any, frequently gives evidence of such a conviction, though he is usually careful to dissociate himself from con-

temporary advocates of natural religion: "Certainly, every Creature shewes God, as a glass, but glimmeringly and transitorily,
by the frailty both of the receiver, and beholder: Our selves have
his Image, as Medals, permanently, and preciously delivered.
But by these meditations we get no further, then to know what
he *doth*, not what he is."[23] Devout Puritans, of course, could
and did say much the same thing; and one of them, Edward
Dering (1540?-1576), managed to say it with considerable
eloquence:

The Lord may hide his face for a while, for a moment in his anger,
as he did from Christ, but he must needes returne unto me with
euerlasting mercies, for the image of his sonne is cleare within me.
A blessed sorrow, and woe: full of happinesse, that fashioneth
these dayes of my vanitie into the similitude of the age of Christ,
that with him at last I might raigne for euer. A precious countenance
it is in the sight of God, that seemeth without beautie in the eyes
of man, and an unspeakeable treasure of joy and gladnes engrauen
in these vessels that are but earth and ashes. When Christ is the
paterne, whose similitude we beare, who can be discouraged under
the crosse?[24]

One may wonder what all this has to do with the interpretation of the works of Shakespeare, who was not a divine and
whose religious affiliation, if any, has been debated inconclu-
sively for many generations. The connection would probably
have been as difficult for most Elizabethans to see as it is now
for us—though for different reasons. First of all, the average
Elizabethan (who was religious and Christian, whatever his
doctrinal persuasions may have been) would probably have sat,
or stood, through a Shakespeare play without noticing the
astonishing number of allusions to Scripture, Prayer Book, and
dogma generally. He would have missed them because to him
they were commonplace; we miss them because to us they are
almost completely foreign, and their strangeness seems but a
part of the general strangeness of an unfamiliar language. With
all our learning, we are likely to be unaware until it is pointed

out to us that Shakespeare more than any other popular playwright of his time had absorbed the language of Prayer Book
and Geneva Bible. Fortunately that much at least *has* been
pointed out to us.[25] What remains to be examined is the way
this assimilated material worked in his art.

The solution most likely to gain acceptance in our time is
one roughly analogous to the position taken by Theseus in
A *Midsummer Night's Dream:* Shakespeare *used* Scripture as
contemporary humanists used their classical allusions, to orna-
ment a tale or to point to some abstract value. It was simply
another way of giving a "habitation" and a "name" to something
not readily apprehended by the senses. Scripture was familiar
to his audiences; therefore Shakespeare used Scripture. This
was one reason why he managed to be popular for as long
as he did: he had his finger on the pulse of the audience; he
himself was uncommitted. Modern interpreters frequently offer
us something like this as the objective point of view—the really
"safe" one—but it leaves too much unexplained. For example,
Miss Helen Gardner, who is well aware of the presence of
typology in Elizabethan devotional literature, argues at some
length that its importance in secular literature is negligible.[26]
She points to a flourishing interest in the literal sense of Scripture, both in Shakespeare's time and earlier, and adds reveal-
ingly, "Neither comedy nor tragedy can exist if the individual
is only valued as illustrative of the general."[27] Of course, it is
quite true that typology could, and occasionally did, degenerate
into little more than an ingenious game of signs and illustrations;
but genuine typology is never merely illustrative. A genuine
typologist regards Scriptural history as sacramental and looks
upon the individual in it as incorporating meaning rather than
pointing to it; and consciously or unconsciously, Shakespeare
was a genuine typologist in his use of Scriptural allusion and
analogy. If he had used Scriptural material only in the way
Miss Gardner thinks it possible for a poet to use such material,
then his allusions to Adam, Cain, Abel, God, and Christ might
have served merely as ornamental signs, illustrative examples,

things to be seen *through*, pointers to something else. Actually, they seldom operate merely in this way.

First, it should be noted that practically all of Shakespeare's allusions, like the allusions of any good poet, tend to earn their way in the context in which they appear. They extend the depth of the play itself; they do not merely point to depths outside the play—in philosophy, theology, politics, or some other more abstract realm of knowledge. The critic who has the courage to remain in contact with Shakespeare's text usually finds that the resources of the metaphors operating within the play are difficult to exhaust. Instead of representing outlets into other realms, they are tributaries flowing in, so that whatever they bring to the play from other literatures or other disciplines becomes known in a new and unique way in the work of art itself. The result is indeed "transfigured so together" that it "More witnesseth than fancy's images, / And grows to something of great constancy." It is, in short, a kind of knowledge that defies restatement in any other terms, but knowledge nevertheless— "howsoever, strange and admirable."

Shakespeare's references to the data of Elizabethan Christianity and his frequent recourse to Biblical analogies have in addition to this ordinary power of metaphor the extraordinarily vital shaping power of typology. If we keep in mind that for Shakespeare's contemporaries everything in Scripture, doctrine, and Prayer Book has one subject only—the eternal presence revealed to the full capacity of human understanding only once in history—then we can begin to understand why a Scriptural reference in Shakespeare often seems to take control of that part of the play in which it appears, and sometimes even takes control of the entire play. All we need to do at this point is to allow Shakespeare creativity, however defined, and allow his Scriptural allusions vitality and power. The rest is demonstration, after which the reader may decide for himself.

In this book the demonstration is focused principally upon twelve plays which, it is hoped, are as representative as any selection is likely to be of Shakespeare's mature work as a whole.

The first four, *Richard II*, *The Merchant of Venice*, and the two parts of *Henry IV* (treated here in a single chapter) show how the Christian aspect emerged in the comedies and history plays that Shakespeare wrote between 1595 and 1600. The next two are "problem comedies" from the period of the tragedies. One of these, *Measure for Measure*, has had frequent public attention from Christian interpreters; the other, *Troilus and Cressida*, has had relatively little.[28] Between these and the treatment of four tragedies—*Hamlet*, *Othello*, *Macbeth*, and *Antony and Cleopatra*—I have included a brief chapter on the Christian interpretation of tragedy. My excuse for this interruption is that it seemed better to answer certain general objections to the Christian interpretation of tragedy all in one place and leave the essays on individual tragedies to stand, if they could, on their own. The last two chapters deal with the so-called romances *Cymbeline* and *The Winter's Tale*, and to the second of these I have appended some brief remarks by way of summary and conclusion.

Two

RICHARD II

*H*OWEVER ONE looks at it, *Richard II* seems to mark a kind
of transition in Shakespeare's development as a dramatic poet.
To his contemporaries it may very well have seemed a relatively
tame performance after the exciting combination of historical
material and Senecan villainy in *Richard III* and the lyrical
movement of his sophisticated *Romeo and Juliet.* For us it is
perhaps easier to see that Shakespeare had reached a terminus
of sorts in both of these early plays. *Romeo and Juliet* is something that we should not willingly part with, but we should be
reluctant to acquire many more like it. For that matter, a play
surpassing *Romeo and Juliet* in its kind almost defies the
imagination. Of possible plays like *Richard III,* also perfect in
its way, one specimen is quite enough. And so it is with plays
like *Comedy of Errors, Love's Labour's Lost,* and *Titus Androni-
cus.* Shakespeare, by the time he came to write *Richard II,* had
proved that he was capable of achieving as much perfection as
was desirable in several of the more important dramatic forms
that his predecessors had sketched out. It remained for him to
show that he had something new to offer, either by producing
a startling innovation in form or by offering a new idea of drama.
We can be grateful that he left the first of these alternatives to

his younger contemporary Ben Jonson, whose surer sense of
formal structure enabled him to produce innovations that found
few imitators because he himself did all that could conceivably
be done with them. Shakespeare's great contribution was the
rediscovery of an ancient and all but forgotten path for drama.
That he too had few followers is regrettable, but hardly his fault.
Even now we come stumblingly to a definition of what it was he
found. Tragedy, since Bradley, looms large in our eye, and we
still tend to define Shakespeare's achievement in relation to
that. The value of *Richard II*, we are sometimes tempted to
say, lies in its anticipations of characterizations yet to come,
Brutus, Hamlet, and Macbeth. So it does, but not exclusively
there. What really sets this remarkable play sharply apart from
Shakespeare's own earlier work and the work of his contemporaries is an approach—demonstrable in most of his later
work quite without regard to formal classification—which reveals
Shakespeare clearly as a poet with a metaphysical turn of mind,
capable of seeing the particular event both as something unique
and as something participating in a universal web of analogy.
We find next to nothing of this in the *Henry VI* plays, in
Comedy of Errors, in *Love's Labour's Lost*, in *Romeo and Juliet*,
or in *Richard III*, which, for all its slick dramaturgy, remains a
play about Richard III, at its farthest conceivable extension a
warning to would-be usurpers and tyrants. It is in *Richard II*, a
play popularly and rightly famous for one passage in glorification
of England, that Shakespeare manages for the first time to extend his field of reference to include everybody.

The kind of seeing which this new approach to material
requires is illustrated in that scene in Act II in which the Queen
betrays an inclination to see more in Richard's going to Ireland
than a mere separation. Bushy, with more commonsense than
foresight, tries to persuade the lady that simple sorrow has
distorted her judgment and made her look upon perfectly normal
situations as if they were ingenious *trompes-l'oeil*,

> ... perspectives, which rightly gaz'd upon
> Show nothing but confusion, ey'd awry

Distinguish form; so your sweet Majesty,
Looking awry upon your lord's departure,
Find shapes of grief, more than himself, to wail;
Which, look'd on as it is, is nought but shadows
Of what it is not.

(II.ii.18-24)

Bushy would have her look squarely at the event and accept it at face value. The Queen, however, is not easily comforted. "It may be so," she replies; "but yet my inward soul / Persuades me it is otherwise." She happens to be right, of course; history makes her right. But Shakespeare gives her kind of vision at least as much vindication as history does. If we may believe some of the critics who have written about it, *Richard II* contains much that is unassimilated, contradictory, and without special significance. That is, if we look at the play "rightly," in Bushy's sense, we see in it at least a partial failure to achieve complete control over the historical materials. Nevertheless, if we take a hint from Richard's Queen and eye the play awry (as, for example, in our recollection of it), it has a way of subtly distinguishing a form that tends to pull all the seemingly irrelevant parts together and make the whole meaningful as no chronicle before it, dramatic or nondramatic, had ever been.

Some writers have attributed this "informed quality" of *Richard II* to Shakespeare's conscious or unconscious dependence upon an analogy with ritual. Among those who have acknowledged the importance of ceremony and ritual in the play is E. M. W. Tillyard, who devotes several illuminating pages of his *Shakespeare's History Plays* to the matter;[1] but Tillyard sees ceremony only as part of the data of the play, an attribute of Richard and his medieval kingship, which Bolingbroke is about to destroy. One might say that Tillyard looks at the play "rightly," in Bushy's sense. J. Dover Wilson, on the other hand, following some remarks by Walter Pater, has observed in his edition that *Richard II* stands so remarkably close to the Catholic service of the Mass that it ought to be played throughout as ritual.[2] Hardier critics than Wilson have

gone still farther and made out cases for relating the play to
ancient fertility rites, some of which, like their Christian
counterparts, present remarkably close analogies with this play.
For example, of the four types of fertility ritual in which F. M.
Cornford found a significant tendency toward drama,[3] three
show a resemblance to the action of *Richard II* which is too
striking to be ignored. In one of these, which Cornford calls
"The Carrying out of Death," the sin of a whole kingdom is
symbolically purged with the death of a single victim. In
another, "The Fight of Summer and Winter," winter personified
as an evil antagonist is defeated by the representative of summer.
In a third, perhaps the most suggestive of all, the old king, or
old year, having grown evil through decay, is deposed and replaced by the new.

Suggestive as all these examples of ritual are, however, they
have no discernible connection with plays of the Elizabethan
theater; for as far as responsible investigators have been able to
tell, the theater which Shakespeare inherited was a lineal
descendant of neither folk rite nor Christian ritual. It is much
more sensible to explain whatever ritual movement we find in
Richard II as something Shakespeare himself achieved—partly by
analogy with existing ritual perhaps, but achieved by himself—in
the process of shaping a particular event from chronicle history
into a living poetic symbol. In that sense, it may be said that
he imported into English drama something that it had not
inherited legitimately—or, to revert to our first metaphor, he
rediscovered for drama an almost forgotten path, impossible for
most but vastly rewarding for those few capable of using it. The
question to be asked and answered is, how did he happen to
stumble upon it? One cannot answer such a question with
finality. Shakespeare's own profound sense of analogy must, of
course, provide nine-tenths of any answer anyone might suggest;
and the presence in England of a powerful Christian ritual,
revitalized by half a century of intermittently vigorous opposition, certainly had something to do with it. But in addition
to these aspects of Shakespeare's achievement, one other, related

to both and yet isolable in its own right, commands attention; and this is his persistent use of Biblical story as analog for his secular fable. In *Richard II* this aspect confronts us from beginning to end.

The most obvious manifestation of it is the identification of Richard with Christ, which happens to be a historical one. Shakespeare makes explicit use of it first in Act III, when he makes Richard refer to Bushy, Bagot, and Green as "Three Judases, each one thrice worse than Judas!" (III.ii.132). In Act IV, of course, there is considerably more of this sort of thing. There the Bishop of Carlisle warns that if Bolingbroke ascends the throne, England shall be called "The field of Golgotha and dead men's skulls" (IV.i.144). And Richard observes of Bolingbroke's supporters:

> . . . I well remember
> The favours of these men. Were they not mine?
> Did they not sometime cry, "All hail!" to me?
> So Judas did to Christ; but He, in twelve,
> Found truth in all but one; I, in twelve
> thousand, none.
>
> (IV.i.167-171)

A bit farther on he calls his enemies by another name:

> . . . some of you with Pilate wash your hands
> Showing an outward pity; yet you Pilates
> Have here deliver'd me to my sour cross,
> And water cannot wash away your sin.
>
> (IV.i.239-242)

This set of allusions, familiar even to casual students of the play, serves admirably to point up Richard's own view of the situation and also to underline effectively the official Elizabethan view that (in the language of the *Homilies*) "The violence and injury that is committed against authority is committed against God."[4] A second set of allusions, equally familiar, begins with

Gaunt's reference to "This other Eden, demi-paradise," which gets its proper qualification somewhat later in the Garden scene of Act III, when the Gardener's man describes England as a "sea-walled garden" choked with weeds and the Gardener himself receives the Queen's rebuke for presuming to accuse Richard of negligence:

> Thou, old Adam's likeness, set to dress this garden,
> How dares thy harsh rude tongue sound this
> unpleasing news?
> What Eve, what serpent, hath suggested thee
> To make a second fall of cursed man?
>
> (III.iv.73-76)

Here with these allusions a second attitude, not exclusively Elizabethan, is underscored: that the king, as himself man, is responsible to God for the right use of sovereignty, both by defending true religion and the honest subject and by punishing the wicked.

Taken together, these two sets of allusions give us a double image of Richard—Richard *microchristus* and Richard *microcosmos*, Richard the Lord's Anointed and Richard Everyman. This, of course, is simply the conventional Elizabethan double image of kingship and would not of itself be particularly startling were it not for the additional suggestion of a pattern that unfolds as the play proceeds. The Golgotha of which Carlisle speaks does indeed come to pass. Richard rides to London with many to throw dust upon his head but none to cry, "God save him!" Despised and rejected, he languishes at Pomfret, only to face his executioners with such a manifestation of regality in death that Exton, like the centurion at the foot of the cross (who said of Jesus, "Truly this man was the Son of God."—*cf.* Matthew xxvii.54 and Mark xv.39), is compelled to acknowledge it:

> As full of valour as of royal blood!
> Both have I spill'd; O would the deed were good!

For now the devil, that told me I did well,
Says that this deed is chronicled in hell.

(V.v.114-117)

Even Bolingbroke, to whom Richard alive was a "living fear,"
is moved to say:

Though I did wish him dead,
I hate the murderer, love him murdered.

(V.vi.39-40)

The twentieth-century reader is apt to miss the full significance
of all this. Undoubtedly a great many Elizabethans, who were
long accustomed to seeing typological interpretations of Biblical
history, saw in this presentation of Richard as a sort of Adam-
Christ a typological interpretation of their own national history.
In Scripture the fall and death of the First Adam is corrected
and atoned for by the sacrificial death of the Second (see Romans v.12-21). That is, Adam's disobedience and death is an
anticipatory realization of a pattern that achieved its complete
historical realization only in the perfect obedience and death
of Jesus of Nazareth, with whose resurrection a way was cleared
for Adam (and all those who had sinned in Adam) to escape
the full consequences of death. From the typologist's point of
view this pattern, perfectly symbolized by one Adam's atonement for the other's sin, is the eternal principle of which all
history is in one way or another but the spelling out. Whether
he realized it or not at the time, Shakespeare, in laying the
outlines of such a complex and richly suggestive symbol against
the surface of his chronicle material, had given to secular fable
a significance that it had achieved only rarely in drama since
the days of Aeschylus and Sophocles. To paraphrase Dryden,
he had affected the metaphysical in his treatment of it. Moreover, having underscored that revolutionary affectation by utiliz-
ing ceremonial in his play, by representing ceremonially much
that was not strictly ceremony, and by frequently alluding to

the symbolic substance of analogous pagan ritual (sun and ice, summer and winter, etc.), he had also produced a work which "eyed awry" presents a ritualistic analogy with the sacrifice on the cross.

Seeing a ritualistic aspect in a play, however, is not the same as identifying it with ritual or attempting to play it as ritual. To see Richard as a ritual type of Adam-Christ is certainly warranted by Shakespeare's text, but to see him exclusively as that is to see Bolingbroke exclusively as Satan-Judas; and this is certainly *not* warranted by the text. The leading question of the play is not simply "What is true kingship?" but "What is the true king? What is the Lord's Anointed?" Mere ritual is powerless to answer this question, and history and the *Homilies* do little better. Shakespeare could expect his audience to know the report of history that both Richard and the Lancastrian usurper in their turns possessed the title of "Lord's Anointed" and could expect them accordingly to stand with Gaunt when he says ruefully near the beginning of the play:

> God's is the quarrel; for God's substitute,
> His deputy anointed in His sight,
> Hath caus'd his death; the which if wrongfully,
> Let Heaven revenge.
>
> (I.ii.37-40)

He could assume that the judgment of York on Bolingbroke in Act II would be accepted as appropriate by loyal Englishmen everywhere:

> My lords of England, let me tell you this:
> I have had feeling of my cousin's wrongs
> And labour'd all I could to do him right;
> But in this kind to come, in braving arms,
> Be his own carver and cut out his way,
> To find out right with wrong—it may not be;
> And you that do abet him in this kind
> Cherish rebellion and are rebels all.
>
> (II.iii.140-147)

Similarly, he could let York's pained acquiescence in Bolingbroke's accession to the throne serve as an appropriate public
moral for the play as a whole: "Heaven hath a hand in these
events, / To whose high will we bow our calm contents"
(V.ii.37-38). Yet there is something less than a martyr's acquiescence in Richard's famous metaphor for the historic turn-
about:

> Now is this golden crown like a deep well
> That owes two buckets, filling one another,
> The emptier ever dancing in the air,
> The other down, unseen, and full of water.
> That bucket down and full of tears am I,
> Drinking my griefs, whilst you mount up on high.

> (IV.i.184-189)

The conclusion startles Bolingbroke into saying, "I thought you
had been willing to resign." And Richard replies with three lines
that would be uncomfortably out of place in a play reduced to
the level of ritual:

> My crown I am; but still my griefs are mine.
> You may my glories and my state depose,
> But not my griefs; still am I king of those.

Here Richard is undoubtedly already thinking of himself as a
betrayed and repudiated Christ, moving ahead to a sour cross
while the Pilates stand about washing their hands. The role
evidently delights him, and he plays it well. Nevertheless, we
should notice that the role is one he has himself discovered,
not one that has come looking for him. We should also notice
that Shakespeare cast Richard initially in quite another role,
which he plays equally well, in spite of himself, and which
temporarily at least disqualifies him as a spotless victim.

The Richard that Shakespeare sets before us at the beginning
of the play is not only God's Anointed but a man guilty,
ultimately if not directly, of his uncle's death. He knows that

no one has proved his guilt, and he thinks that no one, except Aumerle of course, knows exactly what the details of Woodstock's death were. Yet Bolingbroke, in the very first scene, pronounces the murdered man Abel and his murderer by implication Cain:

> . . . like a traitor coward,
> Sluic'd out his innocent soul through streams
> > of blood;
> Which blood, like sacrificing Abel's, cries,
> Even from the tongueless caverns of the earth,
> To me for justice and rough chastisement;
> And, by the glorious worth of my descent,
> This arm shall do it, or this life be spent.

> > > (I.i.102-108)

What Bolingbroke does not realize is that his condemnation and threat of revenge, hurled at the innocent Mowbray, are applicable only to Richard. The Cain he really seeks, however unwittingly, sits on the throne before him and wears the robes of the Lord's Anointed. And ironic as this situation is, it becomes even more ironic when we think of the ancient identification of Abel with Christ and of Cain with the disbelieving Jews who slew him. In Shakespeare's time there was nothing particularly esoteric about such an identification. The New Testament provides ample authority for it (Matthew xxiii.25 and Hebrews xi.4; xii.24); there is a reference to it in the Canon of the Mass; and frequent use of it is made in the writings of the Church Fathers.[5] Among Shakespeare's audience there must have been at least a few who had encountered it in contemporary exegetical works and a great many who knew about it from pictorial representations in the familiar *Biblia Pauperum*. Yet even if the identification of Richard-Christ with Richard-Cain escaped the audience entirely, the primary application of Bolingbroke's allusion to the story of Cain and Abel could hardly have escaped them. They all knew well enough what had happened to Woodstock and who was directly responsible for it, and they could not have missed the implication that Richard secretly bore the curse of Cain. A second allusion to the murder of Woodstock, however, completes the identification. It is Gaunt who makes this one:

> O, spare me not, my brother Edward's son,
> For that I was his father Edward's son,
> That blood already, like the pelican,
> Hast thou tapp'd out and drunkenly carous'd.
>
> (II.i.124-127)

Here we have one of our oldest symbols for the Saviour, the pelican mother who feeds the young with her own blood, inverted by Gaunt to make an accusation against the young king. That is, Richard, who should have been the parent pelican of the figure, prepared to nourish his brood with his own life if need be, is here accused of having caroused on the blood of another (Woodstock). Perhaps Shakespeare's audience missed this allusion too. No one can say for sure about that. The important point is that Shakespeare put it there; and with it the chain of analogies, as Shakespeare conceived it, seems complete: Richard-Christ-antichrist-Cain, all are linked as one.

But what of Bolingbroke, who also assumes the role of the Lord's Anointed before the play is complete? After Cain had killed his brother, God put his mark on the fugitive murderer and decreed that no vengeance should be taken upon him. The traditional Christian explanation for God's prohibition against revenge in this case was that satisfaction for Abel's blood was to be expected only with the advent of "Jesus, the mediator of the new covenant, and . . . the blood of sprinkling, that speaketh better things than that of Abel" (Hebrews xii.24). Bolingbroke, in proclaiming himself the avenger of a murdered Abel, was using a figure of speech, to be sure, but he was nevertheless presuming to make right in his own way something that mere man can never make right. In other words, he was presuming to do something that even as *microchristus* he could not expect

to accomplish without committing the same sin he would
avenge. The place of Bolingbroke in the action of the play is
perhaps clear enough without the use of Biblical allusion, but
such allusion can help us state it: Bolingbroke's story is that of
a man who sets out to slay the murderer Cain and does so, only
to find that he himself has the blood of Abel on his hands.

Richard II, then, if it is to be compared to ritual, must be
compared to some of the pagan rituals we know, and not to any
Christian ritual. The allusions point to a clear, unambiguous
analogy with Christ for neither of the principals. Each is a
microchristus with a specifically human blind spot, a failure to
see that human kingship, unlike the divine kingship of Christ,
involves both a crown and a potential Cain who wears the crown.
Each discovers, among other things, that the crown is never
enough to make the wearer immune to the consequences of
being human, but each finds in his turn that the crown can be
an eloquent teacher. The crown is a well of instruction, and
Richard gets his in the process of descending. From the moment
he sets foot on English soil after his return from Ireland, he
alternately gropes for and rejects the knowledge which he fully
possesses only in the hour of his death at Pomfret. There,
breeding thoughts, setting Scripture against Scripture, and
imaginatively assuming and repudiating all sorts and conditions
of mankind, he comes at last to the flat truth,

> Nor I nor any man that but man is
> With nothing shall be pleas'd, till he be eas'd
> With being nothing.
>
> (V.v.39-41)

The irony of this moment is that here in the recognition of
his physical weakness and his human need for humility Richard
poses his greatest threat to Bolingbroke, who at almost the same
time receives a similar enlightenment on the way up. Up to the
moment of his coronation Bolingbroke has never once thought
of the terrifying efficacy that regal power confers upon human

impulses. As Bolingbroke he could wish Richard dead and bury the guilt of the wish in his own soul. As Henry he must learn that even a whispered wish is a powerful command. That he wished Richard dead is now enough to make Richard dead, and the blood of Richard is upon him. Turning upon Pierce of Exton, who held the actual dagger, he condemns him in the words of innocent Mowbray:

> With Cain go wander through the shades of night,
> And never show thy head by day nor light.
>
> (V.vi.43-44)

But the Mowbray who once left England "To dwell in solemn shades of endless night" (I.iii.177) now rests in Abraham's bosom and was never Cain. The two lines that follow are at once sober and plaintive:

> Lords, I protest, my soul is full of woe
> That blood should sprinkle me to make me grow.

And with these lines we come full circle. The great Biblical-metaphysical framework of allusion that began with Boling-broke's reference to the murder of Abel has encompassed the fable and returned to its starting point. We can now state the questions of the play in terms of the analogies that define them: Who is the Cain? Who, the Christ? Can one avenge Abel without becoming Cain? Can Cain dwell with Christ in the same golden well?

Such questions as these inevitably arise whenever a great dramatic poet lays the relatively clear-cut distinctions of mythic pattern against the disorderly flux of human affairs. It makes little difference whether the poet particularizes his myth and so brings it to the status of history (as the Greeks frequently did) or brings to the particularity of chronicle history the outlines of a more ancient imitation. The result is the same. In either case we find good and evil, innocence and guilt, so inextricably mixed that human ingenuity cannot say where the dividing line is. As in the ancient fertility rites, we tend to find slayer and slain, old king and new king, Cain and Christ, united in one human frame. There is no other solution in purely human terms. And the bewildered protagonist who suddenly sees the unresolvable paradox in his human situation can only cry out, as Bolingbroke does:

> Lords, I protest, my soul is full of woe
> That blood should sprinkle me to make me grow.

Three

THE MERCHANT OF VENICE

THERE IS no doubt about the relevance of Christian materials
to *The Merchant of Venice*. A child with a set of Bible verses
and the memory of his confirmation class could establish that.
But there has always been doubt in the minds of many readers
about the essential Christianity of the play. Even those who
are ready to excuse the "inhuman" treatment of Shylock on
historical grounds tend to find something uncomfortably pious
about Antonio and Portia and stop short of accepting Bassanio,
who has scarcely grown out of his adolescent irresponsibility
by the time the play has ended. Some modern readers find the
play palatable because they can take it as a serious sociological
document; but most, one suspects, prefer to regard it simply as
a romantic excursion in which Shakespeare wandered discon-
certingly out of his depth, digging up muddy issues which he
might better have dealt with in other plays. Most find it safest
to read *The Merchant of Venice* as a gorgeously caparisoned
puppet show, in which a collection of fragile dolls toy superficially and gracefully with the themes of love and friendship
and move to a musical close, at which happy point the sooty
ogre of the preceding acts can be forgotten because he has been
laid away lifeless in his chest to await the next performance.

Yet there have always been those who insist, in spite of the difficulties, on taking the play seriously, all the way through from beginning to end, forgetting nothing and rejecting nothing. One of these was Sir Israel Gollancz, who in some delightfully informal essays, brought together for publication after his death, justified the play as a Christian allegory after the manner of the late medieval morality plays.[1] Gollancz cited two texts as fundamental to the interpretation of the play. The first, "Greater love hath no man than this, that a man should lay down his life for his friend" (John xv.13), relates obviously to the business of the bond; and the second, taken from Ephesians, "Christ also loved the Church and gave himself for it" (Ephesians v.25), has in addition some applicability to the love making, the caskets, and Portia's successful attempt to resolve the moral indebtedness of her husband. Along with J. D. Rea and Hope Traver, Gollancz also saw the bond element of the story as deriving from the medieval versions of the debate of the four heavenly daughters (based on Psalm LXXXV) and the medieval stories about Satan's arraignment of the Redeemer.[2] He hesitated, however, to give Shakespeare full credit for writing an allegory on Christian themes and suggested that the two distinguishable parts of the play—the bond story and the story of the caskets —had been fused and perhaps interpreted together as Christian allegories by Shakespeare's anonymous predecessor, who, according to Stephen Gosson's report in 1579, wrote a play called *The Jew* "representing the greediness of worldly chusers, and the bloody mindes of Usurers."

About the extent of Shakespeare's indebtedness to an earlier play we cannot be sure, since we have only Gosson's ambiguous report and no trace of a play to go by. This much, however, is sure: the play which we do have is a demonstrably Shakespearean entity from first to last. If Shakespeare worked from another play, as he frequently did, he here reworked pretty thoroughly and deserves the credit, or responsibility, for the distinctly Christian aura that hangs about this play. In any case, the aura is what concerns us here, and of that there cannot be much serious doubt. Benjamin N. Nelson, acknowledging Gollancz's work, finds that it makes the play a minor document in the history of the idea of usury. "Antonio's heroic suretyship to Shylock for Bassanio," he writes, "finds its prototype in Christ's act in serving as 'ransom' to the Devil for all mankind."[3] And Nevill Coghill, who has undertaken to develop some of the implications in Gollancz's essays about the medieval background of *The Merchant*, has found the play more fundamentally Christian even than its medieval prototypes. Coghill describes the play as "an *exemplum* in modern dress" on the theme of Justice and Mercy, the Old Law and the New; it asserts the rightness of both principles, be believes, and the need for some sort of compromise between them—justice yielding a little to mercy, and mercy yielding a little to justice.[4] Probably for most readers Coghill has gone as far as is desirable toward pronouncing the theme of the play Christian; yet we can agree with all that he has said, and with all that Gollancz and the others have said, and still hold that the Christianity of the play is largely fortuitous. After all, there are not many themes that cannot be accommodated to Christian dogma in one way or another; and the themes in *The Merchant of Venice* were so accommodated long before Shakespeare got hold of them.

One might, for example, point to the moralized versions of the casket and bond stories in the *Gesta Romanorum*.[5] The moralized version of the bond story, it is true, never found its way into any of the English printed versions of the *Gesta*, but it does appear in an English manuscript version of the fifteenth century and in other versions printed elsewhere. According to the "Moralitee" of this story, the Emperor (corresponding to Portia's dead father) is Jesus Christ, the daughter (Portia) is "the sowle I-made to the similitude of god," the young suitor is Everyman, and the merchant is the Devil. The meaning of the daughter's action to save her husband is given as follows: "we shulde caste fro vs the olde lyf and cloþe vs with a newe, *scil*, goode vertuys, and assende vpon the palfrey of Resoune, and so go forthe to holy chirche, & þere pray god with a fulle herte, & allegge ayenst þe devil, that he sle vs not, by cause that god bowte vs."[6] The casket story was moralized in Richard Robinson's several editions of the *Gesta*, one of which probably served Shakespeare as a source. There we find that "By the third vessell of lead full of golde and precious stones, we ought to vnderstand a simple life and a poore, which the chosen men choose, that they may be wedded to our blessed Lorde Jesu Christ by humilitie and obeysance, and such men beare with them precious stones, that is to saye, faith and hir fruitfull workes, pleasinge to God: by the which at the iudgement day they be espoused to our Lord Jesu Christ and obtaine the heritage of heauen, vnto the which bring vs he that dyed on the Crosse."[7] Such quotations as these, however, suggest only that Shakespeare could not have been unaware that Christian implications had been found in his materials for *The Merchant of Venice*. In themselves they prove nothing about the Christian implications of the material as "transfigured together" within the play.

We need go no farther than Ser Giovanni Fiorentino's *Il Pecorone*, very likely Shakespeare's immediate source for the bond story, to find a version later than the *Gesta* which is not moralized at all.[8] The Emperor, who served in the *Gesta* as a figure of Christ, has disappeared altogether. To the young lover (who originally borrowed the money and also wooed the lady) has been added a bondsman, giving us the two men and the theme of friendship as we have them in Shakespeare. In addition, we have also the business of the ring, which business, for reasons we shall consider presently, Shakespeare doubled. These changes bring us a long way from the stodgy morality of the *Gesta* version toward the seemingly free and easy account that we find in Shakespeare and suggest that the immediate background for the core of Shakespeare's story was romantic and secular and only distantly and collaterally related to such things as *Piers Plowman* and *The Castle of Perseverance*. The proper conclusion would seem to be, as we frequently find it in introductions and commentaries, that Shakespeare completed the secularization of a medieval moral *exemplum*. In at least one respect, however, Shakespeare himself seems to have forestalled this conclusion. The bondsman of *Il Pecorone* (Shakespeare's Antonio) helps bring the story to a satisfactory romantic conclusion by joining hands with the Lady of Belmont's maid-in-waiting (Shakespeare's Nerissa) to make a double wedding. In *The Merchant of Venice* Shakespeare, for reasons that must seem obvious to interpreters like Gollancz and Coghill, keeps Antonio single and clinches his bachelorhood by bringing in a third male principal, Gratiano, to take the hand of Nerissa.

The Renaissance doctrine of friendship, which like the Platonic doctrine from which it is derived exalts love between friends over love between man and woman, does not fully account for what happens here. It is quite understandable in terms of such a doctrine that Antonio, as a Renaissance gentleman bound in friendship to Bassanio, should "only love the world for him" (II.viii.50). It is also understandable that Portia should high-mindedly forgo jealousy and recognize an obligation upon herself to preserve her husband's "higher love" at all costs. The terms in which she expresses her attitude in this matter are as precisely Neoplatonic as one could wish:

> I never did repent for doing good,
> Nor shall not now: for in companions
> That do converse and waste the time together,
> Whose souls so bear an egal yoke of love,
> There must be needs a like proportion
> Of lineaments, of manners, and of spirit;
> Which makes me think that this Antonio,
> Being the bosom lover of my lord,
> Must needs be like my lord. If it be so,
> How little is the cost I have bestow'd
> In purchasing the semblance of my soul
> From out the state of hellish cruelty!
>
> (III.iv.10-21)

Yet by the time that Portia says these lines, the possibility that we are not to take the relation between Antonio and

Bassanio as exclusively the conventional Neoplatonic one has already been introduced into the play. Gollancz, Nelson, and Coghill, who have all seen Antonio as a figure of Christ, the perfect friend who so loved man that he gave himself for him, may be accused of unwarranted spiritualizing or allegorizing; but the analogy that leads them on is substantially supported by Antonio's letter, which Bassanio reads aloud to Portia at the close of the second scene in Act III:

> Sweet Bassanio, my ships have all miscarried,
> my creditors grow cruel, my estate is very low,
> my bond to the Jew is forfeit; and since in pay-
> ing it, it is impossible I should live, all debts are
> cleared between you and I, if I might but see
> you at my death. Notwithstanding, use your
> pleasure; if your love do not persuade you to
> come, let not my letter.
>
> (II.iii.318-325)

We might dismiss as something demanded by the plot Antonio's observation, "my bond to the Jew is forfeit; and . . . in paying it, it is impossible I should live." Nevertheless, it would be difficult to find in all the Renaissance literary examples of perfect friendship a neater statement of a neater parallel to Christ's voluntary assumption of the debt that was death to repay. And one does not find among such examples a satisfactory parallel to Antonio's demand upon Bassanio, which follows immediately: "all debts are cleared between you and I, if I might but see you at my death." Here we are beyond Platonism and completely within the realm of Christian dogma, which holds that the sinner is not ransomed by the death of the Saviour unless he witnesses that death—furthermore, that he is not ransomed unless he witnesses it willingly and out of love for the Redeemer: "Notwithstanding, use your pleasure; if your love do not persuade you to come, let not my letter."[9]

Antonio is not following a Platonic code of friendship here, for that would have required him to show more consideration for

Bassanio's sensibilities. Strictly speaking, he is not even behaving like a Christian, for a Christian is commanded to forgive his debtors and forget the debt. Antonio is saying, in excusable contradiction to all acceptable codes for human behavior, "I will excuse your debt if you will witness my execution. Come and be present at my death, if you love me." And this is the invitation that only Christ properly extends, to the discomfort of many Christians, who turn away at the sight of the cross and grow weary at the thought of trying to repay in love a debt that can never be repaid, in equity or in kind. The parallel continues throughout the trial scene in Act IV. To the Duke, who feels sorry for Antonio's predicament, Antonio says:

> . . . since he stands obdurate
> And that no lawful means can carry me
> Out of his envy's reach, I do oppose
> My patience to his fury, and am arm'd
> To suffer, with a quietness of spirit
> The very tyranny and rage of his.
>
> (IV.i.8-12)

To Bassanio he says:

> I am a tainted wether of the flock,
> Meetest for death. The weakest kind of fruit
> Drops earliest to the ground, and so let me.
>
> (IV.iv.114-116)

Beyond this, of course, the play does not press the parallel between Antonio and a sacrificial victim. It does not show an actual death, or even the shedding of blood; but it does show an Antonio, snatched from the shadow of death, translated into Belmont, where, unlike his prototype in *Il Pecorone*, he remains the good friend, single, and uncommitted to any other human attachment. If Shakespeare at any point in composing this play saw typological significance in Antonio, the odds are that he deliberately departed from his source here in order to maintain it to the end.

Taking Antonio as a figure of Christ, however, raises the question of what to do with Portia; for in the *Gesta* version of the casket story Portia is the Christ, "which the chosen men choose," and in the bond story she is the "daughter" of Christ, "the sowle I-made to the similitude of god." A good deal of this is retained in *The Merchant of Venice*. As the Prince of Morocco so eloquently testifies, Portia is the bride whom all the world desires: "From the four corners of the earth they come / To kiss this shrine, this mortal-breathing saint" (II.vii.39-40). But, more importantly, she is the bride-intended only for the elect. "O me, the word choose!" she complains to Nerissa. "I may neither choose who I would nor refuse who I dislike." Nerissa's reply could stand for the reply of almost any theologian, Calvinist or Catholic, to a catechumen disturbed by the doctrine of election:

> Your father was ever virtuous, and holy men
> at their death have good inspirations; therefore
> the lott'ry that he hath devised in these three
> chests of gold, silver, and lead, whereof who
> chooses his meaning chooses you, will, no
> doubt, never be chosen by any rightly but one
> who you shall rightly love.
>
> (I.ii.30-36)

And, indeed, when the casket story reaches its climax, we are hard put to say who really does choose, so ardent are they both, Bassanio and Portia, in desiring one another. When she discovers, however, that her husband is not really free and cannot be hers until Antonio's debt is paid, she offers "To pay the petty debt twenty times over," and sends him away with "Since you are dear bought, I will love you dear."

At first glance it might seem simpler to leave Portia's analogy with Christ at this. She is Bassanio's bride, and her function, as Jessica puts it, is to make it possible that "The Lord Bassanio live an upright life; / For, having such a blessing in his lady, / He finds the joys of heaven here on earth" (III.v.79-81). Yet,

unless we are careful, taking such a limited view of Portia's
part in the play will put us in the position of regarding her
performance at the trial as an interesting irrelevance. The attempt to see an analogy between her role there and Mercy as
abstractly represented in the old debate of the Four Heavenly
Daughters only makes matters worse; for, in spite of the obvious
relevance of the Four Daughters story to the trial scene, that
story in the form in which we usually encounter it obscures
rather than clarifies the action of the play as a whole. From start
to finish *The Merchant of Venice* is a play about the restoration
of Bassanio; and for as long as we take time out to think of Portia
as a representative of mercy in opposition to Shylock's justice,
we are really thinking of the play as if Antonio were at the center
rather than Bassanio. Furthermore, we are running the risk of
disenchantment when Portia finally wins, not with mercy, but
with a legalistic trick. The triumph of mercy in this play comes
not in Act IV but in the disposition of Bassanio in Act V, where
a young man who has seemingly deserved nothing at last comes
to merit and get everything, all because two people love him and
are willing to give and hazard all they have for him. What we
need to keep clearly in mind throughout the trial scene is that
Portia is as much Bassanio's savior as Antonio is. Her whole
objective in coming to the trial, as her trick about the ring at
the close of that scene shows, is to snare Bassanio, her means
is to rescue Antonio from Shylock's grasp, and her reason for
tolerating in "godlike amity" Antonio's claim upon her husband's affections is that she sees in Antonio the image of herself.
As she tells Lorenzo, who has no inkling of what she is about
to do,

> Antonio
> Being the bosom lover of my lord,
> Must needs be like my lord. If it be so,
> How little is the cost I have bestow'd
> In purchasing the semblance of my soul
> From out the state of hellish cruelty!
>
> (III.iv.16-21)

Antonio, as the play has it, is saved principally for the sake of Bassanio. For without Antonio's initial willingness to give himself, Bassanio could never have come to the lady in the first place; and without the lady's willingness to rescue Antonio from the consequences of his awful hazard, Bassanio, untested by the lady's device at the trial, would have remained unregenerate, simply another adventurer, not worth much to anybody.

The debate of the Heavenly Daughters, however, can help us understand Portia's part in the play provided we do not lean exclusively on late medieval representations of it. In the year of Shakespeare's death the Anglican John Boys published an exposition of Psalm LXXXV, proper for Christmas Day morning prayer, which is much more relevant to *The Merchant of Venice* than are *Piers Plowman* and *The Castle of Perseverance*. Boys begins with the traditional explanation:

In Christ aduent, *Mercy and truth are met together*, righteousnesse and peace haue kissed each other. Bernard hath a prettie dialogue to his purpose, betweene *righteousnesse* and *truth* on the one side, *mercy* and *peace* on the other part, contending about the redemption of mankinde. Christ our blessed Messias and Mediator ended the quarrell at his coming, and made them all exceeding kinde kissing friends: for in giuing himselfe a ransome for all men, he did at once pay both vnto *Iustice* her debt, and grant vnto *Mercy* her desire.[10]

Then he proceeds to amplify, first, with the suggestion that Coghill worked into his interpretation of *The Merchant*: "Righteousness and peace meet in Christ, God and man: for by these two, some Diuines vnderstand the Old Testament and the New." After this, Boys advances a totally new suggestion, which illuminates the play better than any other that has been made so far:

Or by these two vertues vnderstand Christs two natures, his diuine nature by *mercie*, hauing power to forgiue sinnes, and to heale all manner of sicknesse: by *truth* his humane nature. . . . And this exposition is more probable by the next verse [Psalm LXXXV.11]:

Truth shall flourish out of the earth, and righteousnesse hath looked
down from heauen. Christ is *truth,* as he saith of himselfe, *I am the*
way, the truth, &c. and Christ is our *righteousnesse,* I Corinth. 1.30.
Now Christ as man, and borne of the Virgin Mary, *budded out of*
the earth: and as God, he looked down from *heauen.* That men
might be iustified by grace from heauen, it pleased him on this day
to *bud out of the earth.*[11]

As soon as one looks beyond the simple labels *righteousness-truth*
and *peace-mercy* (as applied respectively to Shylock and Portia)
and sees in the trial scene a demonstration of two aspects of a
single motive working to bring about the salvation of a single
unworthy sinner, one is in a fair way to understand and accept
the whole play. Whether or not one accepts as relevant the
analogy suggested by Boys' exposition (Antonio representing
Christ's physical nature, which offered a physical body as sacrifice; and Portia representing Christ's divine nature, offering forgiveness), one is almost bound, it seems to me, to accept the
functional identity of Antonio and Portia. They are united in
opposition to Shylock and united in their effort to claim Bassanio
for their side; they are united, moreover, in their method, which,
as John R. Brown has pointed out in his recent edition of the
play,[12] is that of "giving and hazarding" all they have and expect-
ing nothing in return. They are opposed, however, as truth and
mercy are opposed, or as any two halves of a whole may be said
to be opposed. Each is a partial manifestation of what, according
to the Christian idea of human regeneration, it takes to save a
man. Antonio's friendship, offering living flesh and blood as
payment for what is really his friend's debt, cannot of itself make
Bassanio whole. And Portia's generous offer of undivided love,
to say nothing of her magnificent dowry, can only be disastrous
to him; for, amiable as he is, Bassanio before the first scene is
over is already established as one who habitually draws on the
generosity of others. He means well enough, but he means well
primarily for himself. It takes both friend and bride, working
together, each for the other and jointly for Bassanio, to bring
about a transformation in the young man, and it takes all of

five acts to do it in. The reconciliation of truth and mercy whereby they achieve their aim does not seriously involve Shylock. To be sure, he provides the contextual occasion for that reconciliation, but the reconciliation itself is between Antonio and Portia; and the focus of the reconciliation is in Bassanio and for his sake.

Criticism has struggled with Bassanio for a long time, the problem being to justify the interest that Antonio and Portia take in him. So far the best explanations have said in effect that, since Portia and Antonio find him worthy, he must somehow surely be worthy. That is, they take Bassanio on faith. This is undoubtedly part of the answer, but it needs amplification. In the beginning Bassanio appears to his saviors to be worth saving, not because he has done anything to deserve saving, but because he bears within him their own image. This reason is mildly embarrassing to Portia, who sums it up beautifully in the passage already quoted in which she tells Lorenzo that she loves Antonio because, being Bassanio's friend, he must be like Bassanio and therefore like herself. But, she adds modestly, "This comes too near the praising of myself, / Therefore no more of it." Her reason, however, has also been represented symbolically in the last casket scene, in which Bassanio, moved more by plainness than by eloquence, chooses lead and finds Portia's picture. In the *Gesta* version which Shakespeare seems to have used, the inscription on the leaden casket reads, "Who so chooseth me, shall finde that God hath disposed." Shakespeare has replaced this inscription with one that brings Bassanio's motive in choosing into line with his supporters' motive in giving him the opportunity to choose: "Who chooseth me must give and hazard all he hath." The point to be noticed is that Bassanio here hazards nothing that is his own. Until he opens the casket, he faces the possibility that he will not gain, but there is never for a moment the possibility that he will lose anything more than the right to marry another (a risk that all the choosers face). He has nothing really to lose. What he does show is an instinct for the kind of sacrifice that Portia and

Antonio have demonstrated. He rejects rightly "what many men desire" and (with good sense) "as much as he deserves"; he chooses, without knowing what it means to choose it, the only course that can make him an inhabitant of Belmont. To this choice the necessary sequel is Bassanio's coming to full knowledge through proof, and for that Shakespeare developed the detail of the rings.

The doubling of the rings in *The Merchant of Venice* is simply the natural consequence of Shakespeare's adding Gratiano as a double for Bassanio. Other departures from the ring business in *Il Pecorone* are more significant. One interesting bit is his addition of Portia's request for Antonio's gloves. "I'll wear them for your sake," she says appropriately; for Antonio, unlike his prototype in the Italian story, proceeds to Belmont to enjoy a spiritual bond with the lady, not a betrothal to her maid-in-waiting. Bassanio, like Gianetto in *Il Pecorone*, is asked to give up his ring, and like Gianetto he refuses on the ground that his wife gave it to him. The differences here are two. Gianetto in refusing speaks eloquently of his love for his wife ("I love her better than I love myself. . . . I would not exchange her for any woman in the world"), yet he gives up the ring without any outside prompting (the bondsman is not even present) in apparent recognition of the supreme obligation that he has to the savior of his friend. Bassanio, free and clear, recognizes no supreme obligation. He would give a present of three thousand ducats, but he is by no means prepared to give and hazard all he has until Antonio shames him into it by saying, "Let his deservings and my love withal / Be valued 'gainst your wife's commandment." Worse still, he gives no indication that he cherishes the ring as anything more than a pledge of his newly acquired wealth:

> Good sir, this ring was given me by my wife;
> And when she put it on, she made me vow
> That I should neither sell nor give nor lose it.

> (IV.i.441-443)

Portia's reply is precise and to the point: "That 'scuse serves many men to save their gifts." The important point, however, is that he does surrender the ring. Nevill Coghill, in defending the conversion of Shylock as an act of mercy, comments, "Mercy has triumphed over justice, even if the way of mercy is a hard way."[18] He might have said something like this about Bassanio with equal propriety. Bassanio comes into his reward in the hardest possible way. He gives up his old nature with diffidence and pain. He is among those elect who make it to the table only because they are pushed.

At the table, however, the feast is the same for everybody, and Bassanio takes his seat at it, with his eyes, for the first time, wide open. When Portia charges him with his sin, which properly motivated would have been no sin at all, he shows an understanding of honor and gratitude that were completely lacking at the time of the event:

> I was enforc'd to send it after him;
> I was beset with shame and courtesy;
> My honour would not let ingratitude
> So much besmear it.
>
> (V.i.216-219)

Most important of all, however, is his recognition of what it is that justifies his seat at Belmont:

> *Bass.* Portia, forgive me this enforced wrong;
> And in the hearing of these many friends
> I swear to thee, even by thine own fair eyes,
> Wherein I see myself—
> *Por.*   Mark you but that!
> In both my eyes he doubly sees himself,
> In each eye, one. Swear by your double self,
> And there's an oath of credit.
>
> (240-246)

And instantly Bassanio complies, swearing by his true "double self" the oath that cannot be broken:

> Pardon this fault, and by my soul I swear
> I never more will break an oath with thee.
>
> (247-248)

Beyond this Bassanio cannot go, and Antonio steps in with a reminder that his sacrifice for Bassanio is as eternal as his friendship:

> I once did lend my body for his wealth,
> Which, but for him that had your husband's ring,
> Had quite miscarried. I dare be bound again,
> My soul upon the forfeit, that your lord
> Will never more break faith advisedly.
>
> (249-253)

"Then," says Portia, tying the whole matter up, "you shall be his surety," and she returns the ring to her husband. Bassanio, having acknowledged both agents of his redemption, his friend and his bride, is at last entitled to wear it.

Critics who feel that Shylock is the best thing in *The Merchant of Venice* are not likely to be patient with an interpretation that dismisses him as a "contextual occasion"; yet this phrase was not intended to imply that Shylock is merely incidental or peripheral to the main business of the play. In many respects Shylock is the most fully developed "character" in it; and he is certainly more credible than any of the other usurers and Jews who figure in analogous bond stories. If his ability as a literary creation to survive means anything, it is fair to say that he is the most credible literary Jew of all. Behind him lies the tangle of dead convention that scholars have been at great pains to unravel. He has in him much of the Devil of the *Processus Belial* and the moralized version of the bond story in the *Gesta Romanorum*. He is also the despised Jewish usurer of Mediterranean fable and drama that we encounter directly in *Il Pecorone* and at at least one remove in Marlowe's *Jew of Malta*. He is certainly the comic villain, curiously compounded of a thousand prejudices, legends, stage devices, and straggling

bits of information and misinformation, that Professor Stoll
has presented to us in his lively essay on that subject.[14] In
addition to all these things, Shylock is a human being. It is
irrelevant to suggest, as Professor Stoll has done, that all his lines
can be played for comedy or for an unsympathetic response from
the audience. The same thing is true of Hamlet and Macbeth,
but we come at such conclusions by asking the wrong question.
The question to ask about any dramatic character is, what
interpretations will he legitimately and consistently bear? It is
unfair to Shylock, to say nothing of Shakespeare, to limit him to
the response that an Elizabethan actor might have got from an
Elizabethan audience. For one thing, The Merchant of Venice
is a poem first and a sociological document afterward, if at all.
For another, we, with all our scholarship, can never be absolutely
sure what the Elizabethan response was. The text, however, is
always with us, and the text affords us a Shylock that is beyond
question in many ways human and sympathetic. Moreover, the
traditions that Elizabethans inherited about Jews, about whom
they knew very little from direct experience, give ample reason
to suppose that they as much as any people had very good
grounds for accepting, certainly under the guidance of a con-
vincing playwright like Shakespeare, a serious, complex, and
dignified portrayal of the Jew.

The Elizabethans' primary acquaintance with the Jew was
through Scripture, and the traditions of Scriptural interpretation
which they inherited required them to look at the Jew in two
ways. In the first way, the Jew was the crucifier of Jesus, the
historical fulfillment of the Satanic type Cain, who slew the
spotless Abel. He therefore represented a race to be feared,
despised, and rejected. In another way, thanks largely to St.
Paul's historical interpretation of Christianity, the Jew was
representative of a race to be redeemed. St. Paul's view of the
Jewish race, developed at length in the tenth and eleventh
chapters of Romans, credits the Jew with a "zeal of God, but
not according to knowledge" (Romans x.2). They are a "dis-
obedient and gainsaying people," under correction, not damna-

tion. Some (among whom he includes himself) are not even under that, having seen and acknowledged the Messiah on their own. For the rest, "As concerning the gospel, they are enemies for your sakes: but as touching the election, they are beloved for the fathers' sakes. For the gifts and calling of God are without repentance. For as ye in times past have not believed God, yet have now obtained mercy through their unbelief: Even so have these also now not believed, that through your mercy they also may obtain mercy. For God hath concluded them all in unbelief that he might have mercy upon all" (Romans xi.28-32). It was this way of looking at the Jew, emphasized in the writing and teaching of three generations of English reformers, that had most to do with the return of the Jews to England under Cromwell; and it was this way that made it possible for Elizabethan audiences to see in Shylock a devilish yet thoroughly human creature, on his way in spite of himself, at the end of Act IV, to the baptismal font. The Elizabethans said and wrote a great many uncharitable things about Jews; but, inconsistent as they may have been, they were not necessarily hypocrites at heart. The reader who finds it difficult to square Antonio's demand that Shylock turn Christian with his previous railing upon him as a misbeliever, calling him cutthroat dog, and spitting upon his Jewish gabardine should look carefully at John Foxe's sermon at the baptizing of a Jew, cited earlier in this study.[15] There Foxe, taking his text from the eleventh chapter of Romans, stresses Paul's view that all Israel will eventually be saved, but he also points out that modern Jews, in addition to being descendants of the ones who crucified Jesus, are typological fulfillments of the murderer of Abel, the betrayer of Joseph, the contemner of Moses, the slayer of the Paschal lamb, and the detractors of King David.[16] The thing that makes Shakespeare's Jew difficult to interpret is that he cannot be reduced satisfactorily to conform to any single, simple Elizabethan attitude. He is the complete picture of Jewry in history according to St. Paul—the blind, stumbling Israelite, whose fall is "the riches of the world."

It is in this sense that Shylock is the contextual occasion of Bassanio's coming to Belmont. He is the near-perfect symbolic representation of the historical context, specific and general, in which man's salvation was achieved. From the Christian point of view, Israel, as the Jews understood it, had to be repudiated in order that Israel, as it really is, might be saved. As St. Paul put it, "For if the casting away of them be the reconciling of the world, what shall the receiving of them be, but life from the dead?" (Romans xi.15). As the play ends, Israel has not yet been received at Belmont, but he is on his way. Jessica, who by her very name suggests that part of Israel which St. Paul called "a remnant according to the election of grace" (Romans xi.5)[17] and who, in any event, is a Jewish wife sanctified by her believing husband,[18] has already taken up residence there, there to be instructed by Lorenzo:

> Sit, Jessica. Look how the floor of heaven
> Is thick inlaid with patines of bright gold.
> There's not the smallest orb which thou behold'st
> But in his motion like an angel sings,
> Still quiring to the young-ey'd cerubims.
> Such harmony is in immortal souls;
> But whilst this muddy vesture of decay
> Doth grossly close it in, we cannot bear it.
>
> (V.i.58-65)

Some critics have been disturbed by Jessica's gaiety in Belmont and feel that she ought to show some signs of remorse at having left her father; but such readers need to be reminded that the Shylock she left was an unregenerate Shylock, whose house, with the departure of the "merry devil" Launcelot, was shortly to become an unrelieved hell. What remorse she felt, she felt before she left:

> Alack, what heinous sin is it in me
> To be asham'd to be my father's child!
> But though I am a daughter to his blood,

I am not to his manners. O Lorenzo,
If thou keep promise, I shall end this strife,
Become a Christian and thy loving wife.

(II.iii.16-21)

Upon leaving she took no grief with her, only the clothes
upon her back and a dowry that was modest in comparison
with the fortune she was heiress to. We tend to forget that
Jessica by her sudden leavetaking hazarded as much as anyone
else in the play. For the sake of Lorenzo, whom she had to
take on faith, she gave up wealth, history, and a religion, asking
only his love in return. The miracle for her is that she got, not
only Lorenzo's love, but all the things she had thrown away,
transformed and with interest. It is no wonder that for this
Jessica, for all Jesses and Jessicas, Belmont should be a heaven
for rejoicing—for laughter, music, candlelight, young love, and
dancing—where even the sinful device of usury finds its divine
analog. If one should object that there is still human flesh in
Belmont, that men behave like men there and women like
women, and that therefore we do not honor properly either our
love of life in the play or our love of Christ by bringing the two
things together, we might suggest a speech of Portia's:

A substitute shines brightly as a king
Until a king be by: and then his state
Empties itself, as doth an inland brook
Into the main of waters.

(V.i.94-97)

It is not the business of religion to transform our impression
of this play; it is the play that should transform our impression
of religion, which, until it is fully known, is well served by such
substitutes as this. Puritan piety is an admirable thing, but it
too is a substitute; and even the blackest Puritan knows in his
heart that Saul's daughter was wrong when she scorned David
for dancing before the ark.

Four

PRINCE HAL AND THE EPHESIANS

*A*T THE CONCLUSION of his famous "I know you all" soliloquy in *1 Henry IV*, Prince Hal promises the audience, "I'll so offend, to make offence a skill / Redeeming time when men think least I will" (I.ii.239-240). To almost any reader the phrase "redeeming time" must seem an apt one, but to readers familiar with the Bible it has especial power, suggesting possibly Colossians iv.5, "Walk in wisdom toward them that are without, redeeming the time," and almost certainly Ephesians v.15-16, "See then that ye walk circumspectly, not as fools, but as wise, Redeeming the time, because the days are evil." Of the translations of Scripture that Shakespeare is likely to have known, only the Great Bible of 1539 substitutes another phrase here ("avoydyng occasyon"). The Geneva New Testament of 1557, which seems to have been the version that Shakespeare knew best, has "Redemyng the tyme," as has the Rheims version of 1582. As far as I can tell, the phrase does not turn up significantly elsewhere except in Shakespeare's play; so it is reasonable to suppose that the appearance of it there has value as an allusion. Reading further in Ephesians with the *Henry IV* plays in mind amply confirms that supposition. In fact, reading the plays with Ephesians in mind almost gives one the illusion that Shakespeare set out to confirm St. Paul's epistle. The plays remain, as Shakespeare's plays invariably remain, things of solid flesh, blood, and earth; but they also prove to have the mysterious power to enrich the meaning of whatever Shakespeare has allowed them to touch. One hesitates to say which is more handsomely served by this particular contact, Shakespeare or St. Paul; but fortunately one does not have to say. The purpose of this chapter is simply to describe the contact. As preliminary to that we need to consider briefly what holds these plays together and what keeps them apart.

In any consideration of the unity of Shakespeare's *Henry IV* plays Falstaff comes early to mind as one of the great forces binding those two plays together; so doubtless he is, but it is easy to forget that he never stands at the true center of them, as Hal does. Seeing Falstaff in his proper place and proportion means never losing sight of his primary function in both plays, that of clown. He is a special kind of clown, to be sure, more arresting in some ways than any other character in either play and probably more diverting to us than such real-life clowns as Tarlton and Kemp were to Shakespeare's original audiences. J. Dover Wilson has described Falstaff's inheritance, not exhaustively by any means, by writing that he is heir to the Vice and inheritor of the functions and attributes of the Lord of Misrule, the Fool, the Buffoon, and the Jester.[1] We can see all this conspicuously displayed in Falstaff's repartee with Hal and in his seriocomic "play extempore," to say nothing of his playful threats to all his friends, threatening to beat Hal out of the kingdom with a dagger of lath (*1 Henry IV* II.iv.150-154), threatening to have ballads made upon all his companions at Gadshill "and sung to filthy tunes" (*1 Henry IV* II.ii.47-50), threatening to advertise by ballad his triumph over Sir John Coleville of the Dale if Prince John will not give him proper credit for it (*2 Henry IV* IV.iii.51-59). "I will devise matter enough out of this Shallow," he says at the beginning of the last act of *2 Henry IV*, "to keep Prince Harry in continual laughter the wearing out of six fashions." So it goes. These touches and many more like them all serve to underscore Falstaff's conception of his relation to Prince Hal, which, to put it euphemistically, is that of "companion to the Prince," or, more plainly, that of court fool and jester. In Part I Falstaff embodies in adult flesh a youthful attitude toward the world which at best can serve only occasionally as the mode of an adult's existence. The sad part about Falstaff is that he continually—with charm in Part I and with increasing bitterness in Part II—urges this attitude upon Hal as an all-sufficient one. The best one can say about it is that the Falstaffian attitude deserves to be retained and modified into something more appropriate to Hal's imminent adult station. Hal, still immature and hence unable to make the necessary modifications in that symbol of his greener youth, is driven eventually to try eradicating it altogether, at great risk and with permanent damage to his own moral and spiritual life. Yet even here, where Hal's defective spirit makes the rejection of Falstaff seem almost like vindication for the old man, it is Hal's loss in rejecting Falstaff that distresses us rather than Falstaff's failure to achieve the position of scandalous preferment that he has vainly and pathetically grasped for.

Hal, in fact, holds together the three plays that involve him somewhat better than Falstaff holds together his two. If the reader is willing to make a few reservations, he may find it enlightening to take these three plays as three stages in a young man's struggle toward self-redemption. He does not even have to imagine that Shakespeare planned to do something like this in advance. With the rough outline of the old *Famous Victories* in mind, Shakespeare may have begun simply by projecting a play or plays on the subject of Hal's "coming of age," with perhaps a final play on Hal's "full flowering" contemplated for a projected *Henry* V. The characteristically ironic and near-tragic developments which begin to suggest themselves almost as soon as the first play starts may easily represent Shakespeare's own gradual growth in understanding as well as Hal's. They certainly suggest an honest reluctance to wind up anything with an easy "happily ever after." For example, the tentative reformation of Hal in Part I, though sufficient as it stands to permit a plausible ending of that play, nevertheless leaves one slightly curious about what the boy is likely to do at the next invitation to carouse in Eastcheap; and Part II, though it relieves our uneasiness about Hal's moral decisiveness, raises the even more serious question of Hal's loss of humanity, which continues to haunt us throughout most of *Henry V*. Similarly, the fairytale ending to that last play, admittedly almost a necessity for a play about a young man whom history had given only two more years to live, hardly conceals that even at the end of the story the young man still has a great deal to learn, both about being a king and about being a man. This is probably the main reason why *Henry V* sometimes fails to please us; but it behooves us to be grateful for the artistic honesty that compelled Shakespeare to leave it as he left the others, with something still to be desired.

Taken separately, as one really should take them, each of these plays has its own unity. The thing that holds *1 Henry IV* together is Hal's attempt to define for himself, in spite of the conflicting claims of his father, Falstaff, and young Hotspur, the proper sphere of honor. On this matter of defining the sphere of honor, the King and Hotspur are pretty much in agreement; the only difference between them is that it is to the King's advantage that Hal measure up to their common code, to Hotspur's advantage that Hal fall short. Hal, though apparently seeing the limitations of the code they would measure him by, realizes that he must meet that code on its own terms before he can ever begin to transcend it. He further realizes that by so doing he must necessarily repudiate the easy but cynical alternative (What is honor?) proposed by Falstaff. Hal's confrontation of these views ends in his brilliantly successful encounter with Hotspur at Shrewsbury, and the degree of order restored to England and generated within himself is the measure of his achievement in that action. The whole action of Part I, therefore, can be described as a movement toward order—not just any order, but an order that is both politically acceptable and humane, one that avoids equally the timid conventionality of the King's conception and the deplorable anarchy of Falstaff's.

We can best see the plot of the play as a series of attempts to reach or at least to define this goal of order. Each new attempt is marked by some kind of ritual or ceremonial occasion which symbolizes the order that seems at that moment to be in view; yet with each new symbol of order some new source of disorder also appears, interrupting the ritual and thwarting the completion of the action. For example, in Act I, Scene i, we find the King on the point of making a formal pronouncement of peace to his nobles; but scarcely has he got the words out of his mouth when Westmoreland interrupts with news that rebellion has broken out all over again. A similar ritual occasion in the third scene of that act gets interrupted by Hotspur's defiance of the King's authority. The "play extempore" in Act II, which to be sure is a parody of a formal occasion that has not at that point taken place, looks forward with double vision to Hal's harmonious reconciliation with the King and to an increasingly bitter estrangement from Falstaff. Meanwhile Hotspur, who has achieved an order of sorts among his band of friends and allies, is proceeding to sow seeds of additional disorder for himself and his cause in an explosive exchange with Owen Glendower (III.i). Thus, when we come to the middle of the play, we realize that neither the King nor Hotspur has succeeded in achieving much of that permanent order they so desperately seek; it remains for Prince Hal, who, unknown to any but himself and us, is also committed to the restoration of order, to articulate in his encounter with his father (III.ii) a promise of the only kind of order that can possibly have any lasting value for himself, for the King, and for England. The King gets in this climactic scene what he has been praying for, but he gets it on Hal's initiative and on Hal's terms. When Hal, with perfect decorum, has successfully completed the ritual combat with Hotspur, not even Falstaff's parody of that combat—a baffling irrelevancy to the sober-minded Prince John but not to Hal—can prevent the final realization of order symbolized in the judgment scene at the end of the play.

To define the sphere of honor, then, and to achieve a semblance of order at both the personal and the national levels—these are two ways of formulating the action 1 Henry IV. The third way, which is the primary concern of this chapter, may have developed along with the play as the result of that single happy allusion to a passage in Ephesians. At any rate, that one early allusion helps us to see a great many more to the same epistle, so that in the end we have a new formulation of the action of 1 Henry IV which allows us more confidently than ever before to consider the two parts of Henry IV as a meaningful whole.

Quoting only a few of the highlights of St. Paul's exhortation to the Ephesians should make clear the striking applicability of that epistle to Shakespeare's 1 Henry IV:

in time past ye walked according to the course of this world, according to the prince of the power of the air, the spirit that now worketh in the children of disobedience; Among whom also we all had our conversation in times past in the lusts of the flesh, fulfilling the desires of the flesh and of the mind; and were by nature the children of wrath, even as others (II.2-3). . . . I, therefore, the prisoner of the Lord, beseech you that ye walk worthy of the vocation wherewith ye are called (IV.1). . . . That we henceforth be no more children, tossed to and fro, and carried about with every wind of doctrine, by the sleight of men, and cunning craftiness, whereby they lie in wait to deceive (IV.14). . . . That ye put off concerning the former conversation the old man, which is corrupt according to the deceitful lusts; and be renewed in the spirit of your mind (IV.22-23). . . . putting away lying (IV.25). . . . Let him that stole steal no more (IV.28). . . . fornication, and all uncleanness, or covetousness, let it not be once named among you, as becometh saints; Neither filthiness, nor foolish talking, nor jesting (V.3-4). . . . See then that ye walk circumspectly, not as fools, but as wise, Redeeming the time, because the days are evil (V.15-16). . . . And be

not drunk with wine, wherein is excess; but be filled with the
Spirit (v.18).

All these passages have been set down here because they suggest
in some way Shakespeare's *Henry IV* plays; but one would have
to admit, I think, that they also give, as far as they go, a fair
idea of the general development of St. Paul's epistle. They make
it clear that the kind of order Paul was urging Christians to
exhibit in their lives is the very order which is being sought in
all three of these plays: children obeying fathers, fathers
respecting children, husbands caring for wives, wives submitting
dutifully to husbands, and servants obeying their masters. And
from the achievement of this order the Christian can look
forward to achieving the final thing to be sought, strength to
resist evil, whereupon he may be ready to put on "the whole
armour of God" and "wrestle not against flesh and blood, but
against principalities, against powers, against the rulers of the
darkness of this world, against spiritual wickedness in high
places" (vi.12). Before the achievement of either Christian
order or spiritual strength, however, must come redemption of
the time. This is Hal's immediate objective and his partial
accomplishment in *1 Henry IV*.

His objective in *2 Henry IV* is similar, but it takes there a
slightly different form. The conflict in that play develops from
a tiny seed that sprouted early in Part I when Falstaff made a
mildly rebellious response to Hal's first stirrings toward respectability: "If sack and sugar be a fault, God help the wicked. . . .
Banish plump Jack, and banish all the world" (II.iv.516-527).
At this point Falstaff was only potentially Hal's antagonist, but
his use of the word *banish* implied an unfortunate ultimatum:
Hal had either to embrace the old man who lies, cheats, steals,
drinks to excess, and talks lewdly, or banish that man, reject him
outright. Had Falstaff been another Peto, Bardolph, or Poins,
such an ultimatum would have caused little concern; but Falstaff
is that most monstrous and most human of paradoxes, the full-
fledged sinner who is nevertheless sweet, kind, true, valiant,

and—incidentally—old. By pointing to these claims he manages to put Hal's newly acquired morality to the test. Thus the great question created in Part I and carried over for full development in Part II is not another high-flown query about honor or order but the simple, practical question, "What shall we do with our fat brother Falstaff?"

Hal's answers to that question are not the same as Falstaff's. They include, to use the terms of Ephesians, redeeming the old man as part of the corrupt times; only as a desperate alternative do they include casting him off entirely; and they do not include embracing him as he is. Almost from the moment when he decides to turn toward maturity, therefore, Hal begins to try to salvage his fat knight to be a companion at court and a link with his youth. His first attempt consists of giving his friend a "charge of foot" (III.iii.208-209). Falstaff's reply to this is typical of his resistance to all such efforts: "I would it had been of horse. Where shall I find one that can steal well?" His words to the Hostess after Hal has gone follow the same general line, "Rare words! brave world! Hostess, my breakfast, come. O, I could wish this tavern were my drum." Falstaff, of course, has no intention of fulfilling the trust about to be placed in him. He misuses the King's press damnably and gaily admits as much. Later, on the battlefield, when Hal asks to borrow his sword, he offers instead the loan of his "pistol," which turns out to be the inevitable bottle of sack, accompanied by an impromptu quip, " 'Tis hot, 'tis hot. There's that will sack a city" (V.iii.55-56). As the play draws to a close his anger mounts. He pays no attention to Hal's tenderly sentimental observations on his supposed death, he chooses the most shocking means available to show his contempt for Hal's victory over Percy and his formal code of honor, and he is not even moved by Hal's offer to lie in his behalf (V.iv.161-162). "I'll follow, as they say, for reward," is the beginning of his final comment, which continues, "He that rewards me, God reward him! If I do grow great, I'll grow less; for I'll purge, and leave sack, and live cleanly as a nobleman should do."

The very thought of growing less as he is made to "grow great" creates the angry Falstaff that we see in Part II. Some critics have mistakenly tried to write him off here as a mere boasting coward. The report in Part II is that, in spite of his scandalous behavior at Shrewsbury, he did "some good" there (I.ii.70-72), and throughout much of that play he continues actively to serve the King, though severed from Prince Hal. Here it is that Falstaff's determination not to grow great, not to abandon the role of jesting companion that he feels is his prerogative, not to be soberly wise as kings are, becomes the adamantine rock upon which Hal's intention proves itself and is at length humbled. The Hostess with more overt cause to reject her fat man than Prince Hal ever had, and with considerably more insight than Hal, declares out of Falstaff's hearing, "I have known thee these twenty-nine years, come peascod time; but an honester and truer-hearted man . . ." (II.iv.413-414). And the rebel Sir John Coleville says simply, "I think you are Sir John Falstaff, and in that thought yield me" (IV.iii.18-19). This is the man whom Hal mistakenly tries to flatter into conventional respectability by conventionally dignifying his claim to knighthood. "If the Prince put thee into my service for any other reason than to set me off," says Falstaff to the page thus assigned to him, "why then I have no judgment. Thou whoreson mandrake, thou art fitter to be worn in my cap than to wait at my heels" (I.ii.14-18). The Prince's efforts are doomed to failure; but his motive is clear, as is the significance of the terms in which he sets it forth. For these terms constitute a second binding link with Paul's epistle to the Ephesians, stronger than the first link but, largely because of a gloss common in popular editions, seldom regarded.

In Part II, Hal, newly returned to London and on the point of going in search of Falstaff, says to Bardolph and the young page, after some preliminary banter, "Well, thus we play the fools with the time, and the spirits of the wise sit in the clouds and mock us. Is your master here in London?" The exchange continues (italics are mine):

Bard. Yea, my lord.

Prince. Where sups he? Doth the *old* boar feed in the *old* frank?

Bard. At the *old* place, my lord, in East-cheap.

Prince. What company?

Page. Ephesians, my lord, of the old church.

Prince. Sup any women with him?

Page. None, my lord, but *old* Mistress Quickly and Mistress Doll Tearsheet.

(II.ii.158-167)

Ephesians, the glosses commonly tell us, means here "boon companions." But this is only repeating what the N.E.D. says, and the N.E.D. lists this use of the term as the first in the language in this sense, the only other being that in *Merry Wives of Windsor* IV.v.19. "Boon companions" they certainly are; but the term suggests that they are also companions whose lives need some reforming, just as the Ephesians or Lacedaemonians or whomever Paul's epistle was addressed to might have been expected to need the admonitions that appear in the Epistle to the Ephesians. Moreover, Falstaff's friends are not merely Ephesians but "Ephesians of the *old* church," that is, of the unregenerate. For we are dealing with "old" in the sense that it is used in Ephesians IV.22, "That yet put off concerning the former conversation the old man, which is corrupt according to the deceitful lusts"; and as it is used in Romans VI.6, "our old man is crucified with him, that the body of sin might be destroyed"; and as it is used in Colossians III.9-11, "Lie not one to another, seeing that ye have put off the old man with his deeds; And have put on the new man, which is renewed in knowledge after the image of him that created him." It is the old man, the unregenerate, that is to be either transformed or repudiated here; and St. Paul speaks of this metaphorical man in a tone that makes him quite proper to serve as an analogy for the old boar in the old frank, Ephesian of the old church, and friend to old Mistress Quickly.

We should keep in mind, too, that it was probably Shake-speare who made Falstaff old. Oldcastle died a martyr and, as Jockey in the *Famous Victories of Henry V*, had never been old. Neither was the Oldcastle of the anonymous *Life of Sir John Oldcastle* old, as the prolog to that play makes clear:

> It is no pamperd glutton we present,
> Nor aged Councellor to youthfull sinne,
> But one, whose vertue shone aboue the rest,
> A valiant Martyr and a vertuous peere.

One likes to think that Falstaff's age came about accidentally as the result of Prince Hal's obvious pun in *1 Henry IV* on his friend's original name ("As the honey of Hybla, my old lad of the castle"—I.ii.46-47). His age, as he tells it in the next act, is "some fifty, or, by'r lady, inclining to threescore" (II.iv.466-467). As the Prince, acting in the person of the King, describes it, "There is a devil haunts thee in the likeness of an old fat man" (II.iv.492-493). To this, Falstaff replies, "That he is old, the more the pity, his white hairs do witness it; but that he is, saving your reverence, a whoremaster, that I utterly deny. If sack and sugar be a fault, God help the wicked! If to be old and merry be a sin, then many an old host that I know is damn'd" (II.iv.513-519). By the end of Act II Falstaff is definitely estab-lished as aged.

It is only in Part II that Falstaff's age develops into such a symbol of the reprehensible part of him that he himself would try to deny it. "You that are old," he says to the Lord Chief Justice, "consider not the capacities of us that are young; you do measure the heat of our livers with the bitterness of your galls; and we that are in the vanguard of our youth, I must confess are wags too" (I.ii.196-200). The Chief Justice's reply is devastating:

> Do you set down your name in the scroll of
> youth, that are written down old with all the
> characters of age: Have you not a moist eye, a

dry hand, a yellow cheek, a white beard, a
decreasing leg, an increasing belly? Is not your
voice broken, your wind short, your chin
double, your wit single, and every part about
you blasted with antiquity? and will you yet
call yourself young? Fie, fie, Sir John!

(I.ii.201-209)

Falstaff's defense echoes the wording if not the sense of the
admonition in Colossians III.16 ("Let the word of Christ dwell
in you richly in all wisdom; teaching and admonishing one
another in psalms and hymns and spiritual songs, singing with
grace in your hearts to the Lord") and in Ephesians v.18-19
("And be not drunk with wine, wherein is excess; but be filled
with the Spirit; Speaking to yourselves in psalms and hymns and
spiritual songs, singing and making melody in your heart to the
Lord"). He says: "My lord, I was born about three of the clock
in the afternoon, with a white head and something a round
belly. For my voice, I have lost it with hallooing and singing
of anthems. To approve my youth further, I will not. The
truth is, I am only old in judgement and understanding." Youth,
whatever else it may be, is symbolic of virtue. No one questions
that here. It is only the proof of youth that is in question; and
Falstaff knows only too well the terms in which spiritual youth
must be claimed. But the Chief Justice has denied him that
kind of youth: "Now the Lord lighten thee!" he says, "Thou
art a great fool" (II.i.208-209). Prince Hal, as we have seen,
has called him the "old board of Eastcheap," and the page
pronounced him one with the "old church." Even Doll Tearsheet has said, "Thou whoreson little tidy Bartholomew boarpig,
when wilt thou leave fighting o' days and foining o' nights, and
begin to patch up thine old body for heaven?" (II.iv.250-253).
At last Falstaff himself is forced to admit, "I am old, I am old"
(II.iv.294).

At this point the Prince steps forth to draw the old man out
by the ears and, technically at least, succeeds. He has already

made up his mind that Falstaff and his companions are obdurate
and persistent (II.ii.49-50), that he, Hal, suffers in common
esteem by being "engraffed" to such companions, and that any
traffic with such companions is simply "playing fool with the
time" (II.ii.153-154). He has now only to catch Falstaff in the
appearance of "wilful abuse"—something that turns out to be so
embarrassingly easy to do that even Hal seems glad to find an
excuse to let the matter drop. There is therefore no legal action
—only the rejection of a friend in the name of honor, duty, and
morality: "I feel me much to blame / So idly to profane the
precious time," he says. "Falstaff, good night" (II.iv.390-395).
And there the opposition stands, without hope of reconcilement.
Between this and the final "Fall to thy knees, old man. . . .
How ill white hairs become a fool and jester," there is no
development of the relationship between these two. There is,
however, a great development in our understanding of that
relationship.

For one thing, we see from the start that the Prince has
misgivings about what he is doing. His question to Poins, "Doth
it not show vilely in me to desire small beer?" has been followed
by "Belike . . . my appetite was not princely got" (II.ii.7-12).
Falstaff gets to the root of Hal's trouble when he observes, "His
grace says that which his flesh rebels against" (II.iv.379-380).
Hal, long before he rejects Falstaff, has rejected—or refused to
face squarely—a part of himself. The audience is not asked to
believe with Hal that he was merely dallying with something
he fully intended to put by, as he himself said in the "I know
you all" soliloquy in Part I; nor is it asked to accept Warwick's
suggestion that Hal was merely studying evil as a prince in
order to know it better as a king (2 Henry IV IV.iv.67-69).
Falstaff, for all his villainy and pride (and he has much of both),
stands as a great symbol of common humanity in Part II as in
Part I. He is therefore the "old man" in the sense that he
incorporates many human failings that Hal must learn to
recognize in himself and reject, and he is at the same time the
old man who is still full of life and the love of life and has much

to teach the young Hal about both. Casting Falstaff off and accepting Falstaff are not alternatives between which Hal must choose; he must in all conscience and honesty do something of both. He must "cast off the old man" in the sense that he must recognize and attempt to correct the ancient penchant for sin within himself as well as in those about him; but he must also in charity recognize his own participation with Falstaff in common flesh and accept his own fleshliness as well as that of his friend. Ideally his attitude should be that of 1 Corinthians XII, which includes a recognition that "much more those members of the body, which seem to be more feeble, are necessary"; and his emphasis should be that of Ephesians IV.16, whereby the "whole body fitly joined together and compacted by that which every joint supplieth, according to the effectual working in the measure of every part, maketh increase of the body unto the edifying of itself in love." The truth about Falstaff is aptly summarized near the beginning of 2 *Henry IV* in the opening exchange of Act I, Scene ii:

> *Fal.* Sirrah, you giant, what says the doctor
> to my water?
> *Page.* He said, sir, the water itself was good
> healthy water but, for the party that ow'd it,
> he might have moe diseases than he knew for.

Shortly thereafter Falstaff makes his famous boast: "The brain of this foolish-compounded clay, man, is not able to invent anything that intends to laughter more than I invent or is invented on me. I am not only witty in myself, but the cause that wit is in other men" (I.ii.8-11). Diseases he certainly has; but he also has his claim to uniqueness, to being essential and indispensable. And Hal's unfortunate impulse to condemn the whole man rather than struggle through the difficult course of trying to redeem what is basically good in him is as much the mark of an incipient puritanism as it is of immaturity. Admittedly, he does make a show of trying to remake Falstaff,

but he wants to remake him by ignoring all that makes him
Falstaff in the first place. It is no wonder that Falstaff rebels.

Throughout the rest of Part II, in spite of some unpleasant
things that serve to remind us of Falstaff at his worst, there is
evidence of a serious effort on Shakespeare's part to make Falstaff
more sympathetic than ever. Even his selection of conscriptees,
outrageous on principle, is not without merit; it suggests more
than anything else Gideon's selection of a band to serve the
Lord. Falstaff's "Give me the spirit, Master Shallow" (III.ii.278)
is by no means pure irony. Who in honesty would prefer
Mouldy's constant care for "my old dame" or Bullcalf's "whoreson cold" to Feeble's courageous, "We owe God a death . . .
let it go which way it will, he that dies this year is quit for the
next" (III.ii.251-255)? And as for human sympathy, who does
not wince with Falstaff at the thought than Jane Nightwork,
one of his "bona robas," is "Old, old, Master Shallow" (III.ii.
219)? Or who fails to sense the pathos of "We have heard the
chimes at midnight"? There is pathos, too, in his attempts to
persuade himself that Hal has not forgotten his old friend or
his old friend's uses and pathos in his shaky attempt, as he
stands waiting for the king to ride by, to manufacture reasons
why his sweaty appearance and general breathlessness will be
most likely to please. The rejection, when it comes, hits at
that peculiar combination of the reprehensible and the lovable:

> I know thee not, old man; fall to thy prayers.
> How ill white hairs become a fool and jester!
> I have long dreamt of such a kind of man,
> So surfeit-swell'd, so old, and so profane;
> But being awak'd, I do despise my dream.

> (V.v.51-55)

Some have praised this rejection, but few love it, for it is in
no sense an act of love. There is, in fact, no evidence of love in
anything that Hal says here, no humanity, no recognition of the
beam that makes the mote recognizable. And not only has he

failed to see what is lovable in the man he is repudiating; he has reached a point of blindness where men generally are concerned. Thus at the end of *2 Henry IV* we leave Prince Hal with much to learn. In the last play in this series he does learn some of it, but not until he has known scorn, until, as king, he has known what it is to put off king's robes and wear a servant's cloak, until he has seen men weep and seen men die, and wooed a maid like any other man.

Five

TROILUS AND CRESSIDA

To SURVEY all the things that have been said about *Troilus and Cressida* would be both tedious and needless. It is enough to say that many readers have been intrigued by the play and almost as many repelled by it; for in it Shakespeare had the audacity to do what we do not often allow any playwright to do—that is, to present a tale in which the protagonist finds life both unbearable and inescapable. Troilus' fate is to go on living with nothing left to live for, and that fate is so disquietingly common that most of us derive little satisfaction from thinking about it. Hence there has been a long succession of attempts, from Dryden's time to the present, to explain the play away as something that Shakespeare wrote early, wrote only in part, wrote in sickness, wrote in anger, or perhaps wrote as idle amusement on leftover steam generated for the composition of *Hamlet*. These are undoubtedly comforting suppositions, but it is probably more honest to accept our discomfort and assume that the play means what it seems to mean. "The real problem about the play," writes Kenneth Muir, "is the failure of most critics to appreciate it."[1] We can best attack that problem by divesting ourselves of any trace of the notion that there is something inartistic or second rate about satire. The representation of human folly has as much right to literary respectability as the representation of human dignity or human idealism, folly being both more common than the other two and more likely to be genuine. Muir, who finds the play eminently praiseworthy, may be said to have begun at this point, for he takes the view that the play is in large part an exposure of what commonly passes for idealism; yet he does not see in it any repudiation of genuine human ideals or of genuine human dignity. Cressida, as he observes, may be corrupt, but she does not cancel out Rosalind or Viola, and she does not necessarily stain our mothers. One might make a similar observation about Troilus. We are compelled to recognize that his action in the play is folly and his fate disillusionment; we are also compelled to recognize, I think, that Shakespeare's representation of him is more immediately meaningful to us than his representation of larger heroes like Hamlet or Macbeth. Yet nothing in the play suggests that we are bound to be fools or that the fate of Troilus is precisely representative of what our own is likely to be. It sobers us, but it leaves us with a capacity for hope.

The Biblical allusions in *Troilus and Cressida* are neither so numerous nor so striking as those in the other plays we have considered. Moreover, they do not here readily suggest Biblical analogies with the fable. Yet there is nothing casual or accidental about them. Working as reinforcement for the network of metaphors in the play, they help to establish and define the values that are presented there. They help also to correct the view held by some readers that the play is an outpouring of personal bitterness and disillusionment, that it represents Shakespeare's denunciation of contemporary England, or of his own theatrical world, or of human nature generally. Recognizing these allusions, their Biblical context, and the way they operate within the play enables us to see that the much discussed "bitterness" of *Troilus and Cressida* is not so unrelieved as some critics have supposed.

Preparation for one of these allusions appears in Troilus' soliloquy near the end of the first scene of Act I:

> Tell me, Apollo, for thy Daphne's love,
> What Cressid is, what Pandar, and what we.
> Her bed is India; there she lies, a pearl;
> Between our Ilium and where she resides,
> Let it be call'd the wild and wand'ring flood,
> Ourself the merchant, and this sailing Pandar
> Our doubtful hope, our convoy, and our bark.

> (I.i.101-107)

The allusion itself comes into focus several scenes later when Troilus, attempting to justify the retention of Helen, resorts to some of the same terms:

> Why, she is a pearl,
> Whose price hath launch'd above a thousand ships,
> And turn'd crown'd kings to merchants.

> (II.ii.81-85)

Marlowe is probably responsible for the phrase "launch'd above a thousand ships" here, but *pearl* and *merchant* in both quotations allude to one of Jesus' parables about the kingdom of heaven, as given in Matthew xiii.45-46: "Again, the kingdom of heaven is like unto a merchant man, seeking goodly pearls: Who, when he had found one pearl of great price, went and sold all that he had, and bought it." The "pearl of great price" is almost a dead commonplace with us; and, as Richmond Noble observes, it was a commonplace with Elizabethans too.[2] It is confirmed as allusion here by its use, both times, in conjunction with *merchant*; and as allusion it makes both times an ironic comment on the situation at hand.

The pearl in Matthew's gospel has been variously interpreted as a symbol for Christ's church, for the elect, or for the kingdom within; but pretty clearly it is something worth giving up everything else in the world for.[3] The merchant there is explicitly said to be like the kingdom of heaven. Here the pearls are Cressida and Helen, two ladies whom the Elizabethans considered at best a pair of unusually glamorous whores, to be sought and bought, not figuratively but literally, by someone primarily interested in glamorous whores. The irony for Troilus is that he uses the allusion innocently, under the naive impression that Cressida is really infinitely worth seeking and Helen infinitely worth keeping. Helen, we may be sure, knows precisely where her attraction lies; and Cressida, who seems to have some inkling of the beauty of Troilus' innocence, equally recognizes her own value as that of fleshly merchandise. Her objective is to get, not to give. "That she belov'd knows nought that knows not this," she tells herself privately at one point; "Men prize the thing ungain'd more than it is. . . . Therefore this maxim out of love I teach: / Achievement is command; ungain'd, beseech" (I.ii.314-319). Pandarus, of course, from beginning to end recognizes his office as that of a "trader in the flesh"; and Paris knows that he, too, is of that breed, so that when Diomedes bitterly denounces his Helen as a whore, he can reply in the cant of merchants:

> Fair Diomed, you do as chapmen do,
> Dispraise the thing that you desire to buy;
> But we in silence hold this virtue well,—
> We'll not commend what we intend to sell.
> Here lies our way.
>
> (IV.i.75-79)

Ulysses, who is sometimes credited with giving (in his speech on degree) a lofty philosophical key to the interpretation of this play, behaves and talks as much like a merchant as any of the Trojans. Plotting with Nestor to work upon the basest part of Achilles' nature by having Ajax draw the right to fight Hector, he says:

> Let us, like merchants, show our foulest wares,
> And think, perchance, they'll sell; if not,
> The lustre of the better yet to show,
> Shall show the better.
>
> (I.iii.359-362)

Even the prophetess Cassandra recognizes the level to which men on both sides have descended and urges the course of wisdom upon her brothers in terms they seem most likely to understand. "Let us pay betimes," she pleads, "A moiety of that mass of moan to come" (II.ii.106-107).

Yet Troilus, to whose lips the metaphors of trade come most readily of all, remains, until he is finally outbidden, unaware that he actually is in a kind of trade. He can ask the question, "What is Cressid, what Pandar, and what we?" and not really understand the answers he gives to his own questions (I.i.101-107). He can shock his brother Hector with the question, "What is aught, but as 'tis valu'd?" (II.ii.52) and fail completely to recognize that his implicit repudiation of absolute value where Helen is concerned makes a mockery of the absolute value he has attributed to Cressida. "We turn not back the silks upon the merchant, / When we have spoiled them," he tells Hector, yet he fails to see how the figure might easily come to apply to his own personal situation. And he never dreams how truly he speaks when he says to Cressida on taking leave of her, "We two, that with so many thousand sighs / Did buy each other, must poorly sell ourselves / With the rude brevity and discharge of one" (IV.iv.41-43). Never, that is, until the evidence of his senses forces him to recognize that Cressida is a pearl who will glow brightly for any merchant-lover who happens to possess her; and then with undiminished naivete he repudiates all pearls and all merchantmen, leaving Pandarus to lament, "O world! world! world! thus is the poor agent despis'd!" (V.x.36-37).

This, the story of a young man's disillusionment, is Troilus' story and the story of the play, which belongs primarily to Troilus and not to Hector, Cressida, or some other. It is like the story of Prince Hal in some respects but unlike Hal's story in that the disillusionment of Troilus is never relieved. A more appropriate parallel to Troilus' story, however, exists within the play itself. It is that of Achilles, whom critics have too often been content to describe as the conventionally proud and brutal

Greek hero, untrustworthy in some ways and incorrigibly vain, doting upon a Trojan princess. Shakespeare has surely given us more than this. His Achilles, like his Troilus, is a young man who stumbles over infantile principle, who sees the relativity of other men's values but naively believes that he himself is in possession of an absolute one. Some have designated Achilles' flaw as his lustful passion for Priam's daughter Polyxena, which in Shakespeare's play helps to explain why Achilles has abstained from battle. But love for Polyxena is merely the occasion for Achilles' abstention; it does not really account for it. Achilles is wedded not to lust but to his own sense of greatness, which makes it possible for him to take liberties with military decorum that not even an Agamemnon would dare. This is why there is real pathos in that scene (III.iii) in which Achilles tries to maintain confidence in the security of his greatness against the powerful arguments of Ulysses and the railing of Thersites. He has been telling Patroclus that "greatness, once fall'n out with fortune, / Must fall out with men too"; and then he concludes, "But 'tis not so with me; / Fortune and I are friends. I do enjoy / At ample point all that I did possess" (III.iii.75-89). Even here his confidence has been slightly shaken by the snub that Agamemnon, Nestor, Menelaus, and Ajax have given him; but it disintegrates almost completely before the verbal assaults of Ulysses:

> O, let not virtue seek
> Remuneration for the thing it was;
> For beauty, wit,
> High birth, vigour of bone, desert in service,
> Love, friendship, charity, are subjects all
> To envious and calumniating Time.
> One touch of nature makes the whole world kin,
> That all, with one consent, praise new-born gawds,
> Though they are made and moulded of things past,
> And give to dust that is a little gilt
> More laud than gilt o'er-dusted.

> (III.iii.169-179)

Achilles, now rapidly approaching the point that Troilus will not reach until he has witnessed the exchange between Cressida and Diomedes, tries to make a show of assurance by ordering Patroclus to have Ajax invite Hector to visit the Greek camp; but by the time Patroclus and Thersites have finished their little playlet by way of demonstrating how the stupid peacock Ajax is likely to treat this request, his once superb confidence has been reduced to a tissue of doubts. "My mind is troubled," he says, "like a fountain stirr'd; / And I myself see not the bottom of it" (III.iii.311-312). Polyxena at this point is no part of his distress; nor does thought of her prevent his treating Hector, come to the Greek camp to fight with Ajax, with unpardonable insolence. He stares at the Trojan hero like a merchant appraising a beef —"As I would buy thee, view thee limb by limb" (IV.v.238) —for in the world as Achilles now sees it, greatness is no birthright but something to be bought periodically, as one buys meat and drink. That a letter from Queen Hecuba reminding him of his promise not to fight Hector causes him momentarily to desist in no way alters the fact that he now regards his own greatness as something to be bought by slaying Hector. He is here simply a young man honorable enough to keep a promise —"Fall Greeks; fall fame; honour go or stay" (V.i.48)—and Hector is temporarily spared. A few hours later he is a young man honorable enough to avenge the death of a friend, and Hector dies. In all this swift rush of events Achilles is fundamentally neither lustful nor brutish; he is merely disenchanted. It is disenchantment that has brought him into the conflict as it has also brought Troilus. At the end of the play there is scarcely a hair's difference between Achilles' "Now, Troy, sink down!" and Troilus' "You vile abominable tents / Thus proudly pight upon our Phrygian plains."

If consideration of the play were to stop here, there might be some justification for calling it inconclusive. From the point of view of Troilus and Achilles the world is without real values. War is a meaningless business of buying and selling. Loving is usually a matter of buying and selling too. One gets what one can afford; one has what one can afford to keep; and one repays theft with revenge. Justice is simply a matter of being "even." But Troilus and Achilles, although they are the primary and secondary reflectors for the action of the play, do not have their being merely in the world as they see and understand it. The world about them is much more complex and varied than they realize. It is full of men and women, all more or less capable of embodying such values as love, honor, and greatness and all potentially fallible. Agamemnon knows this:

> . . . every action that hath gone before,
> Whereof we have record, trial did draw
> Bias and thwart, not answering the aim
> And that unbodied figure of the thought
> That gav't surmised shape.
> (I.iii.13-17)

His advice, which Nestor seconds, is to trust in Providence and have faith that "the protractive trials of great Jove" will winnow the light away and leave a mass "rich in virtue and unmingled." Ulysses, who talks more nobly than he acts, takes a more humanistic view of the cosmic order and argues convincingly (who, indeed, could entirely disagree with him?) that the great principle which holds all the universe together is that of degree, without which

> everything includes itself in power,
> Power into will, will into appetite;
> And appetite, an universal wolf,
> So doubly seconded with will and power,
> Must make perforce an universal prey,
> And last eat up himself.
> (I.iii.119-124)

This principle, like Agamemnon's, is sound, though it is questionable whether Ulysses lives by it;[4] and neither principle carries us far enough into the meaning of the play. If divine testing is involved, its principal result here is to winnow out Hector, a more significant "mass of virtue" by far than any other on either side. And if degree has really been shaken by Achilles' temporary defection, it is hardly restored by the manner of his return to battle, which brings power without principle to a consummation in the worst kind of foul play. Both Agamemnon and Ulysses in this scene are dealing in platitudes, one piously and the other with an ulterior motive; and all we can conclude about their platitudes from the events of the play is that the purpose of Jove and the status of his order remain hidden from beginning to end.

The values that are openly exposed to our scrutiny are precisely those that Achilles and Troilus, until it is too late, seek and fail to find—honor, greatness, and love. And for all that we can *see*, it is principally these values that hold the world together and make life bearable. These are no abstractions, though perhaps one could say they are implied in the platitudes of Agamemnon and the philosophical discourse of Ulysses; they are virtues realized in varying degree in many of the characters throughout the play, but to the greatest degree in Hector, who gives the play its norm and its meaning. Hector's recipe for honor is simple and practical: give Helen back to her husband; she is valuable to him but only a condemnation to us. His reply to Troilus, who would divorce princely honor from such practical considerations as this, stems directly from the core of wisdom upon which the play revolves:

> . . . value dwells not in particular will
> It holds its estimate and dignity
> As well wherein 'tis precious of itself
> As in the prizer. 'Tis mad idolatry
> To make the service greater than the god;
> And the will dotes that is inclineable
> To what infectiously itself affects,
> Without some image of the affected merit.

> (II.ii.53-60)

It is possible, as Noble suggests,[5] that this passage has a connection with Jesus' denunciation of the Pharisees in Matthew xxiii.19, "Ye fools and blind: for whether is greater, the gift, or the altar that sanctifieth the gift?" In any event, it carries the same import: honor is not an end in itself, to be maintained abstractly and pridefully for the sake of one who would aspire to possess it; it is inseparable from the honorable deed—here, giving back what has been wrongfully taken. Paris' proposal that they justify dishonorable taking by "honorable keeping her" (II.ii.146-162) prompts Hector to deliver a brief sermon on moral philosophy that parallels, and in practical wisdom goes well beyond, Ulysses' sermon on degree:

> The reasons you allege do more conduce
> To the hot passion of distemp'red blood
> Than to make up a free determination
> 'Twixt right and wrong, for pleasure and revenge
> Have ears more deaf than adders to the voice
> Of any true decision. Nature craves
> All dues be rend'red to their owners: now,
> What nearer debt in all humanity
> Than wife is to the husband? . . .
> If Helen then be wife to Sparta's king,
> As it is known she is, these moral laws
> Of nature and of nations speak aloud
> To have her back return'd. Thus to persist
> In doing wrong extenuates not wrong,
> But makes it much more heavy.
>
> (II.ii.168-188)

Yet Hector's way is too difficult for Paris and Troilus, who seek earthly greatness with their honor, and Hector declines to try to force them to be good:

> . . . Hector's opinion
> Is this in way of truth; yet ne'ertheless,
> My spritely brethren, I propend to you
> In resolution to keep Helen still,

For 'tis a cause that hath no mean dependence
Upon our joint and several dignities.

(II.ii.188-193)

Troilus' callous reply that follows this last announcement betrays
a notion of greatness that is as insubstantial as his notion of
honor:

Were it not glory that we more affected
Than the performance of our heaving spleens,
I would not wish a drop of Troyan blood
Spent more in her defence. But worthy Hector,
She is a theme of honor and renown,
A spur to valiant and magnanimous deeds
Whose present courage may beat down our foes,
And fame in time to come canonize us;
For, I presume, brave Hector would not lose
So rich advantage of a promis'd glory
As smiles upon the forehead of this action
For the wide world's revenue.

(II.ii.195-206)

Yet the greatness Troilus seeks, and naively presumes his older
brother would seek with him, is nothing to the greatness that
has wisely tolerated his folly. Hector, true to his own doctrine,
has not attempted the impossible. Having failed to encourage
greatness of spirit in his brothers, he has not sought to compel
them to do the thing that true greatness would require. Instead
he has taken upon himself the responsibility for their persistence
in folly; and by so doing, he has condemned himself to death.

One might more properly say, however, that it is Troilus who
has here condemned Hector to death; for without Troilus'
eloquent but foolish insistence on continuing, Hector would
very probably have overridden the objections of Paris and
brought the war to an end. The particularly regrettable thing
about Troilus' arguments in that crucial scene (II.ii), however,
is that they derive their fervor, at least partly, from his private

attachment to the fickle Cressida. Troilus here is a young man with a fixation, incapable of distinguishing between what his own will "infectiously itself affects" and what is a true image of the affected merit; he cannot see what Cressida is for the Cressida he wants to see, and he romantically sees in Paris' attachment to Helen an attachment akin to that of his own adolescent imagining. Paris, of course, knows what such attachments as his own are, and describes them as compounded of hot blood, hot thoughts, and hot deeds; whereupon Pandarus, affecting mock surprise at Paris' description, asks these pregnant questions couched in terms curiously reminiscent of Scripture (Matthew XXIII.33): "Is this the generation of love,—hot blood, hot thoughts, and hot deeds? Why, they are vipers. Is love a generation of vipers?" (III.ii.144-146). For Pandarus, this is all there is to love, be it a generation of vipers or of something else; and for Cressida, it is only a little more. She has a faint image of something better than sex, although, as she tells Troilus, she thinks it scarcely possible among men: "you are wise, / Or else you love not, for to be wise and love / Exceeds man's might; that dwells with the gods above" (III.iii.162-164). Troilus' reply, beginning "O that I thought it could be in a woman," is only rhetorically wistful, however; he does believe such love exists in at least one woman and is willing to stake his truth upon it.

Such naivete as this is not altogether a bad thing. Troilus knows very little about the world and the men and women in it. He innocently imagines that honor is more real than being honorable and that loving is ecstatic desiring and possessing rather than giving away; yet, unlike Pandarus and Paris, he has not yet soured into cynicism. His love of honor, of glory, and of Cressida is the raw, selfish love of all adolescence; and that, if it can be preserved through the last storms of the possessor's growing up, may blossom into something lasting and good, like the love of Hector for Andromache at least, and perhaps like his near-divine love for mankind. Troilus, in short, is worth risking a lot for; and Hector, in a tragic action peripheral to the main action of this play, risks his life and loses it in order that his youngest brother may have the occasion for growth that he seeks. One may question whether this is his only motive. Part of his reason for giving in to Troilus is almost certainly a residual lust for military glory not unlike that he would save his brothers from, and the tragedy that results from this confusion of motives within him might have provided the action for another interesting play about the Trojan War. In *Troilus and Cressida*, however, the tragic action is subsidiary, and our attention is focused upon the effect that Hector's action has upon Troilus. The primary action, as we have seen, is the disillusionment of Troilus; or, to be more specific, it is the story of a young man who cherished a false value at the expense of a good one and did not see the folly of his cherishing until he had brought the good one to destruction. Briefly, it is the killing of Hector.

There is something Christlike about this man Hector, though it would be pretentious indeed to treat him as anything so magnificent as a type of Christ. For all his greatness, Hector shares some of the folly and meanness that he would eradicate in others. Once committed, he fights with all the vigor and savagery that are in him, and he dies with blood on his hands. Yet this is the man who would give every other man his due, who would urge his brothers to shun worldly greatness, who would end the war as an encounter unworthy of honest men. He is a man who loves and respects his enemies. His courtesy moves Ajax to say, "Thou art too gentle and too free a man" (IV.v.139). He offends Menelaus and begs pardon for it. He respects Nestor's white hairs and embraces him. He responds to Achilles' insolence with a quick show of anger and then, as quickly repenting, takes his enemy's hand. In the field he can spare Thersites as one unworthy of the effort to slay (V.iv.27-38); and he can spare Achilles when Achilles' arms are momentarily "out of use" (V.vi.13-21). He respects his father and treats his brothers with almost incredible charity. The hotheaded arguments of Paris and Troilus, as we have seen, bring only the mildest of rebukes from him:

Paris and Troilus, you have both said well,
And on the cause and question now in hand
Have gloz'd, but superficially; not much
Unlike young men, whom Aristotle thought
Unfit to hear moral philosophy.

(II.ii.163-167)

He even takes upon himself the responsibility for their folly
and accepts the full consequences of it.

This acceptance he never relinquishes, not even when Andromache and Cassendra do their best to dissuade him (V.iii.1-28);
yet one of his last acts of peace is an attempt to persuade young
Troilus to remain out of the fighting.

> *Hect.* No, faith, young Troilus; doff thy harness,
> youth;
> I am to-day i' th' vein of chivalry.
> Let grow thy sinews till their knots be strong,
> And tempt not yet the brushes of the war.
> Unarm thee, go, and doubt thou not, brave boy,
> I'll stand to-day for thee and me and Troy.
> *Tro.* Brother, you have a vice of mercy in you,
> Which better fits a lion than a man.
> *Hect.* What vice is that, good Troilus? Chide
> me for it.
> *Tro.* When many times the captive Grecian
> falls
> Even in the fan and wind of your fair sword,
> You bid them rise, and live.
> *Hect.* O, 'tis fair play.
> *Tro.* Fool's play, by heaven, Hector.
> *Hect.* How now! how now!
> *Tro.* For th' love of all the gods,
> Let's leave the hermit Pity with our mothers,
> And when we have our armours buckled on,
> The venom'd vengeance ride upon our swords,
> Spur them to ruthful work, rein them from ruth.
> *Hect.* Fie, savage, fie!

(V.iii.31-49)

Troilus has again spoken better than he realizes. It is precisely this "vice of mercy," this "fool's play," that accounts for Hector's honor and greatness and demonstrates the love of humanity that is in him.

Hector's death is only the death of a man, and there is no promise of a resurrection after it; but it is the death of a full man who has realized in his life both honor and greatness. It is, moreover, a sacrificial death, courageously ventured and accepted when it had become apparent that other men would not listen to less wasteful kinds of persuasion. Other men may very well question what good it does. Achilles apparently learns nothing from it; and, for all we know, Paris remains unenlightened. Troilus, however, who has already learned from his uncounter with Cressida that values without embodiment in human flesh are "Words, words, mere words, no matter from the heart" (V.iii.108), seems at least to know that now the world has lost its best hope:

> Hector is gone.
> Who shall tell Priam so, or Hecuba:
> Let him that will a screech-owl aye be call'd
> Go in to Troy and say there, "Hector's dead!"
> There is a word will Priam turn to stone,
> Make wells and Niobes of the maids and wives,
> Cold statues of the youth, and, in a word,
> Scare Troy out of itself. But, march away.
> Hector is dead; there is no more to say.

> (V.x.14-22)

Whether Troilus is now capable of knowing what this action is all about, we cannot say. At the end of the play, however much he may value Hector and what he stood for, Troilus does not yet seem to know that it is he who has killed his brother, just as much as Achilles with his Myrmidons.

The judgment upon the world that this play leaves with us is thus not altogether a pretty one. The best man in the world is dead, and the next best man does not quite seem to know why. Yet it is a familiar judgment. It can hardly be an accident that several of the Scriptural allusions in the play come from a single chapter in the Gospel of St. Matthew, the twenty-third, in which Jesus denounces the Pharisees for much the same reasons that Greeks and Trojans are here to be denounced and in some of the same terms. Jesus is telling the multitude at this point, "All therefore whatsoever they bid you observe, that observe and do; but do not ye after their works: for they say, and do not" (Matthew xxiii.3). This touches at the very core of Shakespeare's play, which is rich in noble sentiments but relatively poor in noble deeds. It is applicable to Ulysses, whose noble sentiments are hardly matched by his crafty maneuvering; to Paris and Troilus, who speak well of honor and glory but would fight in a dishonorable cause; to Cressida, whose love, at least in Troilus' partial view, turned out to be, "Words, words, mere words, no matter from the heart." It is beautifully summed up in Hector's " 'Tis mad idolatry / To make the service greater than the god; / And the will dotes that is inclineable / To what infectiously itself affects, / Without some image of the affected merit" (II.ii.56-60). And this, as we have seen, parallels Matthew xxiii.17. Hector's judgment on the warrior in sumptuous armor, his last victim, "Most putrefied core, so fair without," is a further reflection of the same sentiment and one that has a special parallel in Matthew xxiii.27: "Woe unto you, scribes and Pharisees, hypocrites! for ye are like unto whited sepulchres, which indeed appear beautiful outward, but are within full of dead men's bones, and of all uncleanness." Pandarus' "generation of vipers," moreover, is an allusion to the familiar passage a bit farther on in the same chapter: "Ye serpents, ye generation of vipers, how can ye escape the damnation of hell?" (xxiii.33).

The conclusion of Jesus' denunciation, though not alluded to directly, also suggests Shakespeare's play:

Wherefore, behold I send unto you prophets, and wise men, and scribes: and some of them ye shall kill and crucify; and some of them shall ye scourge in your synagogues, and persecute them from city to city. That upon you may come all the righteous blood shed upon the earth, from the blood of righteous Abel unto the blood of Zacharias son of Barachias, whom ye slew between the temple and the altar. Verily I say unto you, All these things shall come upon this generation.

(Matthew xxiii.34-36)

Troilus and Cressida is not Hector's play, but Hector is the prophet in it, the only man on either side who had the wisdom to see the folly of what both sides were doing. The pathetic thing is that he found no one on either side who was prepared to receive his wisdom, and the war had to go on. Both sides, therefore, bear the responsibility for his death; and Greek and Trojan alike share the consequences of it. With no compelling image of honor or of greatness or of unselfish love left, the world of both is ripe for Pandarus and his kind. We may say, if we like, that Shakespeare meant this as a condemnation of Troilus' world and also meant it to apply to his own, but we probably miss the point of the play if we do. Granted that he did mean in some sense to equate England with the world of Trojans and Greeks, the most we can legitimately say is that he was delivering a warning to it—and delivering a warning, moreover, in compassion and love, just as Jesus delivered his warning to Jerusalem in compassion and love. For it is those allusions to Jesus' denunciation that emphasize the tone of Shakespeare's play and help us avoid jumping to unwarranted conclusions in our judgment of it. There are villains in both camps, to be sure; but most of the principal characters, if studied carefully, evoke our pity rather than our disgust. They are not villains, but men of misdirected good, half-considered motives, and limited vision. In telling how these men forfeited the opportunity that one clear-sighted man made available to them, Shakespeare may very well have meant to equate his own England with the misty world of Trojan and Greek and both, through his allusions, with the Jerusalem of Jesus. If so, he was saying simply what satirists have always said, that the world does not greatly change

from one age to the next, that in any age the world is likely to
have its representatives of Troilus and Pandarus, Agamemnon
and Thersites, and that occasionally it is lucky enough to get
someone like Hector, whom more often than not it either
repudiates or crucifies. This is a sober view, but not necessarily
a bitter one. Thersites is a fool and certainly does not speak for
Shakespeare; and Pandarus, however much he may seem to be
on top at the end, has no guarantee of permanent dominion in
a world that at heart despises him.

Six

MEASURE FOR MEASURE

S INCE THE appearance of G. Wilson Knight's *Wheel of Fire*
in 1930, Christian interpretations of *Measure for Measure* have
appeared with surprising frequency. Among the more interesting
ones that have been put forward are those by R. W. Chambers,
Roy W. Battenhouse, Elizabeth M. Pope, and Nevill Coghill;[1]
and all these writers have based their work upon an assumption,
based in turn upon their consideration of the play, that Shakespeare here studied George Whetstone's *Promos and Cassandra*
(1578) and reworked it in terms of recognizably orthodox
Christian presuppositions. Miss Pope, who examines the play
with reference to Renaissance commentary on some of those
presuppositions, explicitly declines to hazard any opinion about
Shakespeare's private view of them; but the other three interpreters, though somewhat less explicit in this matter, have been
equally cautious. All, including Wilson Knight, have been at
pains to let us see the play as a contemporary of Shakespeare's
might have seen it, or at least to put us in a position where our
view of the play will be unobstructed by the special presuppositions of our own time. As might have been expected, some of
their interpretations have prompted spirited objections. Knight's
battery of Biblical quotations, for example, and Battenhouse's

rich collection of citations from both the Bible and the works of Christian Fathers have often moved objectors to say that Shakespeare could not possibly have had so much in mind. To dismiss the work of these men in this fashion is to miss their whole point. They have not claimed to be giving us source studies. No one has tried to accuse Shakespeare of being a bibliolater or of seeking access to a library of commentaries comparable to that of Professor Battenhouse. The point is that Shakespeare, unlike ourselves, got at sometime during his life the substance of such things as part of his daily intellectual bread. He was habituated to them, as we for better or for worse are not, and could draw upon them unreflectingly as we draw upon the political commonplaces that are fed to us from our infancy.

An alternative to such studies as these, frequently cited as a simple and commonsense one, is the study of the play as play. Miss Helen Gardner recommends it in her high praise of Miss Mary Lascelles' Shakespeare's "Measure for Measure" (London, 1953), in which she finds a commendable concentration upon "the characters in their relation with one another—here conditioned by the given story, there, developing free of it."[2] She adds, "Her reward, and ours, is to be left at the end of her book not with themes and patterns but with the play." This commonsense alternative, however, has grave limitations; it encourages no recognition of the play as poem and leaves us incapable of distinguishing between a rich collection of data ingeniously put together in dramatic form and a dramatic poem richly and truly made, embodying more values than the mere sum of its parts, mysteriously reaching out to re-create, and thus make meaningful, fragments of experience that its author may never have dreamed of. In our saner moments we all admit that our criticism of Shakespeare is poor stuff compared with the plays themselves; and we readily allow that the themes, patterns, and analogs by which some recent critics have oriented their study of Shakespeare's works are not to be taken as the only essential ingredients of his plays. In themselves they are merely modes

of grasping the unifying action by which the play exists as a
living creation. Good critics from Aristotle's time to the present
have known and made use of these modes; but articulate recognition of them is one of the great contributions that modern
critics of poetry and drama have made to the popular appre-
hension of dramatic poetry. We are foolish to reject them
entirely.

One begins the study of a play, naturally and properly, in
the manner suggested by Miss Lascelles and praised by Miss
Gardner, by concentrating upon the characters in their relation
with one another. But if one lets it go at that, if one does not
either intuitively or by conscious analysis arrive at some unifying
action that can show plot, character, and diction all moving
together toward a common end, one has at best a fascinating
study in human relations. Shakespeare gives us such studies,
over and over again in his works; we can take that much of his
offering and feel richly fed. But some, in feeding on this much,
have sensed and found much more. Even in *Troilus and
Cressida*, which unlike most plays presents a seemingly meaningless world for our inspection, it has been possible for sensitive
readers to detect a meaningful shape which belies the desperate
cry of its protagonist. The primary obligation of the critic,
once he has become convinced that a play has such a shape, is
to make it clear to other readers in as explicit terms as he can
find. Sometimes he may feel it necessary to set forth an elaborate
pattern and explain it in detail; sometimes he may find it more
expedient to state what he considers to be the unifying theme
of the play. Sometimes he may make use of analogs or relevant
quotations from other works. The method that he uses is not
half so important as his objective, which must always be to lead
us back to the play and make it possible for us to see it as a
significant whole. Thus Wilson Knight finds in the Scriptural
passage from which the title of *Measure for Measure* seems to
have been taken (Matthew VII.1) words that express briefly the
unity which his own careful reading has caused him to see:
"Judge not that ye be not judged." Feeling the inadequacy

of that (for no formulation is really adequate), he brings up a rich collection of related passages all pointing in one way or another to the same end, and concludes by saying, "The simplest way to focus correctly the quality and unity of *Measure for Measure* is to read it on the analogy of Jesus' parables."[3] Similarly the late R. W. Chambers, in a less elaborate presentation of the results of his reading, chose another passage from the Gospel of St. Matthew as the best approximation of what he felt to be the unifying principle of the play: "He that findeth his life shall lose it; and he that loseth his life for my sake shall find it" (Matthew x.39).[4] Battenhouse, going at the problem in a slightly different fashion from either of these, suggests that the play be read as if it were itself a parable, one illustrating the Christian story of the Atonement with all its mystery and paradox.[5] And Nevill Coghill suggests that we read it in the light of the paradox of the fortunate fall, the test by which man perennially fails being contained in Jesus' injunction, "Let your light so shine before men that they may see your good works and glorify your Father which is in heaven" (Matthew v.16).[6] To borrow a phrase from Wilson Knight, one might best call all these studies attempts at "reconstruction of a vision,"[7] observing that to call them attempts is not to belittle them. None of these is complete or finally satisfying, nor should any be expected to be; for, no matter how clever the critic is, he always leaves something unexplored in the play to mock his themes, pattern, analogies, or even analyses. For that reason I venture here to suggest still another formulation of the action of *Measure for Measure*, one that takes into special account some of the human relationships that commonsense critics would have us observe.

Let us consider first the character of Duke Vincentio, for it is his action that prompts and defines all the others. He is, of course, a human being, a man of flesh and blood, differing only in degree from the other human beings in the play. He claims for himself that sum of human virtues, completeness. When Friar Thomas asks whether he has come to the monastery to assuage the pangs of love, he replies:

No, holy father; throw away that thought.
Believe not that the dribbling dart of love
Can pierce a complete bosom.

(I.iii.1-3)

Escalus, who knows him better than any of the others, apparently agrees. To the Duke in disguise he describes his lord as
"Rather rejoicing to see another merry than merry at anything
which profess'd to make him rejoice; a gentleman of all temper-
ance" (III.ii.249-251); and on the same occasion he ascribes
to him the inevitable corollary of completeness, the quest for
self-knowledge: "One that, above all other strifes, contended
especially to know himself" (III.ii.246-247). As might be expected, the Duke is a man who loves solitude better than
assemblies (I.ii.8-9), but he has never made a practice of selfishly
absenting himself from his people, whom he genuinely loves,
not for their adulation but for themselves (I.i.68-71). He has
been diligent in their service for fourteen years according to his
own testimony (I.iii.21—though Claudio says nineteen, I.ii.172);
he has ruled them like a fond father, with laws meant for their
own good but too often used only to threaten them (I.iii.23-31);
and he has seen them run with the liberty he has given them
straight toward their own destruction:

> . . . I have seen corruption boil and bubble
> Till it o'er-run the stew; laws for all faults,
> But faults so countenanc'd, that the strong statutes
> Stand like the forfeits in a barber's shop,
> As much in mock as mark.

(V.i.318-324)

He knows what they are, yet he loves them; and he has set
about in his own way, which is no usual way, to bring them back
to moral and spiritual health.

To Escalus, who does not recognize him and hence misses
much of the import of what he says, the Duke states his objection in riddling fashion: "there is so great a fever on goodness,

that the dissolution of it must cure it" (III.ii.235-236). This reflection of the paradox of the fortunate fall, coming from the lips of one who is presumably in holy orders, passes as a bit of conventional Christian sententiousness, and the Duke concludes by making an even more sententious general application of it, "Much upon this riddle runs the wisdom of the world. This news is old enough, yet it is every day's news" (III.ii.242-244). Holy orders or no, the Duke could not have spoken much better, or given a better formulation of the action of the play. Vienna cannot get well without coming to recognize her own incompleteness, and she cannot recognize that incompleteness without passing through a nightmarish corruption of what goodness she has. Her destiny differs in no essential way from our own in that we, though we are continually enjoined to be good, are continually advised that we cannot be good of our own will to be good. Jesus' command is pertinent here: "Be ye therefore perfect, even as your Father which is in heaven is perfect" (Matthew v.48). This does not suggest that we can reach sinless perfection on our own, but it does require of us the essential effort toward maturity of righteousness without which we cannot possibly know our limitations as creatures. Thus "Be ye perfect" represents the Duke's goal for Vienna, for Angelo, and for all the others. He knows that all of them must come to see that the innate corruption of their goodness, like that of the world at large, can be cured only by their recognition of the utter inability of human goodness to stand alone; he does not expect them to achieve this recognition without a good deal of his own private maneuvering in their behalf. The encompassing action of the play is the achievement of goodness, but it is in no sense an achievement by way of simple purgation. Mariana makes the classic statement of the principle involved. "They say," she observes, "best men are moulded out of faults, / And, for the most, become much more the better / For being a little bad" (V.i.444-446). This, whether intentionally Christian or not on Shakespeare's part, is the design he has allotted to the Duke, who is largely his own creation, for the regeneration

of Vienna. And it works, to perfection. We may take the
success of this design as further evidence of the Duke's completeness as a man, and as evidence also of Shakespeare's acceptance
of it as a legitimate solution for the problems of his plot.

All the other characters in the play must be measured by the
Duke. Some of these do not measure up at all—young Dizzy
perhaps, Master Starvelackey the rapier and dagger man, young
Drop-heir that killed Lusty Pudding, and others among Pompey's
friends in prison. Pompey measures up slightly better than
these, having been diligent in at least a "stinking trade" and
showed a willingness to change for a more respectable one.
Mistress Overdone has at least enough charity to see that Lucio's
bastard is taken care of, and Barnardine has grace enough to
know when he is unprepared to die. These last three represent
the lower extremity of the range of the salvageable, but they
are worth working and hoping for. Juliet and Mariana, passive
victims of the carelessness or indifference of others, are much
higher in the moral scale; and Mariana in the end manages to
leave her passiveness and plead actively for the pardon of one
who has her love but has not deserved it. Much higher still are
Escalus and the Provost, men of limited vision and almost no
imagination, but temperate, full of respect for their lord's law,
and loyal to a fault. In all these we see a representation of the
majority of Vienna's inhabitants in cross section, but they do
not represent her best hope.

Of those who do represent her best hope, Claudio is the least
significant. Yet it is he who stands throughout most of the
play in danger of his life, and it is through him that we see the
stages whereby one comes to know that to preserve life is not
necessarily to have life. He begins by commendably recognizing
that he has abused his God-given freedom:

> . . . too much liberty, my Lucio, liberty.
> As surfeit is the father of much fast,
> So every scope by the immoderate use
> Turns to restraint. Our natures do pursue,

Like rats that ravin down their proper bane,
A thirsty evil; and when we drink we die.

(I.ii.129-134)

He is willing to acknowledge that his sin may be called lechery (I.ii.143-144). He acknowledges, too, the "enrolled penalties" by which he stands condemned; but he betrays his human frailty when he murmers that Angelo "for a name, / Now puts the drowsy and neglected act / Freshly on me. 'Tis surely for a name" (I.ii.173-175). This unsatisfactory state of mind he betrays to the Duke, disguised as Friar Lodowick. "The miserable have no other medicine / But only hope," he says. "I've hope to live, and am prepar'd to die" (III.i.2-4). He needs medicine of another sort, and the Duke administers it at once in the form of his "Be absolute for death" speech (III.i.5-41), which is so familiar that it scarcely needs quoting here. The important things to note about this speech are that it is a collection of truisms and that, as medicine, it does not work; for Claudio at this point scarcely comprehends the fate that seems certainly in store for him. Almost as soon as Isabella has delivered her report about Angelo's proposal, he falls again into the fear of death, this time a real fear bordering on despair, and delivers his own famous setpiece ending,

> The weariest and most loathed worldly life
> That age, ache, penury, and imprisonment
> Can lay on nature is a paradise
> To what we fear of death.
>
> (III.i.129-132)

It remains for the Duke, with a charitable white lie about Angelo's intentions toward Isabella, to remove Claudio's discreditable hope that he may receive a pardon as a result of his sister's shame and bring him face to face with the fact of death, so that Claudio can finally say, this time with real conviction, "Let me ask my sister pardon. I am so out of love with life that I will sue to be rid of it" (III.i.173-174).

Whether Claudio can or will develop beyond this point toward a state of completeness like the Duke's is a question not explored in this play; but his seesaw development in that direction illustrates the pattern by which the growth of the other two principals will proceed, and his predicament provides the occasion for growth for both of them. When we first see Isabella, she has turned her back upon the world and is about to enter a nunnery. Even Lucio's extraordinarily serious plea on Claudio's behalf at first only moves her to say, "Alas! what poor ability's in me / To do him good?" (I.iv.75-76). A bit later, having agreed to "see what she can do," she pleads but weakly until Lucio prods her to a tack that catches her imagination and makes her plead in earnest:

> I would to heaven I had your potency,
> And you were Isabel! Should it then be thus?
> No; I would tell what 'twere to be a judge,
> And what a prisoner.
>
> (II.ii.67-70)

What she is really trying to tell him is what it means to be a complete man. When Angelo tries to take refuge in the law, the preservation of which he has mistakenly taken to be his sole function as deputy ("Your brother is a forfeit of the law, / And you but waste your words"), she reminds him of one who was the fulfillment of law:

> Why, all the souls that were were forfeit once;
> And he that might the vantage best have took
> Found out the remedy. How would you be
> If He, which is the top of judgement, should
> But judge you as you are? O, think on that;
> And mercy then will breathe within your lips,
> Like man new made.
>
> (II.ii.73-79)

Angelo continues to avoid the implications of her point: "It is the law, not I condemn your brother" (II.ii.80). But she will not let him rest. Enforcement of the law will deter future misdeeds, he argues; and she reminds him of pity. Pity and justice are the same, he replies; and she accuses him of tyranny. Her final thrust is the most effective of all, and it brings results:

> Go to your bosom:
> Knock there, and ask your heart what it doth know
> That's like my brother's fault. If it confess
> A natural guiltiness such as is his,
> Let it not sound a thought upon your tongue
> Against my brother's life.
>
> (II.ii.136-141)

This speech should immediately call to mind Matthew v.28, "But I say unto you, that whosoever looketh on a woman to lust after her hath committed adultery with her already in his heart"; and a similar passage in the Gospel of St. John (viii.7), in which Jesus rebuked those who would condemn the woman taken in adultery, "He that is without sin among you, let him first cast a stone at her." It is, moreover, the same kind of appeal as Jesus'; for it is an appeal to Angelo to recognize and accept the full range of his humanity. That it works to Isabella's immediate disadvantage is beside the point; it works according to the pattern she herself has suggested ("And He that might the vantage best have took / Found out the remedy"), subtly turning Angelo inward to depths within his soul of which she in her naivete is unaware, so that he may eventually know he stands in need of forgiveness and mercy.

At any rate, Isabella's first encounter with Angelo is something of a moral victory; and when we next see her, her self-confidence betrays her into a remark scarcely worthy of her calling. Angelo, unknown to Isabella, has decided to act according to the baser elements of his nature and immediately begins a riddling assault upon her chastity that succeeds in trapping her before she realizes what is happening. "It were as good," he says, "To pardon him that hath from nature stol'n / A man already made as to remit / Their saucy sweetness that do coin Heaven's

image / In stamps that are forbid" (II.iii.42-46). Her reply
is as startling as it is indefensible: "'Tis set down so in heaven,
but not in earth." This is precisely the attitude that the Duke
in allowing Angelo's legalism full play has been at pains to
eradicate. To say that mercy transcends the law is one thing;
to say that human deviation from the law is excusable is quite
another. Isabella, in her attempt to defend Claudio, has here
slipped to his level; and Angelo takes advantage of her slip to
come into the open with his bargaining. It is incorrect to say
that he asks her to do no more than Claudio did; he asks a
great deal more. Claudio and Juliet loved one another and
lacked only the formality of a proper marriage. Angelo lusts
after chaste flesh, and Isabella as far as we know lusts not at all.
Nevertheless, Isabella, having wandered onto shaky ground,
resists her would-be seducer with shaky argument. "Lawful
mercy," she goes so far as to say, "Is nothing kin to foul redemption" (II.iv.112-113). Angelo quickly recognizes that this is the
same error that he himself made in their previous meeting and
teases her for trying to circumscribe mercy by the law. Isabella
is now on the defensive:

> O, pardon me, my lord. It oft falls out,
> To have what we would have, we speak not
> > what we mean.
> I something do excuse the thing I hate,
> For his advantage that I dearly love.
>
> > (II.iv.117-120)

"We are all frail," replies Angelo with misplaced sententiousness.
His is a frailty for men to deplore; Isabella's, a frailty coupled
with a recognition of her human tendency to err and a request
for pardon.

As the play proceeds, we come to wish that she would not lose
sight of this human tendency. Her behavior in the scene with
Claudio, however understandable, is regrettable. Claudio has
barely tasted the sweetness of life and for that taste stands to

lose all the rest of it. His youthful plea for preservation at any cost hardly deserves the bitter condemnation that his sister gives it:

> O you beast!
> O faithless coward! O dishonest wretch!
> Wilt thou be made a man out of my vice?
> Is't not a kind of incest to take life
> From thine own sister's shame?
>
> (III.i.136-140)

Her spiritual nadir and his coincide as she concludes:

> I'll pray a thousand prayers for thy death,
> No word to save thee. . . .
> Thy sin's not accidental, but a trade.
> Mercy to thee would prove itself a bawd;
> 'Tis best that thou diest quickly.
>
> (III.i.146-151)

It remains for the Duke to bring her back to spiritual sanity by reminding her that chastity and goodness are not attributes of her own devising:

> The hand that hath made you fair hath made
> you good; the goodness that is cheap in beauty
> makes beauty brief in goodness; but grace, be-
> ing the soul of your complexion, shall keep
> the body of it ever fair.
>
> (III.i.184-188)

This softens her pride but does not altogether cure it. When the Duke asks her what she will do next, she says that she will go back and "resolve" her brother, adding:

> I had rather my brother die by the law than my
> son should be unlawfully born. But, O, how
> much is the good Duke deceiv'd in Angelo! If

ever he return and I can speak to him, I will
open my lips in vain, or discover his government.

(III.i.194-199)

Revenge thus remains just below the surface of her consciousness
for most of the rest of the play—a fact that the Duke recognizes
when, as Friar Lodowick, he tells her that her brother is dead
and advises her as follows:

> If you can, pace your wisdom
> In that good path that I would wish it go,
> And you shall have your bosom on this wretch,
> Grace of the Duke, revenges to your heart,
> And general honour.

(IV.iii.137-141)

Nevertheless, it is not Isabella who brings herself back to
health, but the whole operation of the Duke's design: Claudio's
supposed death, Angelo's exposure and condemnation, and,
above all, Mariana's active defense of Angelo with her simple
enunciation of the great truth upon which the action of the play
turns:

> They say best men are moulded out of faults,
> And, for the most, become much more the better
> For being a little bad; so may my husband.

(V.i.444-446)

To this Isabella "lends a knee" and on her knees faces the whole
truth, about Claudio, about Angelo, and about herself:

> Most bounteous sir,
> Look, if it please you, on this man condemn'd
> As if my brother liv'd. I partly think
> A due sincerity govern'd his deeds,
> Till he did look on me. Since it is so,
> Let him not die. My brother had but justice,
> In that he did the thing for which he died;

For Angelo,
His act did not o'ertake his bad intent,
And must be buried but as an intent
That perish'd by the way. Thoughts are no
                                        subjects;
Intents, but merely thoughts.

(V.i.448-459)

We may be reminded that Jesus condemned the thought as much as the deed, but Isabella is not Jesus. She is, moreover, arguing before a court of civil law. Thus she follows Jesus' command to mortals, from which the title of this play is taken: "Judge not, that ye be not judged. For with what measure ye mete, it shall be measured to you again" (Matthew vii.1-2). In the course of things she has condemned, or judged, both Claudio and Angelo; now with the charity proper to mortals she refrains from judgment, leaving the exercise of mercy, which she humbly requests, to a higher power. From this point on, she is worthy to share the dukedom, if she will, and all its benefits.

Angelo's story begins earlier and ends later than either Claudio's or Isabella's; and he begins, moreover, with a full complement of talents—election by his lord, rule of Vienna, with mercy and mortality combined in one dominion (I.i.45). That he himself does not know the range of his potentialities and innocently confounds mercy with mortality, eventually becoming indifferent to mercy and contemptuous of the law he himself has imposed, is no discredit to Duke Vincentio's superior wisdom. The Duke has "with a leaven'd and prepared choice" proceeded to Angelo, and he knows what Angelo will do:

There is a kind of character in thy life,
That to the observer doth thy history
Fully unfold.

(I.i.28-30)

That is, to an observer like the Duke. For the Duke knows Angelo's formidable limitations, which the others do not suspect,

as well as his impressive virtues. Yet Angelo is "a man of
stricture and firm abstinence" (I.iii.12), and the Duke needs
just such a man to act as Vienna's scourge. Moreover, as he
further points out, Angelo's virtues need exercise:

> . . . for if our virtues
> Did not go forth of us, 'twere all alike
> As if we had them not. Spirits are not
> finely touch'd
> But to fine issues, nor Nature never lends
> The smallest scruple of her excellence
> But, like a thrifty goddess, she determines
> Herself the glory of a creditor,
> Both thanks and use.
>
> (I.i.34-41)

It is as important to Angelo as it is to the Duke and Vienna that
his special virtues be allowed to develop and mature.

The Duke sees well enough the Angelo whom most of the
world sees, one whom Lucio ignorantly describes as

> a man whose blood
> Is very snow-broth, one who never feels
> The wanton stings and motions of the sense,
> But doth rebate and blunt his natural edge
> With profits of the mind, study, and fast.
>
> (II.i.57-61)

He can appreciate the estimate of Escalus, who says, "my brother
justice have I found so severe, that he hath forc'd me to tell
him he is indeed justice" (III.ii.266-268). To this the Duke
replies simply, "If his own life answer the straitness of his
proceeding, it shall become him well; wherein if he chance to
fail, he hath sentenc'd himself" (III.ii.269-271). But the Duke
also knows an Angelo whom Lucio and Escalus have missed,
so that when Isabella reports on Angelo's attempt to seduce her,
he expresses no surprise: "The assault that Angelo hath made to

you, fortune hath convey'd to my understanding; and, but that
frailty hath examples for his failing, I should wonder at Angelo"
(III.i.188-191). This is the Angelo who has by this time
experienced dismay at the discovery of the corruptness of his
own nature:

> It is I
> That, lying by the violet in the sun,
> Do as the carrion does, not as the flower,
> Corrupt with virtuous season. . . .
> What dost thou, or what are thou, Angelo?
> . . . Ever till now,
> When men were fond, I smil'd and wond'red how.
>
> (II.ii.165ff)

This is the Angelo who has lost the knack for prayer (II.iv.1-5),
who has found in his heart only the "strong and swelling evil of
his conception" (6-7), and who has learned that his much
vaunted gravity is really no better than "an idle plume / Which
the air beats for vain" (11-12). Ironically, this is the same
Angelo who in the beginning begged the Duke to make some
test of his metal "Before so noble and so great a figure / Be
stamp'd upon it" (I.i.50-51). This request of Angelo's is as
human as everything else about him. It is the perennial request
of uninitiated human beings, who know original sin only from
their catechism and who allow readily that completeness is
everything but naively imagine that it can be achieved by simple
addition. "What figure of us think you he will bear?" asks the
Duke of Escalus and attendant lords (I.i.17), but he does not
need to test Angelo in order to find out the answer. *Measure for
Measure* is not a play about human testing in this sense. It is a
play about human perfecting, and the method of that perfecting
is at least as old as Adam.

Angelo's course exhibits the same seesaw movement as the
others. He comes out of the first encounter with Isabella
knowing that he is corrupt, yet in the second he behaves more
abominably than ever. When Isabella seemingly grants his

request of her, he breaks faith with her and tries to kill Claudio
with all possible haste. When he thinks Isabella deflowered
and Claudio dead, he not only wishes the deeds were undone but
sees clearly why they were done: "Alack, when once our grace
we have forgot, / Nothing goes right; we would, and we would
not" (IV.iv.36-37). Yet even this does not prevent his accepting
the Duke's invitation to try Isabella on charges that he thinks
to be false (V.i.163-167), and it does not prevent his hypo-
critically putting on his old gravity to denounce Mariana, the
truth of whose story he undoubtedly sees:

> I did but smile till now.
> Now, good my lord, give me the scope of justice.
> My patience here is touch'd. I do perceive
> These poor informal women are no more
> But instruments of some more mightier member
> That sets them on. Let me have way, my lord,
> To find this practice out.
>
> (V.i.233-239)

And the Duke gives him "way" to pursue the matter to the end.
   The thing that makes Angelo salvageable is that when he
comes really to know his lord, he does not try to lie to him. His
first words after Lucio has pulled aside the friar's hood are:

> O my dread lord,
> I should be guiltier than my guiltiness,
> To think I can be undiscernible,
> When I perceive your Grace, like power divine,
> Hath look'd upon my passes. Then, good Prince,
> No longer session hold upon my shame,
> But let my trial be mine own confession,
> Immediate sentence, then, and sequent death
> Is all the grace I beg.
>
> (V.i.371-378)

From this point on, Angelo is all contrition and obedience. To
make what amends he can, he marries Mariana, he accepts the

sentence of death imposed upon him, and he confesses his faults to his brother deputy, Escalus (V.i.479-482). His completeness at what he presumes to be the end of his life merits for him the renewal of his life, not as a matter of right but as a gift of mercy. The dissolution of Angelo's "goodness" thus has cured the evil that made that goodness accursed. "Well, Angelo," says the Duke, "your evil quits you well" (V.i.501). In him the ancient paradox of the fortunate fall has been proved once more; and if we reject that, we must also reject Shakespeare's play.

"And yet there's one in place," continues the Duke, "I cannot pardon." That one, of course, is Lucio, who has long stood as something of a problem for critics. Nevill Coghill makes the interesting suggestion that Lucio has about him overtones of Satan the tester as he appears in the Book of Job.[8] Lucio's principal business in the play, Coghill says, is to lead Isabella into temptation; thereafter he devotes most of his attention to being rude to the Duke, about whose disguise he seems to know something that the others do not. In Act III he says pointedly to the disguised Duke, "It was a mad fantastical trick of him to steal from the state, and usurp the beggary he was never born to" (III.ii.98-100). And at the end of the play, after the Duke has condemned him for slander, he says, "Faith, my lord, I spoke it but according to the trick" (V.i.509-510). The point to be made here, however, is not that Lucio has *known* the Duke in disguise all along but that he has half *suspected* him all along. Thus if Lucio is really the tester, it is only the Duke whom he tests in this play; and Lucio does not get his answer until he rips away the friar's hood. He begins with pointed questions, follows these with his cryptic remark about "beggary he was never born to," and, when that produces nothing, proceeds to make cutting remarks about Angelo. These the Duke as friar rejects with, "You are pleasant, sir, and speak apace" (III.ii.120). Seeing that these too have failed, Lucio makes his assault upon the character of the Duke, first with a lie about the Duke's inclination toward women and then with a whole pack of lies, ending with "A very superficial, ignorant, unweighing fellow"

(III.ii.147-148). To this the Duke replies with a judgment that grows heavier as the play and Lucio's lying proceed:

> Either this is envy in you, folly, or mistaking.
> The very stream of his life and the business he
> hath helmed must, upon a warranted need, give
> him a better proclamation. Let him be but
> testimonied in his own bringings-forth, and he
> shall appear to the envious a scholar, a states-
> man, and a soldier. Therefore you speak un-
> skillfully; or if your knowledge be more it is
> much dark'ned in your malice.
>
> (III.ii.149-157)

There are several escape holes for Lucio in this speech, but he rejects them all:

> *Lucio.* Sir, I know him, and I love him.
> *Duke.* Love talks with better knowledge,
> and knowledge with dearer love.
> *Lucio.* Come, sir, I know what I know.
>
> (III.ii.158-161)

With these affirmations, in themselves lies, he stands condemned. Thereafter he follows Friar Lodowick about, sticking like an unwelcome burr, irritating as he goes (IV.iii.189-190). The Duke, who in all the action of this play is forced to deal with problems of seduction, murder, and frail despair, is moved to complain only once, and that once about just this sort of thing:

> O place and greatness! millions of false eyes
> Are stuck upon thee. Volumes of report
> Run with these false and most contrarious quests
> Upon thy doings; thousand escapes of wit
> Make thee the father of their idle dream
> And rack thee in their fancies.
>
> (IV.i.61-65)

These are indeed the burrs that stick and are no good to anyone. They are condemned here, in Lucio their present exemplar, just as they are condemned by Jesus in the last chapter of the Bible: "For without are dogs, and sorcerers, and whoremongers, and murderers, and idolaters, and whosoever loveth and maketh a lie" ((Revelation xxii.15). For Lucio and his kind there is recognition of their lord but no knowledge of him, no pardon, and no place hereafter in his dukedom. Whether Satan or not, Lucio is the incorrigible maker of lies; and from such evil as his no good can possibly come.

The decision of the Duke to return and make himself known to those who truly love him is marked by one of the most beautiful passages in the play. Having shown the Provost his seal and persuaded him to delay the death of Claudio, he observes:

> Look, the unfolding star calls up the shepherd.
> Put not yourself into amazement how these
> things should be. All difficulties are but easy
> when they are known. . . . Yet you are amaz'd,
> but this shall absolutely resolve you. Come
> away; it is almost clear dawn.

> (IV.ii.217-226)

Battenhouse cites as a pertinent parallel to this passage Romans xiii.11-12, which, as he notes, announces the beginning of Advent in both the Roman and the Anglican uses: "And that, knowing the time, that now it is high time to awake out of sleep: for now is our salvation nearer than when we believed. The night is far spent, the day is at hand: let us therefore cast off the works of darkness, and let us put on the armour of light."[9] I have quoted a bit more here than Battenhouse quotes because I find, not only these two verses, but the entire thirteenth chapter of Romans particularly relevant to *Measure for Measure*. It was a chapter especially dear to English rulers, clerical and secular, because it advised obedience to proper authority as the starting point of Christian ethics. "Let every soul be subject unto the higher powers," it begins. "For there is no power but of God; the powers that be are ordained of God." Four more verses in this vein are followed by two verses (6-7) exhorting men to "Render therefore to all their dues," after which come a summary of the Commandments and a statement and amplification of Jesus' second commandment: "Thou shalt love thy neighbour as thyself. Love worketh no ill to his neighbour: therefore love is the fulfilling of the law" (9-10). This is the preamble to those verses already quoted as a pertinent parallel to the Duke's observation about the approaching dawn. The conclusion of the matter, in Paul's words (verse 14) is, "put ye on the Lord Jesus Christ, and make not provision for the flesh to fulfill the lusts thereof." Bishop Hooper of Gloucester, writing in 1551, explained as follows his reason for requiring the ministers at his cathedral to teach the thirteenth chapter of Romans in its entirety once a week:

First, St. Paul perceiveth that the grace and promises of God cannot be known of man, until such time as he be brought to acknowledge and displeasure of his sins. The physician and physic be unprofitable unto such as know not that they be sick, as Christ said, "I come not to call the just, but sinners to repentance." Therefore we must know the wound of our souls and the sickness of sin, before we can get any profit by the grace of God. We must confess that all men and women, except Christ, are born the children of ire and of God's displeasure; and that we bear about in us sin, that always repugneth the Spirit, whereby we are ascertained that we be always subject unto sin; as St. Paul saith, "He concluded all men under sin, because he might have mercy upon all." Seeing we be all sinners, and "the reward of sin is death," St. Paul's conclusion, where he saith "We are born all the children of God's displeasure," is true. How then may we be delivered from this great ire and displeasure? By the mercy of God the Father towards us, that first loved us, ere we loved him, whiles we were yet his enemies.[10]

Bishop Hooper's preamble is in itself an apt statement of the central theme and action of *Measure for Measure*. It is a collection of commonplaces, to be sure; but it is a Christian collection and one that should make us additionally cautious about dismissing entirely the view that Shakespeare here recast a stodgily moralistic story in the context of an orthodox Christian vision. For all its secular interest, Shakespeare's play is the story of a ruler who concluded all his subjects under sin, so that those who would might come to recognize the wound of their own souls, cast off the works of darkness, and know by experience their need for his abounding mercy. As such, *Measure for Measure* is distinctively Christian, as *Promos and Cassandra* is not.

"It is open to us to see what analogies we care to see," writes Miss Gardner;[11] but she says nothing about those analogies that cry out for our attention. To Miss M. C. Bradbrook the play suggested the moralities,[12] and no wonder. The composite story of Claudio, Isabella, and Angelo is the medieval story of *humanum genus* re-created in particular flesh and blood with an appropriate time and setting. To Battenhouse, whose training in theology has made him sensitive to nuances of meaning that most of us would have missed, it participates by analogy in the timeless story of the Atonement, never ceasing to be a tale of Vienna but always suggesting a great deal more. And part of that "more" is certainly the whole range of historical time itself, as Christians in Shakespeare's day understood it and as many Christians still understand it: the stage whereon man falls from grace, comes to know himself under the dispensation of Mosaic law, and finds redemption at last under a dispensation of grace with the return of his Lord in the full light of morning. Most men in our time would not write such a play as this one; but then, most men in Shakespeare's time did not write such plays either. Whetstone's unperformed *Promos and Cassandra*, which suffers by comparison with what Shakespeare made of it, remains for us an interesting but impotent antique. Shakespeare, who at least ever since *Richard II* had been using analogies to ring into his work an increasingly wide range of human awareness, here came incredibly close to encompassing the whole scope of man's moral development. He had already done something of this kind in *The Merchant of Venice*. Later, in *The Winter's Tale*, he was to make still another story serve as an analogy for much the same field, with more sublety and even more effectiveness. Critics, on the whole, have been kinder to these two plays than they have to *Measure for Measure*, perhaps because they find it easier to read them as pleasant romances. The story of Duke Vincentio's transformation of his sinful Vienna is neither pleasant nor romantic; but met on its own terms, it can move us as few non-Shakespearean plays have the power to do.

Seven

A NOTE ON CHRISTIAN TRAGEDY

*A*NYONE WHO attempts a Christian interpretation of Shake-spearean tragedy must be prepared to answer a special set of objections. The modern reader is not usually averse to every suggestion of a divine analog for comedy or to the tracing of providential maneuvering in a history play, but he is likely to insist that Christianity and tragedy are incompatible. Sylvan Barnet in an essay on Christian interpretation gives a representative statement of this point of view:

Christianity is dramatic, but it is not tragic, for, as historians from Raleigh to Hegel have realized, Christian teleology robs death of its sting. . . . Shakespeare's plays have been analyzed not merely in ethical terms, but in terms of Christian theology. This procedure is harmful because the business of tragedy, unlike that of a religious system, is not to explain the world, but to portray an aspect of it. Tragedy does not claim to offer the whole truth, nor does it require an act of faith to be believed. It sets forth a kind of experience which every man knows, presenting suffering and death as the hard facts which most men feel them to be. If it presented the death of a good man in medieval Christian terms, i.e., the release of a man from this realm to his eternal reward, it would cease to be tragic.[1]

The view of Christianity implied here is, of course, a limited one; but it would be foolish to deny that a good many professing Christians share it. It would be equally foolish to deny that any literary work restricted by such a view had better be called something other than "tragedy." Yet few Christians are so saintly as to go through life without fears and doubts about the hereafter, and perhaps fewer still die without them. For all but the exceptional Christian, as for anyone else, death is still "the undiscover'd country from whose bourne no traveller returns." The Christian may learn from the image of the man on the cross to strengthen his faith in what he has been told about that country; but from that same image he daily discovers his own unworthiness as creature to merit any reward in it. Death, when it comes to the Christian, is thus accompanied by a double-edged kind of knowledge which makes it as potentially tragic to the observer as any pagan's death. The image of Jesus, which has provided a model of perfection throughout the Christian's life, at his end serves as a measure by which to tally up his own appalling shortcomings and general incompleteness. The result of that tally is never comforting; this is what the writers of our old moralities were trying to say when they represented Death as a shaggy specter and the dying Christian as a conscience-stricken wretch pleading for time. Moreover, when St. Paul wrote, "O death, where is thy sting?" (I Corinthians xv.55), he was referring not to the sting of dying but to the sting of sin, whereby the unbeliever is doomed to *eternal* death. The sting of dying remains with Christians as part of the penalty of sin; it is not deadened by the faith but made sharper than ever. One might observe that Stoicism, which frankly offers the oblivion of eternal death, is said to allow a much less painful passing.

Our modern notions about tragedy are sometimes as limited as our notions about Christianity. Barnet may be right when he says that tragedy "sets forth a kind of experience which every man knows," though this would seem to bring the experience close to some kind of lowest common denominator. He is certainly wrong if he would limit tragedy to the mere representation of "the hard facts of suffering and death." In themselves these hard facts are meaningless, and to insist upon their significance would leave us in the sad but sentimental posture of Willy Loman's widow at the grave of her salesman husband. The common element of all true tragedies, Christian and non-Christian, is the knowledge or vision that suffering brings to a sensitive protagonist. Without this knowledge we have only melodrama, regardless of how pathetic or how terrifying the suffering may be. A platitude tacked on at the end will not suffice; the knowledge must be legitimately earned. The most terrifying spectacle in all Shakespeare is probably the blinding of Gloucester at the hands of Cornwall and Regan, but it misses tragedy by a mile; for Gloucester emerges from his ordeal with the feeble "As flies to wanton boys, are we to th' gods, / They kill us for their sport," which shows him no more knowledgeable than he was before. He is the same insensitive Gloucester who taunted his own son with bastardy. If the suffering really brings the victim to knowledge, however, we can endure almost any spectacle. For example, none of us really enjoys seeing a blinded and bleeding Oedipus on the stage, but most of us consider that sight preferable to the spectacle of an overconfident Oedipus at the beginning of the play, blind in his ignorance. We feel that Oedipus, though at a fantastic cost, has gained a measure of self-knowledge that is worth having. For the same reason most of us prefer the Othello of Act V, who at last knows what wasteful rage he is capable of, to the Othello who exudes sweet reasonableness before the senators of Venice, and even that shattered and all but defeated Macbeth with the certain knowledge of at least one quality in which he is steadfastly good, to the earlier Macbeth who is superficially complete yet vulnerable to every wind of temptation. The insight into the human situation that these protagonists have acquired by means of their ordeals and that we have acquired by watching them makes these terrible actions tragedies; the special nature of that insight makes them Christian.

Christian tragedy presupposes a world similar in many ways

to that of Sophoclean tragedy, but it emphasizes the elements of it differently and gives them different names. It also adds something. In the Sophoclean cosmos disorder is both natural and inevitable. Order is there, too; but a well-ordered, rational universe is merely a rationally perceived norm, desirable in its way but untrue to the nature of things. In fact, order and disorder presuppose one another; both are to be found in the animate world of nature, in the institutions of society, and in man himself. Wisdom means accepting the fact of one's own participation in this natural scheme of things, but the rational part of man balks at what seems to be an inconsistency in the world about him and tries to deny part of it. He may simply shut his eyes to what he does not want to see, or he may try to change what he does not like, or he may refuse to admit that he himself is involved in the more disagreeable part. In any case, his arrogant denial is what the Greeks call *hubris*, and it usually gets him into trouble. If the trouble brings him to the point of wisdom, or at least sets him on the right path, we call his action a tragic one. Ideally, he comes to know what his world is really like and also to know that he with his divided essence is a mirror of the mysterious world about him.

In the Christian universe God is order and goodness, and his manifestation of that goodness is the created world. Nowhere does God's goodness shine forth more clearly than in man, and nowhere in man more clearly than in his Godlike freedom of the will. It is in this freedom, given first to the angels and then to man, that we find the origin of disorder, or estrangement from God, which God in his omniscience foresees and in his wisdom permits. Like Greek tragedy, Christian tragedy focuses upon a division in man himself, but Christians see that division as a partial distortion of a once undistorted image of God, the result of man's ancient and willful estrangement from his maker. The first tragedy, that of Adam, began when God and man were still in a good relationship. The question was (though with God, of course, there was no question) whether this good man, knowing God's will and free to choose, would maintain his will in perfect alignment with the will that had made him. The partial answer is clear to everybody. Adam disobeyed, came to know his creatureliness the hard way, and suffered death. There is a tragedy in this brief sketch of the Genesis story, but it is not yet Christian tragedy. For Christians the primal question remains; and the complete answer to it is a divine comedy involving both the fall of the first Adam and the miraculous triumph of the second. That comedy with its mystery and its revelation provides the modification which makes Christian tragedy what it is; it in no way cancels out the tragedy. Man, Christians believe, can never return to his original perfection without some outside help; yet having the will God gave him, he can still will to be like God, and can still fall as Adam fell, with the same consequences. The Christian's fall, however, is far more tragic than Adam's, for as a result of the incarnation of God in Jesus he can see more clearly the image of the creator in his own flesh and in his own actions. Christian tragedy thus discovers what remains of the divine image in man and contrasts the original perfection of that image with man's present fallen state.

The subject matter of Christian tragedy is the same as that of any other kind of tragedy. It may be historical, quasi-historical, or fictional. Puritan reformers sometimes insisted that stage representation would not be altogether bad if it limited itself to "true" history, which, being an illustration of the workings of Providence, might conceivably be edifying; they insisted further that fiction, being a lie, was the Devil's work—at best frivolous, at worst dangerous. Shakespeare clearly did not share this simple-minded view. With *Richard II* his treatment of historical material became as flexible as his treatment of any other source. Like a thoroughgoing sacramentalist, he could regard history as a meaningful but frequently enigmatic concatenation of events, all participating by analogy in a single vastly complex divine action; and like Dante, he could regard the poet's fabrication of events as a secondary kind of creation, the result of the divine will working through a creature who had received a part of its own creative impulse. Sidney, in making this view explicit, suggested that some might find it "saucy" and admitted that few would understand it:

Neither let it be deemed too saucy a comparison to balance the highest point of man's wit with the efficacy of Nature; but rather give right honor to the Heavenly Maker of that maker, who, having made man in His own likeness, set him beyond and over all the works of that second nature. Which in nothing he sheweth so much as in poetry, when with the force of a divine breath he bringeth things forth surpassing her doings, with no small arguments to the incredulous of that first accursed fall of Adam,—since our erected wit maketh us to know what perfection is, and yet our infected will keepeth us from reaching unto it. But these arguments will by few be understood, and by fewer granted; thus much I hope will be given me, that the Greeks with some probability of reason gave him the name above all names of learning.[2]

Shakespeare, who may never have stated this view explicitly either to himself or to anyone else, put it into practice. That is why Shakespeare's use of Biblical analogies and analogies with Christian fable like that of the Four Daughters of God is especially important to us. If the sense of analogy was weakening in his day, it is all but lost in ours. Most of us get back to it only by an effort of historical reconstruction; and the analogical use of Scripture, simply because it happens to be well documented in a variety of sources, provides one of our firmest clues to a mode of thinking that at one time was habitual with a great many people. To one who has the habit of analogical thinking, any matter that is matter for a tragedy can be matter for a Christian tragedy.

One thing that does survive from Shakespeare's time, though certainly not from the better poets and writers of that time, is the popular view that Christianity is simple. Though knowledge necessary to salvation is undoubtedly simple enough to be communicated to young children, a full knowledge of the faith is too much for any man to acquire in a long lifetime; and there is therefore no reason to assume, as do some readers, that a Christian interpretation of any poem or play will necessarily result in oversimplification. Most modern readers are understandably and properly wary of drawing analogies between Shakespeare's works and the English moralities with their dramatized abstractions, just as they are wary of accepting some of the easy moralizations of Shakespeare that older critics have left with us. But the Christianity of Shakespeare is not of the order of any of these. More than any other English poet, he confronts life in its complexity, sees the latent goodness that characterizes creation, and dramatizes the process whereby creation is redeemed. Thus, whenever in the interests of explication we simplify his insights and reduce the action of his plays to formulas, we run considerable risk of obscuring the very thing that makes Shakespeare's work enduring and great. All criticism of Shakespeare's work runs this risk to some extent, and the four essays on tragedy that follow are no exception. For that reason they need to be supplemented by all readings that call attention to Shakespeare's careful and vastly detailed examination of men's ways and motives.

Eight

HAMLET

$\mathcal{I}$T HAS BEEN a long time since Shakespeare's *Hamlet* had a proper audience, if indeed it ever had one. The principal difficulty in our time seems to be the readiness with which various logically coherent aspects of the action sliver off from the whole and relate themselves, sometimes with incredible neatness, to our own areas of experience. During the past fifty or sixty years so many interpreters have recognized so many different things in the play that modern readers often despair of distinguishing the central light from the multitude of reflectors that have been set up around it. Professor Tillyard, for example, was plainly embarrassed by the "abundance of things presented" in *Hamlet*. It has too much "sheer explication," he said, and explication obscures "the startlingly clear and unmistakable shape" which one has a right to expect in ideal tragedy.[1] Yet the shape is there, and it may be that at last we shall see it come clear. Several more or less recent studies have proved unusually helpful. One that antedates Tillyard's by three years is Msgr. I. J. Semper's *Hamlet without Tears*, which emphasized the authority of the purgatorial ghost and thus the validity of Hamlet's appointment to avenge the death of his father and showed, partly by citing illustrative comment from St. Thomas Aquinas, that Hamlet's dilemma was to execute divine vengeance without reference to his personal motive.[2] After that came G. R. Elliott's more lengthy study, which followed a similar line but used the terms *right vengeance* and *revengefulness* and emphasized Hamlet's responsibility as a "complete gentleman" to subordinate the latter.[3] More recently we have had Fredson Bowers' article in *PMLA*,[4] which asserts that Hamlet, having been given a commission as Heaven's minister to kill the usurper without incurring guilt, grew impatient at Heaven's delay, impetuously stabbed at what he thought was Claudius behind the curtain, and thus became Heaven's scourge, eventually to do the appointed act but with stain upon his hands. These studies are by no means in complete agreement, and Bowers especially differs sharply from the other two in insisting that the closet scene is the climax of the play; but they are in general agreement about the nature of Hamlet's dilemma, which has been a serious stumbling block since the criticism of *Hamlet* began, and their contribution in this regard has been of major importance.

The study that has done more than any other to spell out the unity of the play as a piece of dramatic writing, however, is Francis Fergusson's *The Idea of a Theater*.[5] Fergusson has identified the central theme as the purgation of Denmark, and he has shown the structure of the play to be an interweaving of numerous analogous and ironic versions of that central theme, accompanied by a movement of Pirandelesque improvisation. In addition he has put his finger on the reason why *Hamlet* tends to fall apart beneath the scrutiny of the modern reader. "*Hamlet* can be regarded," he writes, "as a dramatization of the process which led, in the Renaissance, to the modern world and its fragmentary theaters."[6] One can go farther than this, I believe, and say that *Hamlet* represents a desperate, if unconscious, attempt by one artist to arrest that process of fragmentation—to hold together for one moment more the essential parts of a synthesis that was disintegrating before his eyes. But the moment has now passed, and the disintegration has occurred; and subsequent anatomizations of *Hamlet* have made it difficult to

consider the play as anything but a collection. The "vast and
intricate web of analogies" which Fergusson has seen as the
essential nature of the play no longer converges for most of us
in a central "o," as a spider's web does, but spreads into a vast
maze, with intriguing but meaningless complexity. With the
initial problem of the play defined, as I take it to be, and with
the dramatic structure of the play satisfactorily explained, we
may now go far toward recovering *Hamlet* from the category of
"problem play" into which Tillyard, however mistaken he may
have been, was honest enough to put it. The interpretation
which follows is offered as a step in that direction.

The analogies which Fergusson considers are those which
illuminate Shakespeare's conception of plot, and they mainly
involve scenes, situations, and relationships within the play.
Fergusson observed at the end of his study, however, that
Hamlet has the mysterious property, once ascribed by Mark Van
Doren to *The Tempest*, of "lighting up" almost any set of
symbols that happens to be moved near it. In this chapter I
shall explore the implications of a special set of symbols that
Shakespeare himself moved into the electrical field of his version
of the Hamlet story, one that had been created largely by
Christian commentators out of the Genesis account of Cain
and Abel.

As we have already seen in the examination of *Richard II*,
which makes use of the same Biblical analogy, Abel had long
been considered a prefiguration of Christ: he kept sheep, made
a perfect sacrifice, and suffered death innocently at the hands
of his brother, Cain. "The voice of thy brother's blood crieth
unto me from the ground" (Genesis IV.10) was the Lord's
rebuke to Cain; and in that cry Christian exegetes had often
heard an anticipation of the cry of Jesus' blood against the
disbelieving Jews. God let Cain live, they said, because it was
his will that Cain should prefigure the Jews, who likewise lived
on after their murder of Christ as universal objects of mockery
and scorn. Furthermore, they pointed out, the only proper
avenger of Abel was Christ, who was without sin, who suffered

death and sacrifice in his own person, and who did indeed avenge not only his own death but the death of Abel and of all mankind by defeating the Devil in Hell and by confounding both the Devil and the Jews in his bodily resurrection. In *Richard II* Shakespeare drew principally upon the mysterious figure of Cain, which he used as a link to reinforce the analogy between Richard and Bolingbroke suggested by his own metaphor of buckets in a well. In *Hamlet* he made use of the whole story, for in the Hamlet tale he could begin with an actual fratricide, show an Abel's blood literally crying out from the ground, define his Cain with precision, and concentrate upon the dilemma of a mortal prince trying to play the role of divine avenger.

Shakespeare's first demonstrable attempt to link the two stories is one that modern readers would be likely to overlook if editors did not call attention to it in their footnotes. It comes at that point in Act I, Scene ii, at which Claudius publicly rebukes his new stepson for unbecoming sobriety:

> ... 'tis unmanly grief;
> It shows a will most incorrect to heaven,
>
> . . . . .
>
> A fault against the dead, a fault to nature,
> To reason most absurd, whose common theme
> Is death of fathers, and who still hath cried,
> From the first corse till he that died to-day,
> "This must be so."
> (I.ii.94ff)

Even supposing that Claudius' linking of his dead brother here with the murdered Abel is inadvertent, it would be unreasonable to suppose that the allusion failed to impress a good many members of the Elizabethan audience, who not only knew the story of Hamlet perfectly well but also knew without stopping to think about it that Abel was the first corpse and his innocent death the first concrete proof that part of the

penalty for Adam's fall was to be physical death for all mankind.
If the death of the elder Hamlet, thus, was to be thought of as
a parallel to the death of Abel, Claudius was a parallel to Cain;
and Hamlet, who was to be about the business of revenge before
the end of the act, would have to stand as a parallel to whoever
killed Cain, or to the sinless avenger Christ, or perhaps to both.
If the audience got even a fraction of all this, they must have
experienced no surprise at all upon hearing Claudius in Act III
lament his inability to pray: "O, my offence is rank, it smells to
heaven; / It hath the primal eldest curse upon't, / A brother's
murder" (III.iii.36-38). It must have seemed altogether fitting
that Claudius, the villain, the Satanic representative in the piece,
should at this climactic point be aware of the age-old significance of his role. For Claudius' awareness is not the half
hopeful but guilt-ridden awareness of tragic mankind but the
utterly hopeless awareness of one who considers himself damned.
A more important point about this scene, however, is Hamlet's
patent unawareness either of the significance of his uncle's role
or of the significance of his own. Because of his own willful
blindness Hamlet is capable of knowing here only that Claudius
is in some sense his enemy; he does not yet know fully *why*
Claudius is his enemy. And that blindness is the ground of his
tragedy. Later, when his eyes have been opened, he can watch
the singing gravedigger flip up an anonymous skull and observe,
"How the knave jowls it to the ground, as if it was Cain's jawbone, that did the first murder!" (V.i.84-86), and go on to
remark how this skull might have belonged to a politician or a
courtier and how another might have belonged to a lawyer or
a buyer of land. By the beginning of Act V Hamlet's recognition
of his situation has brought with it the recognition that common
humanity shares the curse of Cain, the responsibility for his
action though not necessarily his fate.

All these allusions suggest that Shakespeare in reworking the
story of Hamlet imitated an action which in the life of Christ
found perfect realization in history but which elsewhere, imperfectly realized, is the perennial subject of myth and ritual.

Any revenge story could probably be made to reflect something of this action, but of course few revenge stories do. Kyd's *Spanish Tragedy*, for example, contains no hint of it and for that reason, among others, remains merely melodrama. One may guess that Kyd's *Hamlet* was equally melodramatic. At any rate, it was probably Shakespeare with his infinite sense of analogy and his almost otherworldly (one might say medieval) sense of unity who first saw the timeless significance in this familiar material and freed it from the temporality of a particular revenge in a particular country. His treatment of the barbaric Hamlet story stands in the same relation to the action of Christ as does the Old Testament story of Cain and Abel. To use the terminology of medieval theologians, they have a common allegory. If we take Shakespeare's allusions to Cain and the murder of Abel at face value and consider the murder of the elder Hamlet as a repetition of the first murder—consider it so, moreover, with all the implications that one brought up in the old-fashioned tradition of exegesis would regard as self-evident —we can begin to see Prince Hamlet as the human, fallible, blind, tragic counterpart of the Christ who was knowingly both the scourge of evil and the sacrificial victim who willingly took that evil upon himself. In such a light the full meaning of the play begins to emerge.

Hamlet, as Shakespeare presents him in the opening scenes of Act I, is thoroughly qualified to be the hero of a Christian tragedy. In his virtuous fortitude we see the divine image with a clarity that will enable us to recognize later, at his fall, the imperfection of such an image in even the best of men. His suffering has already been great. He has had to endure the double shock of seeing his uncle assume not only the throne but also the role of husband to the widowed Queen; and in his mind these acts constitute an offense to the dead and possibly incest, not to mention usurpation. Yet neither the spectacle of Claudius' brutishness nor the even grosser spectacle of his mother's infidelity has moved him to vengeful action. For he sees, as no one else is able to see, that their behavior merely makes explicit the rottenness of Denmark, of the world in general, the "unweeded garden," which is his soil as well as theirs. Any corrective action on his part, therefore, must begin and end in equal wickedness. To escape from Denmark, he knows, would solve nothing, and to escape from the world is impossible; flesh is a prison that does not simply melt away, and the Everlasting has fixed his canon against self-slaughter. Thus Hamlet stands at an impasse, and he has the special grace to know that he stands there. Even the suggestion of a solution must come to him as a further gift of grace, and that is where the Ghost fits in. It is the function of the Ghost to provide the revelation which will make it possible for this good man to take extraordinary steps to correct an extraordinary situation.

The appearance of the Ghost presents the matter over which nine-tenths of all *Hamlet* criticism has fretted. For readers familiar with the history of Elizabethan drama, the most compelling temptation is to explain his presence as a convention of the Senecan-Revenge genre; he is a literary catalyst and need not be accounted for in any of the important equations. Thus it is sometimes said that Shakespeare inherited his ghost along with the Hamlet story; audiences expected him to be there (perhaps even expected to laugh at his antics in the "cellarage"), and we of a more sophisticated age must accept him as a quaint literary device for getting the action of the play going. This point of view makes sense only if we happen to be considering a character like Andrea in the *Spanish Tragedy*, who does belong to the convention and who has almost nothing to do with the play in which he appears; but it does more harm than good in the study of *Hamlet*. Among other things, it has helped produce the numerous case histories of Hamlet, which have confused tragedy with psychological analysis and brought Shakespeare a good deal of dubious credit for being ahead of his time. A more profitable assumption is that the Ghost is an important factor in *all* the important equations and therefore needs to be studied carefully. From this assumption it follows for a number of critics that the Ghost must be precisely in accord with some

accepted pneumatology of Shakespeare's time. Thus we have
J. Dover Wilson's orthodox Catholic ghost from a Catholic
purgatory and Roy W. Battenhouse's paganesque ghost from a
non-Catholic purgatory, to say nothing of the possibility of a
devil in disguise as suggested (not seriously) by Robert H.
West.[7] West's great service here has been to remind us that
very few of the men of Shakespeare's time were self-assured
pneumatologists: "The action in which King Hamlet's ghost
takes part emphasizes its tenuity, its frightfulness, its special
knowledge, and the dubiety of its nature and purposes. Unless
we insist on taking the ghost's word for it, we can never feel
sure of that nature and those purposes. Shakespeare strongly
asserted the reality of the supernatural, and he recalled to his
audience some current explanations of it; but in sum he left
the apparition almost as mysterious as he found it."[8] This stage
ghost is credible to us precisely because he leaves us, as he
obviously leaves Hamlet, with the same mixture of terror and
doubt that any supernatural manifestation would presumably
generate in us. We know what he seems to be, and we do not
seriously doubt his story about the murder. What troubles us
is his cry for revenge, which hardly befits a ghost from a Christian
purgatory. As West has pointed out, no other Elizabethan
ghost, in drama or out of it, comes from purgatory and makes
such a demand.[9]

A solution to this problem can be found, I believe, in the
commission which the Ghost delivers, provided we examine it
closely enough. Initially this commission appears to be a
simple stimulus to revenge: "If thou didst ever thy dear father
love . . . Revenge his foul and most unnatural murder. . . . If
thou hast nature in thee, bear it not" (I.v.23ff). Yet the
caveats with which the commission concludes (and which
really justify our calling it a commission) radically alter its
complexion. These caveats are two:

> 1. But, howsoever thou pursuest this act,
>   Taint not thy mind,

2.   nor let thy soul contrive
Against thy mother aught. Leave her to heaven,
And to those thorns that in her bosom lodge
To prick and sting her.

(I.v.84-88)

The second of these, though important, is the less important
of the two. As has often been observed, Hamlet is gravely
concerned about his mother's trespass—so gravely, in fact, that
it tends to replace all other considerations in his mind. And,
like Hamlet, the Ghost seems to be almost more shocked by
Gertrude's complaisance in the affair than by the actual murder.
This warning, therefore, serves as a reminder to both Hamlet and
his father that Gertrude's fault is not at the center of the evil
and that for Hamlet it constitutes a potentially dangerous
distraction. The most important part of the Ghost's injunction
is in the first of these appended warnings, "Taint not thy
mind."[10] For here we have our clue to the authority of the
Ghost and to the nature of the role that Hamlet is being asked
to assume.

It is well known that revenge in Shakespeare's time was a
business without legal sanction, ecclesiastical or civil. Privately,
of course, the Elizabethan could and did view revenge sym-
pathetically under certain circumstances. He could, as we can,
deny a man any legal or ethical right to kill the slayer of his
father or the violater of his sister and yet tolerate the avenger
in such cases and inflict only a nominal punishment for his act
of murder. Still, the Christian prohibition against personal
revenge is unmistakable. The warning of Ecclesiasticus xxviii.1
is repeated throughout the New Testament as well as the Old:
"He that seeketh to revenge himself, shall find vengeance from
the Lord." And Christ's abrogation of the Old Testament
principle of talion (Matthew v.38-39) is too explicit to leave any
doubt. A genuine Christian, however tolerant he may be toward
his neighbor's act of vengeance, cannot take conscience-free
refuge in popular mores. Nevertheless, it is possible for a human

being to execute "virtuous vengeance" under certain very special circumstances, and *Hamlet* deals with those circumstances. As Semper has already pointed out,[11] St. Thomas Aquinas' explanation of them cuts straight to the bone of Shakespeare's play.[12] In the first place, the avenger must be divinely appointed: "He who takes vengeance on the wicked in keeping with his rank and position does not usurp what belongs to God, but makes use of the power granted him by God. For it is written (Rom. xiii.4) of the earthly prince that *he is God's minister, an avenger to execute wrath upon him that doeth evil*. If, however, a man takes vengeance outside the order of divine appointment, he usurps what is God's and therefore sins." It may be noted here that even the principle of talion was, at least originally, to be applied by the judge as an agent of divine authority, not by the ordinary individual. Secondly, the wrong to be avenged must not be merely a personal wrong: "Sometimes a wrong done to a person reflects on God and the Church: and then it is the duty of that person to avenge the wrong. . . . But in so far as the wrong inflicted on a man affects his person, he should bear it patiently if this be expedient." Within the limits imposed by these two conditions lies the authority for Hamlet's taking virtuous revenge upon his father's murderer. He is, in the eyes of Heaven (and of Laertes, too, for that matter; see I.iii.16-24) heir to his dead father and King of Denmark; he is therefore "God's minister . . . to execute wrath upon him that doeth evil." The evil that confronts Hamlet, moreover, is without question one that reflects on God, however deeply it may affect him personally; for the murdered man was also God's minister. Thus the question at issue in the play is not whether Hamlet *may* execute revenge on his uncle, but whether he can execute it without reference to the wrong inflicted upon his person. Here lies the whole force of the Ghost's injunction, "howsoever thou pursuest this act, / Taint not thy mind." As Aquinas explains it (the italics here are mine), "Vengeance consists in the infliction of a penal evil on one who has sinned. Accordingly, in the matter of vengeance, *we must consider the mind of the avenger.* For if his intention is directed chiefly to the evil of the person on whom he takes vengeance, and rests there, then his vengeance is altogether unlawful: because to take pleasure in another's evil belongs to hatred, which is contrary to the charity whereby we are bound to love all men."

Hamlet's human impulse to seek personal revenge appears almost as soon as he learns the true manner of his father's death: "Haste me to know't," he tells the Ghost, "that I, with wings as swift / As meditation or the thoughts of love, / May sweep to my revenge" (I.v.29-31). He is indeed, as the Ghost puts it, "apt" for the business he is to do; yet he is equally "apt" to do it for the wrong reason. The function of the warning "Taint not thy mind" is to make possible the only solution that will punish the usurper, preserve the punisher, and restore health to the infected state of Denmark—that is, the only solution that will effect all three of these. That Claudius is to be punished and that Denmark is to be restored are matters patently within the limits of God's will; with or without Hamlet, these things are to be done. The conditional matter is the preservation of the agent Hamlet, and it is conditional upon nothing more or less than Hamlet's own free will. The questions to be answered by the play (and by any Christian tragedy) are, first, will the protagonist acknowledge his dependence upon God for perfection and do the thing God's way? and, second, if he will not, what then? To do the thing God's way, Hamlet must be willing to kill Claudius only as his wrong reflects upon God, bearing the sword only with a sense of duty and loving the sinner upon whom it must fall. He must also be willing to resist the temptation to chastise his mother for her domestic sin, which Heaven has elected to punish in some other way. All that is required of him is that his will be so aligned; if it is, Heaven will provide occasion for the deed that he is to do and lead him away from temptation to do the deed that is forbidden. Hamlet's opportunity is an extraordinary one: his hand is to be the hand of Heaven, and what his flesh would do "naturally," to its own corruption and possibly damnation, Heaven will accomplish *through* his flesh and leave no blemish. Yet it is an opportunity that requires on Hamlet's part extraordinary Christian—or rather, Christlike—fortitude.

Whereas previously Christian conscience and humility have required only passive endurance of Hamlet, the commission of the Ghost now demands Christlike action. It imposes upon him a crucial test which he does not pass. Indeed, he seems to be totally unaware that he has been tested, but takes the qualified commission as a private dispensation to even a private score. One might observe that the fault is scarcely Hamlet's. He is after all human, not divine; and the Ghost does begin with "Revenge!" and end with "Remember me." Hamlet can hardly be blamed for failing to catch the force of "Taint not thy mind" and "Leave her to heaven," prefaced as they are by such a terrible recital. The proper answer to such an observation is that God's revelation of his will to man seldom comes without temptations to circumvent it. It is the pattern of revelation established with the prohibition in the Garden: the command to Lot and his family not to look back at Sodom, the command to Balaam to go to Balaak, the command to Moses to *speak* to the rock (when he had previously struck it with excellent results), the command to Jonah to make a patently useless trip to Nineveh. The good man is seldom tempted to rebel against God's will; he is merely tempted to modify it to suit circumstances that God apparently did not foresee. As a matter of fact, Hamlet is at least partially aware how he is supposed to do what he is to do. This much is clear from at least two things that he says in Act I. First, we have his outburst as the Ghost departs: "All you host of heaven! O Earth! what else? / And shall I couple Hell?" It is the cry of one who can scarcely believe that such a commission has been thrust into his hands. He does halfway believe it, however, for his comment at the end of that act is unequivocal: "The time is out of joint;—O cursed spite, / That ever I was born to set it right!" (I.v.189-190). Yet the agonized "And shall I couple Hell?" (I.v.93) is followed by a very human "Oh, fie!" and some bitter, but equally human,

comments on the villainy of his uncle and the perfidy of his
mother. These remarks, like virtually everything else in the
first half of the play, serve to underscore the fact that Hamlet's
initial understanding of his situation after the Ghost's visit is
only partial; and even that understanding tends to become
obscured or to disappear altogether in the course of his humanly
ingenious attempts to hide behind the cloak of feigned madness
and to prove the validity of the Ghost's message by the device
of the mousetrap. In fact, of all the conclusions that he might
have drawn from the success of the mousetrap device, he blindly
and perversely chooses the irrelevant one. As far as Hamlet is
concerned, the Gonzago play proves only that Claudius murdered
his father. He does not stop to ask whether it proves the
authority of the Ghost as well. Thus he gloats like a Kydian
Hieronimo:

> 'Tis now the very witching time of night,
> When churchyards yawn and hell itself breathes
> Contagion to this world. Now could I drink
> > hot blood,
> And do such bitter business as the day
> Would quake to look on.
> > (III.ii.406-410)

Thus he goes to his mother "to speak daggers to her," though
he will use none. And thus he comes upon the King at prayer.
   The prayer scene constitutes the climax in the action of the
play. What happens there is both the logical consequence of
Hamlet's faulty understanding of the business he is about and
the immediate cause of everything that comes afterward. On his
way to his mother's chamber, Hamlet sees his uncle on his
knees, trying to beg forgiveness for the sin that has marked him
a new Cain; Hamlet pauses briefly but does not kill him. The
question that inevitably arises at this point is: Why does he
forbear? But there is really no puzzle here. Hamlet's answer
that to kill the King at prayer would not be revenge is the answer
that makes the play a tragedy. It makes the play a tragedy,

however, only for the critic who has first asked the basic question: Ought Hamlet to have killed the King at this point? The answer to that must be *yes*. Bowers, who has helpfully emphasized the difference between divine and human vengeance in his distinction between scourge and minister, declares this answer indefensible.[13] Missing the whole point of the prayer scene, he writes: "an opportunity is given him for private revenge in the prayer scene, but one so far different from divinely appointed public vengeance that Heaven would never have provided it for its minister, a sign that the time is not yet."[14] There is no opportunity for a true private revenge here, or at any rate Hamlet does not think so; and one wonders just why divinely appointed vengeance should necessarily be public.

We must remember that this is the first time Hamlet has seen the King since the Gonzago play proved conclusively to him the validity of the Ghost's story and validated—or should have validated—the Ghost's commission; and for several reasons this meeting provides the ideal solution toward which the action has been tending. For one thing, it provides an occasion whereby Claudius may die in the midst of an act of contrition. The irony of it—the tragic irony of it—is that Hamlet sees this clearly, but still is so blind to the nature of his mission that he does not see it as desirable:

> Now might I do it pat, now he is praying;
> And now I'll do't—And so he goes to heaven;
> And so I am reveng'd. That would be scann'd.
> A villain kills my father, and for that
> I, his sole son, do this same villain send
> To heaven.
> Oh, this is hire and salary, not revenge.

(III.iii.73-79).

This, of course, is precisely the point. Hamlet's action ideally should be a sort of hire and salary, a deed analogous to that committed without conscience by a paid executioner, not a deed of revenge.

Another reason why the meeting with Claudius provides an ideal solution for the action with which Hamlet has been entrusted is that it gives him a chance to submit to the "divinity that shapes our ends" and thus avoid any further reflection of the kind that must bring into play motives to condemn him. Unfortunately Hamlet has already reflected too much; the motive for personal revenge has crowded everything else out of his mind, and by the time he gets his opportunity to kill Claudius with impunity, he has forfeited the right to desire it. Instead he blindly kills Polonius. Later, of course, Hamlet does learn what submission to divinity means:

> Rashly,—
> And prais'd be rashness for it; let us know
> Our indiscretion sometimes serves us well
> When our deep plots do pall; and that should
> > teach us
> There's a divinity that shapes our ends,
> Rough-hew them how we will,—

> (V.ii.6-11)

This rashness that comes of submitting to divinity is the rashness that enables him to cut short the trip to England and return safely to Denmark, untroubled by his peremptory disposal of Rosencrantz and Guildenstern. It is the same rashness, the same avoidance of plotting and thinking too precisely upon the event, that characterizes the fulfillment of his mission in the unpremeditated murder of Claudius at the dueling match. By contrast, the rashness that leads him here in Act III to spare Claudius at prayer and kill the hapless Polonius is the product of much plotting and precise thinking and the consequence of submitting to the most savage of human passions.

Another irony of Hamlet's decision to forbear appears when we consider the contrast between his elaborate device of the play, which he has contrived in order to justify his cause, with the simple, almost obvious occasion which providence presents for the same purpose. His failure to recognize the occasion that providence has provided is, of course, completely human, but it is always human failure which marks the tragic discrepancy between the human punisher and the sinless punisher, Christ. By this decision Hamlet has blindly chosen the way of corrupt humanity rather than that of divinity, and the consequence is simply that Heaven takes his choice at face value. To be sure, he does ultimately fulfill the central part of his commission: he does kill the King and purge Denmark of its evil. But he fulfills it within the pattern of God's human and sinful scourges, who in doing his will execute also their own punishment. As he proceeds to violate the explicit command of the Ghost and stand in judgment upon his mother, he inadvertently commits the murder of Polonius and thus brings upon himself the punishment that traditionally befalls such scourges, blow for blow, eye for eye, tooth for tooth. As Hamlet says later of Laertes, "by the image of my cause I see / The portraiture of his" (V.ii.77-78). Here in Act V he speaks with better knowledge than Laertes; he himself is no longer the personal avenger that he was when he stabbed Polonius. But no amount of knowledge can relieve him of responsibility for that earlier sinful act, which was no better, and perhaps far worse, than the one young Laertes is seeking to commit.

Hamlet's understanding of the situation into which his false step has taken him comes gradually in the play, but enough of it comes in the scene with his mother to justify one's calling it a recognition scene. The last lines that Hamlet speaks in his mist of error are those with which he implores the departing Ghost:

> Do not look upon me,
> Lest with this piteous action you convert
> My stern effects; then what I have to do
> Will want true colour, tears perchance for blood.

(III.iv.127-130)

Here we have irony on the same level as his remark about "hire and salary." Tears instead of blood are exactly what Heaven demands of the avenger who will sinlessly purge the evil of the world. Yet Hamlet has begun to understand when he turns again to his mother and urges her to accept his charges against her but to pardon his "virtue." Consciousness, if not understanding, of error is manifest in his concluding words to her, "Once more, good night; / And when you are desirous to be blest, / I'll blessing beg of you" (III.iv.170-172). His next remark shows some recognition of where he stands and where he is going:

> For this same lord,
> I do repent; but Heaven hath pleas'd it so,
> To punish me with this, and this with me,
> That I must be their scourge and minister.
> I will bestow him, and will answer well
> The death I gave him. So again, good night.
> I must be cruel, only to be kind.
> Thus bad begins and worse remains behind.
>
> (III.iv.172-179)

That is, Hamlet now realizes that what is to follow—though for him "bad" by the standards of the world (tragic in the popular sense)—will constitute a far greater good than anything that has gone before. Worse remains behind; ahead is something better, not only for Denmark, but for his own soul.

What we see in the last two acts of the play is Hamlet's growth in wisdom and understanding, culminating in his attainment of that grace which can be reached only through insight into the nature of evil and realization of man's tragic involvement in it. Act IV is largely concerned with the development of Laertes as Hamlet's foil and scourge, but it does show Hamlet ironically answering to the King for a murder by which he bought the King's reprieve and sealed his own punishment. It also shows Hamlet meditating upon the professional "hire-and-salary" murders that Fortinbras' men will commit in Poland and determining to profit by these "examples gross as earth" and proceed quickly with his own bloody business. Thus it shows us Hamlet at last setting out in the right direction. He is growing in understanding, but he carries upon his back a load of personal guilt for which he must pay. In a sense he is like Samson, who, having perceived the folly of the blindness that he stumbled in when physical sight was still with him, was finally permitted to do the Lord's will—in the right way, humbly and submissively—but was required at the same time to pay for his own folly and perish in doing it.

It is in Act V that we see Hamlet stand forth as a tragic hero in the humility and dignity of complete understanding. He no longer sees himself pridefully as a man set apart by superior knowledge and a dispensation from heaven. He is now Hamlet the Dane, a man, corrupt like any of his subjects. In humility he stands with gravediggers as equals and rebukes the snobbish Osric for doffing his hat. Man "the quintessence of dust" has become loam to stop a beer barrel, Alexander's skull would be indistinguishable from Yorick's, and the unidentifiable jawbone from the pit could be Cain's as well as anyone's. Hamlet's humility has bred in him a new human sympathy. His earlier "man delights not me" remains, but with a difference. He is no longer above man, but with him. And he can profess openly his affection for particular men—for Yorick, for Ophelia, and for Laertes. Coupled with these new insights about man's nature has come another that is still more important, about man's destiny. For now he sees that man's destiny is simply God's will and that neither is to be divined by man's impotent rationality. The fullness of knowledge comes to him now as an illness about the heart, "such a kind of gain-giving as would perhaps trouble a woman" (V.ii.225-226). And in the two speeches that follow, all the wisdom that Hamlet and the play have to offer are symbolized.

The first of these bespeaks the resignation of Gethsemane: "If it be now, 'tis not to come. . . . The readiness is all. Since no man has aught of what he leaves, what is't to leave betimes? Let be." The second speech is even more revelatory of Hamlet's fullness of understanding; for it shows that he now sees that his earlier "sanity" hidden under the cloak of pretended madness was merely the wisdom of the world and God's foolishness, the worst sort of madness that man falls heir to.

> Was't Hamlet wrong'd Laertes? Never Hamlet!
> If Hamlet from himself be ta'en away,
> And when he's not himself does wrong Laertes,
> Then Hamlet does it not, Hamlet denies it.
> Who does it, then? His madness. If't be so,
> Hamlet is of the faction that is wrong'd;
> His madness is poor Hamlet's enemy.
>
> (V.ii.244-250)

The best that Hamlet can now claim for himself is the absence of intent, and in pleading this he disclaims the role of Cain.

At the same time, however, he describes his own fate in a way which suggests still another allusion to the story of Cain and Abel:

> Let my disclaiming from a purpos'd evil
> Free me so far in your most generous thoughts,
> That I have shot mine arrow o'er the house
> And hurt my brother.
>
> (V.ii.252-255)

This is strangely reminiscent of the legend of Lamech, the great-great-great-grandson of Cain.[15] Peter Comestor, professing to follow Jewish sources, wrote in his *Historia Scholastica* that it was Lamech who, blind with age, shot the arrow that killed the hated Cain, when the young boy who was serving him as a spotter mistook Cain for a beast in the bush.[16] Lamech in his horror slew the young boy who had thus made him incur the sevenfold vengeance of God, and then lamented that his impetuosity had only increased the spread of that sin: "If Cain shall be avenged sevenfold, truly Lamech seventy and sevenfold" (Genesis IV.24). It was this spreading of sin, said some, that brought about the deluge and the purging of mankind; and the one English cycle that makes a play of the subject of Lamech so treats it.[17] There is no clear evidence, of course, that Shakespeare thought of the legend here; but the consonance of that legend with *Hamlet* as regards the spread of sin, the blindness that precipitates the catastrophe, and the catastrophe that purges is a further indication of the general background against which Shakespeare wrote his play. Like Lamech, Hamlet sees the errors of his own blindness as spreading the corruption which will end in a bloody catastrophe.

In any case, the scene with Laertes must inevitably sharpen the sense of what we call original sin in the minds of those who see the play from a Christian perspective. The fault which has brought Hamlet to his tragic pass differs in no essential way from the fault that cost Adam his Paradise and brought death into the world, and it differs in no essential way from the countless repetitions of the Fall that take place daily in men's insubordinate lives. Hamlet participates in an action for which the human analogies are endless—Adam, Moses, Samson, every man. But the analogy that unites them all and gives them all significance is the timeless and perfect sacrament of the Cross. This play, like any true tragedy, presents the paradoxical nature of man and his destiny; but it does so from a Christian perspective, showing the human action as implicitly suggestive of a complete action that is beyond tragedy.

What Shakespeare has done here is to take a bloody fable of a barbaric and pagan world and hold it up to the norm that makes possible the Christian view of man's situation as tragic; in it we see not only what we are but the potential perfection which we have missed, marred, or otherwise turned willfully away from. The character in the play who comments most persuasively upon this aspect of the action is Ophelia, who in her madness becomes the Cassandra of the piece. All her lines in Act IV, Scene v, are riddling lines and are meant to be; they reveal a mind in which coherence has vanished and only the disjointed elements remain, loss of a father and loss of a lover mingling in one undifferentiated sense of loss. But the result of this mingling is a recognition that sanity would probably have denied her. In her madness she sees, as no one else in the play sees, Hamlet's role as the savior of Denmark and her own role as that of one who rejected him.

Ophelia's first line in the "mad scene" is as ambiguous as everything else she says there.[18] "Where is the beauteous majesty of Denmark?" she asks as she enters, though it is fairly certain she is not asking for Claudius. Her words here can mean either, "Where now is the glory of this Kingdom?" or "Where is Denmark's king?" They can and do mean both, and everything she says afterward answers this ambiguous question in one way or another. First, she sings a ballad in which an unnamed maid laments the death of a pilgrim lover she has allowed to escape her, "How should I your true love know." The image of Hamlet, who is both the only "true love" she has ever had and the only beauteous hope that Denmark has had since the accession of Claudius, obviously lurks in her mind at this point. Her next words, a reply to the King's "How do you, pretty lady?" are startling indeed:

> Well, God 'ild you! They say the owl was a
> baker's daughter. Lord, we know what we are,
> but know not what we may be. God be at
> your table!
>
> (IV.v.41-44)

Claudius' "Conceit upon her father" is ostensibly a feeble irrelevance; she is certainly not thinking of Polonius here. There is a sense in which what he says is true, but Claudius is now incapable of grasping even as much of the truth as his own lips may shape. Ophelia's allusion is, of course, to the familiar legend of the baker's daughter who failed to recognize that she was entertaining the Saviour and would have given less than generously to him. Freed of her "common sense," she sees herself as having played a baker's daughter who entertained her Lord unawares and who would have given, if at all, with due respect for propriety. "God be at your table," she is saying to the King, "as he was at mine." Thus to Claudius' reference to

Polonius she replies with a rebuke, "Pray you, let's have no words of this, but when they ask you what it means, say you this," and then continues with her ballad for Saint Valentine's day, which symbolizes perfectly the kind of selfless love which she would recommend to all who entertain a Saviour but which she herself has only too late proved capable of.

Ophelia's conceit upon her father Polonius is certainly involved in her mental wanderings in this scene, but it usually merges with conceit upon her Lord Hamlet. Even her line "I cannot choose but weep to think they should lay him i' the cold ground" need not be exclusively a reference to Polonius; for Hamlet is as much the victim of Polonius as Polonius is the victim of Hamlet, and Hamlet, as far as her life is concerned, died when he killed her father. The songs that characterize her second appearance in the scene are similarly ambiguous. It was Polonius whom they literally "bore . . . barefac'd on the bier," but Ophelia interrupts to say, "Fare you well, my dove!" Perhaps the ballad is meant to include this interruption as a last line; in either case it suggests Hamlet, not Polonius. And what are we to make of her last two songs? There is nothing of Polonius in "For bonny sweet Robin is all my joy," of which she sings only the single line. As for the final song, "Go to thy death bed; / He will never come again, / His beard as white as snow, / All flaxen was his poll," there is nothing in this that cannot fit equally well the aged Polonius and the fair-haired Hamlet. But Ophelia has lost something more than two men in her life; she has lost a rare opportunity. "They say the owl was a baker's daughter. Lord, we know what we are, but know not what we may be." She now sees herself as the owl and in her madness knows what she might have been. This, her last scene, prepares us for the scenes that follow, in which Hamlet, in cold sanity, comes to understand his own failure. The play provides nothing like this for the Queen or for Claudius. They do not understand Ophelia, and they do not understand Hamlet. Most important of all, they do not understand themselves.

Anyone can understand the story of Hamlet as a pathetic

and terrible tale; but to understand the Christian tragedy that Shakespeare made of it, one can hardly do better than begin by contemplating Ophelia's, "Lord, we know what we are, but know not what we may be." From beginning to end Shakespeare's transformation of his material was creative and revelatory in the way in which the act of a Christian poet is always creative and revelatory: he remade his own world in the image of an ancient fable and by holding it up to the Light showed that world patterned to perfection but flawed. A satirist might have held out the hope that most of the flaws are correctable. Shakespeare has brought us face to face with our limitations and left us there. Most of us, we see, perennially run the risk of becoming baker's daughters. The best of us must accept the sober truth that even in the role of savior we must play both minister and scourge. In the Christian drama of redemption there is no tragedy, but sacrament, a covenant fulfilled. Christian tragedy reveals the divine image in man and his falling short of the perfection that that image implies. In that drama we see at once the pathos, the terror, and the glory of man's situation: his pathetic weakness and his blind pride, the independence he foolishly yearns for, and the utter dependence on superhuman aid that he may come by grace to acknowledge.

Nine

OTHELLO

$\mathcal{N}$ OWHERE IN Shakespeare does the presence of some kind of Biblical analogy suggest itself more readily to the receptive reader than it does in *Othello,* especially when the reader learns of some of the changes Shakespeare made in the tale by Cinthio from which he got his story.[1] That Iago has been blackened, that Othello has been turned into a paragon of simple virtue, that Desdemona has been transformed from a Venetian lady capable of carrying on an intrigue with a young married captain to a sweet innocent who can scarcely pronounce the word *whore* —such facts as these, readily gleaned from a comparison with Cinthio's version, serve to confirm an impression that Shakespeare here worked toward something of considerably more definite significance than his fuzzy original; and writers have suggested that the temptation plot as Shakespeare eventually worked it out reflects the struggle between Satan on the one hand and the two great victims of temptation, Adam and Judas, on the other.[2] This suggestion is interesting, profitable, and valid, as far as it goes; and the reader will decide for himself whether or not it carries this sort of interpretation quite far enough for *Othello.* Two objections to it are that it leaves Cassio out of account and that it does not account for Shakespeare's creation of Roderigo, both of whom are surely something more than supernumeraries.

The interpretation of *Othello* to be given in this chapter finds a place for both of these characters, but it possibly courts other objections, among them one that such an interpretation forces the play into blasphemy. In anticipation of that objection, one needs only to cite the "blasphemy" of St. Augustine's famous interpretation of the account of Noah's drunken shame and the sin of Ham (Genesis ix.20-27).[3] Augustine takes Noah's nakedness in this episode to be a mystical representation of the passion of Christ, which followed our Lord's drinking the wine of death (or of our sins), made from grapes of his own vineyard (Israel). The whole episode, says Augustine, citing II Corinthians xiii.4 and I Corinthians i.25, signifies the "infirmity and foolishness of God," which are far stronger and wiser than anything the best of man can boast. Shocking as this kind of interpretation was to some Protestant reformers, who tended on the whole to admire Augustine, it was consistent with his conviction that all things, however valued, declare in some way an aspect of their Creator. Augustine's conviction continues to be shared, moreover, right down to the present, by those who hold to the broad, catholic view that God is good and has created all things good. As a besotted Noah can and does show forth the glory of God, so does a murderous Othello. At any rate, such is the thesis of this chapter, that Othello in this play reflects, if anything, the office of God and that Cassio, not Othello, stands as Shakespeare's figure of Adam.

We may recall that in Genesis the serpent, traditionally assumed to be acting as the tool of Satan, is given no motive for his mischief except that he was "more subtil than any beast of the field." Among Renaissance commentators, however, there was the view that Satan attacked innocent Adam and Eve because of envy: God had chosen to exalt a new creation, man, even to the point of allowing his own Son to take that form; and Satan, being an "angel of light," had declined to accept such an exaltation of the inferior order. Arnold Williams in his

Common Expositor[4] calls attention to the prevalence of this view, which Calvin, incidentally, rejected, and observes that an early version of it appears in the ancient *Vita Adae et Evae*.[5] A brief, convenient Elizabethan statement of the view appears in a sermon that Lancelot Andrews wrote more than a decade before *Othello* appeared:

For so soone as God had said, *Let vs make man in our likenes*, that word was straight a whetstone to the diuells enuie. And after the fall, when the seede was promised, that was, and is the cause of all the diuells enmitie, *Gen. 3. 15.* So when the promise was reiterated, *Genes. 22. 18.* that was the cause he so turmoyled all the Patriarchs.[6]

That Shakespeare had some such version of man's ancient and eternal temptation in mind when he wrote *Othello* seems more than probable when we reflect that the ensign he found in Cinthio's *Hecatommithi* had only sexual jealousy as a motive for his enmity against the *capo*, Cassio's prototype. That ensign's jealousy, moreover, was justifiable, Desdemona being, as they say, "no better than she should be." By contrast, the sexual jealousy of Shakespeare's Iago, such as it is, is utterly baseless; and Shakespeare accordingly has represented it as only a secondary motive, uncertainly entertained by Iago (I.iii.392-396, II.i. 300-311, and II.i.316) and finally pooh-poohed completely by Emilia (IV.ii.145-147). As for the Moor in Cinthio's *Hecatommithi*, he has merited no enmity at all from the jealous ancient and becomes merely an unwitting tool in the ancient's hands. Shakespeare's ancient, however, has a palpable if immoral reason to hate his general; his primary motive in the play, like that of Satan in the old *Vita Adae et Evae* and in the writings of Renaissance commentators on Genesis, is wounded self-esteem (I.i.8-33), which leads the possessor of it to cause, first, a weaker creature (Cassio) to fall, and second, that weaker creature's creator (Othello) to slay a spotless victim in consequence. In orthodox Christian doctrine, of course, God did not slay the spotless victim; he permitted wicked men to do that. But Othello is a man, not God; his adversary is also a man, not a fallen angel; his victim is his innocent wife. The action in which these participate, however suggestive of the divine comedy which redeems fallen humanity, is the action of fallen human beings—clearly damnatory for Iago and pathetic for Desdemona, but tragic for Othello, who presumptuously takes upon himself the full office of God.

In line with this general interpretation Act I of *Othello* seems almost like a Prologue in Heaven, wherein Cassio is created lieutenant, Desdemona is exalted through adoration of her lord, and Iago formulates—or articulates—the enmity that is shortly to bring about the great human disaster. Cassio and Desdemona are for all practical purposes purely passive here. Although presented in all their innocence and manifest loyalty to Othello, they stand for the moment in relative perfection, neither creative nor destructive. The action of this act belongs to Othello and Iago: first to Othello because, having for love of Desdemona put his "unhoused free condition . . . into circumscription" (I.ii.25-27), he humbles himself further to the point of begging passage for her to Cyprus that he may continue there "to be free and bounteous to her mind" (I.iii.266); secondarily to Iago, because Iago, although he continually moves in one kind of activity or another, always does so contingently and blindly. Like the damned soul that he suggests (we may recall where Dante put those disloyal to their benefactors) or the Devil whom he typifies, Iago revels in his "own gain'd knowledge" (I.iii.390) and thinks it sufficient. He knows his own price (I.i.11); and, judging by his remarks on love (e.g., I.i.38-40), he thinks he knows the value of other people as well. He disavows loyalty (I.i.58-60) and declares himself a liar (I.i.65). If this were not enough to mark him Satanic, he demonstrates even in the face of his vigorous assertion of the independence of the will (I.iii.322ff) that action for him is always dependent upon what Othello, Cassio, and Desdemona do. His will is sufficient to "engender" a plot; Hell and night are sufficient to bring it forth (I.iii.409-410); but all these must prove powerless if Othello has no love and Cassio and Desdemona have no loyalty. The shape of the sort of thing he is about to do must always await the shape of some positive occasion; thus at no point can Iago ever clearly foresee the conclusion of his plotting. His hope can never be to destroy love, but to trick love into turning from a creative force into a destructive one. He must wait for the good action or motive to show itself and then try to pervert it. As his behavior with Roderigo in Act I clearly shows, his method is that of the tempter—that is, making others misuse their will and become as blind as he is.

Cassio's part in Act I is slight but important, and we learn certain things about him from it. "A fellow almost damn'd in a fair wife," says Iago of him enigmatically (I.i.21); and this very likely refers, as Professor Sisson has suggested,[7] to a dangerous tendency to let women distract him from devotion to duty. At any rate, Cassio seems to be a gentlemanly kind of soldier, better suited to diplomacy and theoretical problems of broad strategy than to rough and ready field tactics, good natured and congenitally naive about the potentiality for evil in others. When Iago observes disrespectfully that Othello "tonight hath boarded a land carack" (I.ii.50), Cassio, it appears, is genuinely puzzled; he simply does not know what Iago is talking about. Yet his kind of innocence, commendable in a child, strikes one as being potentially dangerous in a mature man and trusted lieutenant. Cassio, we may say, is innocent to a fault. In Desdemona, as she appears in Act I, however, innocence is less obviously mixed with naivete. What emerges from her here is the kind of defenseless intelligence that we associate with Spenser's Una. "I did love the Moor to live with him," she says frankly; "I saw Othello's visage in his mind, / And to his honours and his valiant parts / Did I my soul and fortunes consecrate" (I.iii.249-255). This is commendable insight, and Desdemona never swerves from it, calling him "kind lord" with her last breath. Desdemona sees more of Othello's potentiality for evil than anyone else in the play but, with the utmost sophistication, preserves throughout the image of Othello's potential perfection that grows dimmer in the Moor's own dusky countenance as the play proceeds. As Othello bends more and more under Iago's insistent twisting and becomes correspondingly less acceptable as a man and husband, Desdemona steadfastly continues to provide, even after her death, the suggestive image of perfection whereby he can turn again to the light of truth and see himself "as one whose hand / Like the base Indian, threw a pearl away / Richer than all his tribe" (V.ii.346-348). One might add here that this speech marks the first time Othello has really seen Desdemona for what she is. There is no doubt in Act I that Othello values, honors, and prizes his young love; but there should also be no doubt there that he does not fully realize her worth. "She wish'd / That Heaven had made her such a man [as I]" (I.iii.162-163) is his version of her claim to more than ordinary feminine intelligence. Taken at the purely literal level of the play, this is a dangerous attitude with which to begin a marriage.

Cassio, at any level, knows Desdemona and himself better than this—almost from the first. Yet if we grant that Act I suggests allegorically a Prologue in Heaven, we shall see that Act II suggests even more strongly that fresh, fatal morning in Paradise when Adam saw as much truth as it has even been given mere man to see and then turned away. The storm has passed. Cyprus is no longer the focus of a war but an island of peace. Cassio has just arrived safely on it, and Desdemona and her lord are shortly to follow. To the retiring governor, who asks whether General Othello has a wife, he replies (in the words of the Folio):

> He hath achiev'd a maid
> That paragons description and wild fame;
> One that excels the quirks of blazoning pens,
> And in th' essential vesture of creation
> Does tire the Ingeniver.
>
> (II.i.61-65)

Editors have worried these lines into an unnecessary puzzle. "Tire" does not mean "weary" or "exhaust," as many have thought, but, as Sisson has suggested, "attire."[8] The passage may be glossed: "He has achieved a maid that excels the descriptions and extravagant reports of her, one that surpasses in delicacy the flourishes of pens that write her praise, one that clothes the Creator in the essential vesture (that is, earthly matter) of creation." In short, Desdemona is the ideal—truth, goodness, beauty—made flesh, an incarnation of her Creator's ideal excellence. The lines that follow bear out this interpretation nicely. To a second gentleman Cassio points out that Iago's ship could not have helped having a safe passage:

> Tempests themselves, high seas, and howling
> winds,
> The gutter'd rocks and congregated sands,
> Traitors ensteep'd to enclog the guiltless keel,
> As having sense of beauty do omit
> Their mortal natures, letting go safely by
> The divine Desdemona.
> (II.i.68-73)

In the next line he is calling her "our great captain's captain," and a few lines after that, as the lady herself sets foot on shore, he says:

> You men of Cyprus, let her have your knees.
> Hail to thee, lady! and the grace of heaven,
> Before, behind thee, and on every hand,
> Enwheel thee round!
> (II.i.84-87)

In sharp contrast to this business is Iago's parody of praising, which follows immediately. The whole exchange between Iago and Desdemona here is witty and on the surface not very serious, but we ignore it or treat it lightly to the detriment of our understanding. Joking or not, Desdemona points to the central fact about Iago, his ignorant perversity, when she says to him, "O heavy ignorance! thou praisest the worst best" (II.i.144-145), and to Emilia, "Do not learn of him . . . though he be thy husband" (II.i.162-163). The ironic aptness of her judgment is soon borne out all too well by Iago's serious observations to Roderigo, who shares Cassio's estimate of the lady and dislikes Iago's slanderous insinuations about her. "She's full of most bless'd condition," he says, to which Iago replies, "Bless'd fig's-end! The wine she drinks is made of grapes" (II.i.254-257). But for Iago, one might add, all wine is merely fermented grape juice. To one of his kind, matter is always matter, and there is no such thing as sacrament.

Iago's immediate business is to engage Roderigo in a plot against Cassio; and in this temptation of this weak but not unattractive young man, he plays the role of Satan suborning the serpent. What follows, most naturally, is the fall of man. Othello, now lord of the isle, has retired with his beloved, leaving his lieutenant, Cassio, in charge. His general instruction to the islanders has been that each man shall follow his inclination in a night of pleasure; his one prohibition to Cassio, "not to outsport discretion" (II.iii.3). It is interesting to note that Iago first tries here to seduce Cassio by the same means that he has successfully used on Roderigo, that is, by seeking to inflame him with salty talk about Desdemona. Iago's remarks run racily on with such spices as "sport for Jove . . . full of game . . . parley to provocation . . . alarum to love." But Cassio's remarks remain unobjectionable: "most exquisite lady . . . most fresh and delicate creature . . . right modest . . . She is indeed perfection." Having failed in this, Iago turns to a tack that goes better, "Well, happiness to their sheets! Come, lieutenant, I have a stoup of wine." In short, he hits upon the one thing that will cause Cassio, if he does it, to disobey Othello's injunction "not to outsport discretion." And Cassio, at his friend's insistence, drinks the second cup that is, for him, an abandonment of discretion and fatal disobedience. Maudlin in his cups, he mulls over the doctrine of election, "Well, God's above all; and there be souls must be saved, and there be souls must not be saved," adding, "I hope to be saved"; and more pridefully in answer to Iago's "so do I too," "Ay, but, by your leave, not before me; the lieutenant is to be saved before the ancient" (II.iii.105-114).

Thus is Cassio undone. The brawl, of which he remembers only indistinct fragments afterward, is the trivial consequence of his fall. The serious consequence which Iago develops into full-blown tragedy is pronounced by Othello, "Cassio, I love thee; / But never more be officer of mine" (II.iii.248-249). This Cassio interprets as loss of reputation, a second death, worse by far than death of body. The line "Reputation, reputation, reputation!" is frequently cited as Cassio's reaction to his fall, but even more revealing are the words defining reputation which follow: "I have lost the immortal part of myself, and what remains is bestial." Being bestial henceforth, being mortal hereafter, and being meanwhile subject to "one unperfectness" after another—these are the only things that Cassio has to look forward to, until Iago suggests a plan of salvation.

There is nothing at all wrong with the course Iago suggests. He is never more right than when he says in soliloquy:

> ... this advice is free I give and honest,
> Probal to thinking and indeed the course
> To win the Moor again.
>   (II.iii.343-345)

If Desdemona is indeed, as Iago says, the general's general, what more proper than to seek her intercession?

> ... confess yourself freely to her; importune
> her help to put you in your place again. She is
> of so free, so kind, so apt, so blessed a disposi-
> tion, she holds it a vice in her goodness not
> to do more than she is requested. This broken
> joint between you and her husband entreat her
> to splinter; and, my fortunes against any lay

worth naming, this crack of your love shall
grow stronger than it was before.

(II.iii.323-331)

The plan is proper and right. The only difficulty is that, however
much Cassio may participate in the flesh and mortal sin of
Adam and however deeply involved Iago may be in the Devil,
Desdemona is only a human intercessor and Othello is not God.
This is the difficulty, however, that makes *Othello* tragedy
rather than morality. Christian tragedy gets its force from the
ironic casting of semidivine mankind in the divine patterns.
Othello's glory is that he so beautifully, with his free and open
nature, shows forth the divine office. His tragedy is that, in
spite of this glory, he is far short of being divine and must, in
doing his best, come out a fool. Cassio (being mortal like
Adam) is the only one who is perfectly apt for the role he plays
in this pattern. And because all the exemplars are, after all,
only human beings, the "Divinity of Hell" is able to turn
Desdemona's goodness into pitch, "And out of her goodness
make the net / That shall enmesh them all" (II.iii.367-368).
Iago's hellishness succeeds, evil comes out of good, and the
human agents who play the divine roles are disastrously en-
meshed.

Tragedy, except in the minds of people like those medieval
commentators who compared it to a goat (bearded at the
beginning and bare at the end), never ends in the mere hopeless
fact of death. Although it does not deal in mathematical
retribution, it always suggests or expresses some hope of a
mysterious divine justice over, above, and beyond all the particulars of human history whereby right may be vindicated and
evil known. Though it is not the function of tragedy, whether
Sophoclean or Shakespearean, to define the good, it is blindness
to assert that tragedy denies a good. The greatness and the
paradox of tragedy is that it discovers in human madness, in
human senility, and even in humanity's bestial wickedness the
glimmer of a transformed humanity that is dignified and noble

and perhaps just barely possible. Christian tragedy shows us this by showing man, sometimes even at his human worst, participating by analogy in the office of divinity.

Othello, as I have already suggested, participates in many ways. He participates generally by giving commands and by delegating authority, by being first the military deliverer of Venice and later military governor of Cyprus. He participates more specifically, as we have seen, by his exaltation of Desdemona and by incurring the enmity of his ancient when he exalts Cassio. Of these two particulars, the first, one notes, is a purely private matter; the second, however, is part of his public duty. Othello's story, then, is no simple domestic tragedy of a man who spoke well in the Forum and came home to play the fool before his wife. It is the story of a man who displayed his nobility and folly equally at home and in the decisions of his public office. He loved Desdemona, he says, not wisely but too well, and so he did. For he loved her for what she saw in himself, and love of this kind not to be fatal must be wholly divine. His astounding aside over the sleeping body of Desdemona— "This sorrow's heavenly; / It strikes where it doth love" (V.ii. 21-22)—suggests as has often been noted, Hebrews xii.6, "Whom the Lord loveth he chasteneth." Yet one should note, too, that the same sentiment lurks beneath Othello's seemingly charitable dismissal of Cassio, "Cassio, I love thee; / But never more be officer of mine" (II.iii.248-249). Othello always tends to incorporate his love of others within a broad love of the good qualities in himself—a godlike tendency, but limited and damnable in men. Hence, one feels something less than pity at the extravagance with which Othello displays his first grief at the loss of his first and most dearly beloved: "O heavy hour! / Methinks it should be now a huge eclipse / Of sun and moon, and that th' affrighted globe / Did yawn at alteration" (V.ii. 98-101). Only one death ever got so much notice, and that death was followed by a physical resurrection. The physical Desdemona, as far as Othello knows at this point, is irremediably dead.

There are some who profess to see a kind of regeneration in Othello; others who see him damned. All one can be sure of is that Othello dies in possession of genuine knowledge. His life has been a "vain boast." "Who can control his fate?" he cries (V.ii.265).

> . . . O ill-starr'd wench!
> Pale as thy smock! when we shall meet at court,
> This look of thine will hurl my soul from heaven,
> And fiends will snatch at it. Cold, cold, my girl!
> Even like thy chastity. O cursed, cursed slave!
> Whip me, ye devils,
> From the possession of this heavenly sight!
>
> (V.ii.272-278)

Whether this is for him regenerative knowledge and whether, if it is regenerative, he has gained it in time, is not for us to ask. The point is that Othello has achieved for us all a partial recognition of the blindness that besets us.

Desdemona's participation in the pattern dovetails with Othello's, yet it has its own special quality. Her function is to be innocent, in deed as in her own opinion. "A guiltless death I die," she says at the end; but she speaks once more in answer to Emilia's query about who did the murder. "Nobody; I myself. Farewell! / Commend me to my kind lord." Here she shows more knowledge than some have given her credit for. Desdemona accepts the office of intercessor for Cassio, carelessly or forgetfully neglects to pick up the fatal handkerchief, and lies venially when she cannot remember what she has done with it. In Act IV, Scene ii, Othello charges her histrionically with the role of whore; and in that same act Desdemona accepts her role, willfully yet humbly, not dreaming why she must do so. "'Tis meet I should be us'd so, very meet," she tells Emilia. "How have I been behav'd, that he might stick / The small'st opinion on my least misuse?" (IV.ii.107-109). The act she denies; the word she cannot bring herself to pronounce. "Beshrew me," she says, "if I would do such a wrong / For the whole world"

(IV.iii.78-79). And yet she goes so far as to defend her husband's displeasure, first directly,

> My love doth so approve him,
> That even his stubbornness, his checks,
>   his frowns,—
> . . . have grace and favour in them.
>
> (IV.iii.51-53)

and then inadvertently, though perhaps with subconscious intent, in Barbary's Willow Song:

> "Sing all a green willow must be my garland.
> Let nobody blame him, his scorn I approve,"—
> Nay, that's not next.
>
> (IV.iii.19-21)

The words have slipped out, but she means them; and in the last act, she dies by them.

It is at this point, with Desdemona's death and Emilia's entry, that Cassio's survival comes to light. This is the Cassio, we recall, whose virtue Othello saw as being like his own, whose virtue so attracted Desdemona that she pleaded for him and so charmed Iago that he was forced to say, "He hath a daily beauty in his life / That makes me ugly" (V.i.19-20). This Cassio lives because Desdemona, who enlightened the black-amoor, attracted the serpentine Roderigo and made him jealous, and caused envy to spring up even in the devil Iago, died bearing unjustly upon her bosom the sin of intemperate disobedience of which that same Cassio was justly accused. Thus through Shakespeare's tragedy of an honest Moor shine most of the details in Milton's divine comedy: God's creation of Adam, God's election of the Son, Satan's jealousy and seduction first of the serpent and then of mankind, man's fall and search for a mediator, the mediator's intercession and death, and the restoration of fallen man. Shakespeare's play, however, is not merely a reflector or a transparent transmitter of an ultimate truth. Primarily, it is a story at the literal level of a Moor who killed the dearest thing on earth to him, who "Like the base Indian, threw a pearl away / Richer than all his tribe" (V.ii.346-347). We should see that first, and only that for a long time.

Ten

MACBETH

$\mathcal{U}$NLIKE *Hamlet* and *Othello*, *Macbeth* is not only a tragedy but a history play with obvious and significant implications for Shakespeare's audience. Like the *Henry IV—Henry V* plays it says something important about the reign in which it was first produced. We are shown, among other things, how Scotland in days gone by was purged so that she might in time produce a monarch worthy to wear the triple crown. We are assured, moreover, that all this was providentially directed. But no matter how one looks at it, whether as history or as tragedy, *Macbeth* is distinctively Christian. One may simply count the Biblical allusions as Richmond Noble has done;[1] one may go further and study the parallels between Shakespeare's story and the Old Testament stories of Saul and Jezebel as Miss Jane H. Jack has done;[2] or one may examine with W. C. Curry the progressive degeneration of Macbeth from the point of view of medieval theology.[3] Roy Walker goes so far as to say, "If we are willing to admire *Macbeth* only on the understanding that the play must not be made too Christian we shall never know the tragedy that Shakespeare wrote."[4] And Miss Jack has written, "The explicitly Christian quality of *Macbeth*, the fact that it is an imaginative exploration of evil in Biblical terms, is the key to the tragedy."[5] This chapter, which is indebted to all these investigators in one way or another, focuses attention on the nature of Macbeth's wickedness. It also rests upon the assumption that the comprehensive action of the play is Christian.

The one who has done the most to clarify the action of *Macbeth* for us is Francis Fergusson,[6] who, as we have seen, performed a similar service in his essay on *Hamlet*. By action Fergusson means the motive or intent which defines not only the leading character's mode of being but the shape and texture of the entire play. If a play is truly unified, it has for its soul a unifying action, which makes plot, characters, and imagery all appear to spring from a single inspiration. The unifying action in *Macbeth*, he believes, is best expressed in a phrase that Macbeth uses in Act II, Scene iii, when he excuses his murder of the grooms by saying that his love for Duncan "Outran the pauser, reason." Fergusson's essay is easily available and should be read carefully. There is space here only to reproduce his statement of what outrunning the pauser, reason, means:

To "outrun" reason suggests an impossible stunt, like lifting oneself by one's own bootstraps. It also suggests a competition or race, like those of nightmare, which cannot be won. As for the word "reason," Shakespeare associates it with nature and nature's order, in the individual soul, in society, and in the cosmos. To outrun reason is thus to violate nature itself, to lose the bearings of common sense and of custom, and to move into a spiritual realm bounded by the irrational darkness of Hell one way, and the superrational grace of faith the other way. As the play develops before us, all the modes of this absurd, or evil, or supernatural, action are attempted, the last being Malcolm's and Macduff's acts of faith.[7]

It is difficult to imagine a better statement of the action of *Macbeth* than this one. It is also difficult to imagine a statement more in accord with the essence of Christianity. One is reminded both of the Psalmist's, "The fool hath said in his heart, There is no God" (Psalms xiv.1; liii.1), which speaks of the irrational darkness of the damned, and of St. Paul's description of the wisdom by which the world perishes and the "foolishness" by which it may be saved:

> For the Jews require a sign, and the Greeks seek after wisdom: But we preach Christ crucified, unto the Jews a stumblingblock, and unto the Greeks foolishness; But unto them which are called, both Jews and Greeks, Christ the power of God, and the wisdom of God. Because the foolishness of God is wiser than men; and the weakness of God is stronger than men.
>
> (1 Corinthians i.22-25)

Indeed these two passages from Scripture can help us to understand the situation in which Macbeth finds himself at the beginning of the action.

Like Banquo, Macbeth has been given the special privilege of participating knowingly rather than unknowingly in that part of nature's "reasonable" order which concerns his own destiny. Thus he begins one step beyond what constitutes the boundary of "reason" for most of us and stands on the threshold of that spiritual realm of which Fergusson speaks, at the point where the irrational path to Hell and the suprarational path to Heaven diverge. All that is required of Macbeth is that he stand there. He has no command to do anything or even to be anything other than what he has always been; if he should act upon his special knowledge, he must take upon himself full responsibility for the consequences. Macbeth knows this. He knows that the witches have correctly identified him as Thane of Glamis and correctly, though in anticipation of his own knowledge, called him Thane of Cawdor; he even entertains the hope that they have correctly prophesied the "swelling act / Of the imperial theme" (I.iii. 128-129). Yet he also recognizes that he does not know who the witches are or by what authority they prophesy, and thus the most he allows to them is a knowledge of "chance": "If chance will have me King, why chance may crown me / Without my stir" (I.iii.143-144). In these two lines, however, he comes close to stating the principle that leads him a few hours later to oppose Lady Macbeth's frantic urging with, "Prithee, peace. / I dare do all that may become a man. / Who dares do more is none" (I.vii.45-47). Unfortunately, he forgets to stand upon this admirable principle and instead, by acting as if he were the sole author of his action, becomes involved in a chain of atrocities so frightful that we sometimes wonder whether Shakespeare did not hide a monster rather than a tragic hero under Macbeth's initially amiable exterior. Mere acting, we observe, need not have involved him in such wickedness. Thus two questions confront us: first, what is the nature of Macbeth's extraordinary villainy? and second, what justification can we find for calling the story of such a man a tragedy?

One interpretation of the play virtually forces a negative answer to the second question. Roy Walker has written that Macbeth is a man "by nature predisposed to evil."[8] If we take this point of view in its naked simplicity (and Walker does not quite ask us to do that) we cancel out the emphasis of tragedy, which is always on the protagonist's freedom, and always on his gain as well as on his loss. On the other hand, G. R. Elliott, in trying to rescue Macbeth from his latter-day "blackeners," gives a great deal of attention to Macbeth's essential goodness,[9] which he finds to be very much like that tragically limited humanity, or "fellow-feeling," that characterizes the average man. Elliott's corrective was needed, and we should be grateful for it; but we should ask ourselves whether in a somewhat different way it too does not tend to cancel out tragedy. All tragic heroes are like us in some respects; otherwise we should not be interested in them. But their virtues and their vices are also pitched at a level considerably above our normal one. Macbeth throughout this play is presented as a man of uncommon potentialities. His potentialities for evil are, of course, easiest to see, and they are so fully demonstrated as the play progresses that we tend to overlook the proof of his extraordinary potentialities for good. It is with proof of these that the play begins.

At the start Macbeth is a man of great physical courage. Aside from the third witch's passing reference, the first thing we

hear about him is the bleeding sergeant's account of how "brave
Macbeth" unseamed the merciless Macdonwald and then went
on with Banquo at his side to fight

> As cannons overcharg'd with double cracks; so they
> Doubly redoubled strokes upon the foe.
> Except they meant to bathe in reeking wounds,
> Or memorize another Golgotha,
> I cannot tell.
>
> (I.ii.37-41)

If we do not take one sergeant's word for it, we can certainly
take Ross' word, which is that every post during the day has
brought Macbeth's praises in the kingdom's defense "thick as
hail" (I.iii.97-100). Duncan acknowledges not only Macbeth's
valor but his continuing loyalty when he makes him Thane of
Cawdor; and, what is more important, the witches, who are
truthful prophets whatever else they may be, have seen in
advance his election to be King. The wave of temptation that
sweeps over Macbeth as he meditates upon their announcement
does not argue him so much predisposed to evil as predisposed
to be ambitious and, moreover, predisposed to further his ambition with his greatest natural endowment, "bravery":

> This supernatural soliciting
> Cannot be ill, cannot be good. If ill,
> Why hath it given me earnest of success,
> Commencing in a truth? I'm thane of Cawdor.
> If good, why do I yield to that suggestion
> Whose horrid image doth unfix my hair
> And make my seated heart knock at my ribs,
> Against the use of nature? Present fears
> Are less than horrible imaginings.
> My thought, whose murder yet is but fantastical,
> Shakes so my single state of man that function
> Is smother'd in surmise, and nothing is
> But what is not.
>
> (I.iii.130-142)

The significant thing here is that Macbeth recognizes the temptation for what it is—a temptation to pit two of his great virtues,
physical courage and loyalty to his King, against one another—
and, for the moment at least, can be horrified at the suggestion.
Any temptation at all, even one to commit murder, would have
argued Macbeth merely human; but this is an extraordinary
temptation, born of what he has reason to believe is genuine
foreknowledge, and Macbeth meets it on its own terms: "If
chance will have me King, why chance may crown me / Without
my stir." Then he adds, "Come what come may, / Time and
the hour runs through the roughest day" (146-147). For the
moment this is enough.

The next temptation proves that Macbeth is still a babe with
far more knowledge than is good for him. Duncan's quixotic
transfer of Cawdor's honors to Macbeth can only have suggested
to him that all the fulfillment of prophecy will be as rapid as this
part of it, and Duncan's announcement almost immediately
thereafter that Malcolm is Prince of Cumberland and heir to
the throne strains Macbeth's newly achieved accommodation of
will and foreknowledge to the breaking point. His "black"
meditation at this point marks a revival of his tendency to fall
back on a support which he has proved by long testing—his own
physical prowess and resourcefulness:

> The Prince of Cumberland! That is a step
> On which I must fall down, or else o'erleap,
> For in my way it lies. Stars, hide your fires;
> Let not light see my black and deep desires;
> The eye wink at the hand; yet let that be
> Which the eye fears, when it is done, to see.
>
> (I.iv.48-53)

Lady Macbeth is right when she says in the next scene that
Macbeth is "not without ambition, but without / The illness
should attend it" (I.v.20-21). By "illness" she undoubtedly
means evil or cruelty, and her strategy is to add evil to a
composition that does not have very much of it. Inadvertently

she succeeds, but not by adding something. When she advises him to "beguile the time" by looking like the time (I.v.64-65), she unwittingly urges him to abandon his conviction that "Time and the hour runs through the roughest day"—in short, to make Time his fool. And when Macbeth tries to do that, he implicitly denies God and His providence—outruns the pauser, reason—and becomes himself a fool. Thereafter he has no choice but to be evil.

One brief reminder of his human insufficiency might have saved Macbeth at this point, but faulty human rationalization undoes him. We see what is happening to him in the opening soliloquy of Scene vii:

> If it were done when 'tis done, then 'twere well
> It were done quickly. If the assassination
> Could trammel up the consequence, and catch
> With his surcease success; that but this blow
> Might be the be-all and the end-all here,
> But here, upon this bank and shoal of time,
> We'd jump the life to come.
>
> (I.vii.1-7)

Whereas only shortly before in his thinking Heaven and earth had been interpenetrated, now they are widely separated. Life on earth is one thing; life hereafter, another. And since the second life is largely conjectural, one may conceivably take the chance that it does not exist at all. If Heaven does not control Time, then Macbeth may safely venture to make Time his fool and fulfill the prophecy of the witches himself. We note that Macbeth here suggests four admirable reasons for not killing Duncan: Duncan is a kinsman, he is a king, he is a guest, and he is a good man (I.vii.13-25). But none of these moral reasons can have much force against a powerful ambition newly fortified by a denial of God, and in Scene vii Lady Macbeth's suggestion of ways and means proves too much for Macbeth's naked human morality to stand. In the last four lines of the scene (I.vii.79-82) he sums up his decision and his total defection from truth.

"I am settled," he says, "and bend up / Each corporal agent to this terrible feat." There is no invocation of chance or Providence here, only a fool's reliance upon the power that his material body can supply. The concluding couplet completes the demonstration of his folly:

> Away, and mock the time with fairest show;
> False face must hide what the false heart doth
> > know.
> > (I.vii.81-82)

Time, as the rest of the play amply demonstrates, is not mocked; and Macbeth's heart, now false indeed, has no longer any true knowledge at all.

I have used the word *forget* to describe Macbeth's defection, but there is nothing accidental about what he does. He neither forgets nor disbelieves what the witches have told him, but he "forgets" about Providence when he decides to usurp the role of Providence, bring to pass that part of the prophecy he wants fulfilled, and frustrate all the rest of it. His will is very much involved here; he chooses a course that is opposed to his earlier and better judgment and "settles" himself in it. Christian doctrine has a word for this kind of defection, *apostasy*. Apostasy is said to be the sin against the Holy Ghost. It involves coming into full knowledge and then falling away. Several passages in the Bible refer to it, but the one most commonly cited is in Hebrews:

For if we sin wilfully after that we have received the knowledge of the truth, there remaineth no more sacrifice for sins, But a certain fearful looking for judgment and fiery indignation, which shall devour the adversaries. He that despised Moses' law died without mercy under two or three witnesses: Of how much sorer punishment, suppose ye, shall he be thought worthy, who hath trodden under foot the Son of God, and hath counted the blood of the covenant, wherewith he was sanctified, an unholy thing, and hath done despite unto the Spirit of grace?

(Hebrews x.26-29)

Ministers nowadays do not spend much time warning their congregations against apostasy, but the ministers of Shakespeare's time warned against it frequently.[10] One of them, John Dennison, in "A Sermon: Wherein the Sinne against the Holy-Ghost is plainely described," characterizes it as a "witting, willing, malicious, and total" abandonment of the truth whereby the offender continues in his way and endures while still on earth the torment of the damned.[11] Dennison's references in the course of his sermon to vexation of soul and vain knocking at the door suggest, though probably by accident, a comparison with *Macbeth*:

when men *are forsaken of God, they are deliuered to the Diuell*: not for the destruction of the flesh, *that the spirit may be saued in the day of the Lord, as the Corinthian was.* But to be vexed in soule and body hereafter as *Saul* was. And then what followes our Sauiour shewes in the persons of the blasphemous Pharisees: *When the vncleane spirit hauing beene cast out returneth, he brings with him seauen spirits worse then himselfe, which doe enter and dwell there* and taking vp their habitation, doe shut fast the doore of the heart, so that, albeit the *spirit* of God doe *knocke* againe and againe, yet can it finde no entrance, and that causeth such a lamentable effect, The latter end of that man is worse then the beginning.[12]

The point is sometimes made that apostasy is the sin for which no pardon is possible. Roman Catholics and Anglicans alike deny this view. God alone may pardon it, say the Romans, but there can be no doubt that God *will* pardon it, provided the sinner makes a proper repentance.[13] Similarly, Anglicans insist that God will receive *any* repentance for *any* sin and cite the sin of apostasy as the extreme example. The statement given in the Elizabethan *Homilies* is as follows:

the final falling away from Christ and his gospel . . . is a sin against the Holy Ghost, that shall never be forgiven, because they that do utterly forsake the known truth, do hate Christ and his word, they do crucify and mock him, (but to their utter destruction,) and therefore fall into desperation, and cannot repent.[14]

Total apostasy, by definition, is unforgivable only because it precludes repentance, without which forgiveness is impossible. The questions which the observer can never answer with finality have to do with the degree of apostasy (which God alone knows) and the possibility (never to be ruled out) of a merciful dispensation of grace sufficient to enable the sinner to repent at his last moment.

Apostasy, says Dennison at one point in his sermon, is precisely analogous to the revolt of a soldier in the field against his colors and his captain. This, interestingly enough, is the analogy that we see between the first Thane of Cawdor and his successor, Macbeth. Like Macbeth, the earlier Thane was a "prosperous gentleman" (I.iii.73) who abandoned his loyalty, became a traitor, and paid the penalty. The apparent difference between the two lies in the earlier Thane's satisfactory repentance:

> . . . very frankly he confess'd his treasons,
> Implor'd your Highness' pardon, and set forth
> A deep repentance. Nothing in his life
> Became him like the leaving it. He died
> As one that had been studied in his death
> To throw away the dearest thing he ow'd
> As 'twere a careless trifle.
>
> (I.iv.5-11)

The difference, for all we know, may be more apparent than real. All we really know about the Thane of Cawdor is that he rebelled against Duncan and repented of his mistake. Macbeth's rebellion was not primarily against Duncan but against a higher power than Duncan, and to that power he had to repent directly, if at all; his murder of Duncan followed as the first, but most important, of a series of consequences.

At the beginning of Act II we find Macbeth firmly settled in his plotting and sure of his course. To Banquo, who has had a similar gift of foreknowledge and similar temptations (II.i.7-9) but still has the grace to admit as much and ask for divine help, he callously lies that he has not thought of the weird sisters

(II.i.21) and deviously proposes further discussion of the matter. When the dagger appears to him a few minutes later, he puzzles briefly about the nature of it and then observes that it "marshall'st me the way that I was going, / And such an instrument I was to use" (II.i.42-43). With the blindness that is characteristic of apostasy, he neither sees nor cares about anything except the operation of his own will and the direction it has chosen. Shakespeare, however, has made it possible for us to see something that Macbeth is not able to see, and he has done this by pointing up the analogy between the murder of Duncan and the crucifixion. We note that the fantastic storm which accompanies the murder has not actually begun when Macbeth ascends the stairs; it is presumably in progress as he descends. As the Old Man in Scene iv says, "this sore night / Hath trifled former knowings" (II.iv.3-4), but Shakespeare has managed to pack into the various reports of it a suggestion of all the details that St. Matthew reports about the storm that followed the death of Jesus:

And behold the veil of the temple was rent in twain From the top to the bottom; and the earth did quake, and the rocks rent; and the graves were opened; and many bodies of the saints which slept arose.

(Matthew xxvii.51-52)

Macduff reports the murder thus:

> Confusion now hath made his masterpiece!
> Most sacrilegious murder hath broke ope
> The Lord's anointed temple, and stole thence
> The life o' th' building.
> (II.iii.71-74)

Lennox tells of many strange reports, among them one that "the earth / Was feverous and did shake" (II.iii.65-66). Macduff rouses Banquo, Donalbain, and Malcolm by calling them to reenact the same anticipation of Judgment Day that caused the saints in Jerusalem to leave their graves:

> Shake off this downy sleep, death's counterfeit,
> And look on death itself! Malcolm! Banquo!
> As from your graves rise up, and walk like sprites,
> To countenance this horror! Ring the bell.

(II.iii.81-85)

And Lady Macbeth, entering, completes Macduff's metaphor with, "What's the business, / That such a hideous trumpet calls to parley / The sleepers of the house?" (II.iii.86-88). These reminders of crucifixion and Judgment Day linked by the common detail of the resurrection of the dead bring back to mind the words of the bleeding sergeant in Act I, when he said of Banquo and Macbeth that "they meant to bathe in reeking wounds, / Or memorize another Golgotha" (I.ii.39-40). Macbeth has now literally done both of these things and justified the sergeant's hyperbole. The little world of Inverness, where only shortly before "heaven's breath smelt wooingly" (I.vi.5-6), now bereft of its King and shortly to be abandoned by its saints, already has become the hell that its porter drunkenly has imagined it to be.

The easiest interpretation to put on all this is that Macbeth has here delivered himself over to the Devil or to diabolical powers. In a sense this is true. Macbeth is certainly diabolical, and he does the Devil's work; but like the Devil he has willed himself into his desperate position, and he is captive of nothing except the Providence he chose to ignore. The precise term for him is still *apostate*, as another quotation from Hebrews makes clear:

For it is impossible for those who were once enlightened, and have tasted of the heavenly gift, and were made partakers of the Holy Ghost, And have tasted the good word of God, and the powers of the world to come, If they shall fall away, to renew them again unto repentance; seeing they crucify to themselves the Son of God afresh, and put him to an open shame. For the earth which drinketh in the rain that cometh oft upon it, and bringeth forth herbs meet for them by whom it is dressed, receiveth blessing from God: But that which beareth thorns and briers is rejected, and is nigh unto cursing; whose end is to be burned.

(Hebrews vi.4-8)

Shakespeare's treatment of the murder of Duncan as an analog to the crucifixion puts the state of Macbeth precisely in line with the central point of this passage: Macbeth, by analogy, has crucified his Lord afresh and put him to an open shame. And this grave sin is both the consequence of his deviation and penalty for it. Henceforth he will be "nigh unto cursing" (which is not *quite* the same as being absolutely accursed) and will live out the rest of his life, as far as we are allowed to see it, in a hell of his own making.

Macbeth's hell has three significant characteristics: first, a growing recognition of his predicament; second, a patent inability to get out of it (he cannot repent); and, third, a general restlessness which commits him alternately to fits of tedium and to senseless and frequently murderous acts of desperation. No sooner has he murdered Duncan than he finds himself troubled (somewhat naively, it must appear to us) about why he cannot say "Amen" to the sleeping groom's "God bless us!"

> But wherefore could not I pronounce "Amen"?
> I had most need of blessing, and "Amen"
> Stuck in my throat.
>
> (II.ii.31-33)

Although a few lines farther on he says that he is afraid to think what he has done (51), by the end of the scene he knows well enough what he has done and wishes it were undone:

> To know my deed, 'twere best not know myself.
> Wake Duncan with thy knocking! I would
>   thou couldst!
>
> (II.ii.73-74)

In Scene iii, with the confusion swirling about him, he comes privately to an acknowledgment of where he now stands:

Had I but died an hour before this chance,
I had liv'd a blessed time; for, from this instant,
There's nothing serious in mortality.
All is but toys; renown and grace is dead;
The wine of life is drawn, and the mere lees
Is left this vault to brag of.

(II.iii.96-101)

This recognition suggests a condition so "nigh unto cursing"
that one might almost be justified in pronouncing it spiritual
death and completely accursed. But there is more to Macbeth's
punishment than this.

The Hebrew proverb says of the man who has preserved the
wisdom of the Lord in his life, "When thou liest down, thou
shalt not be afraid; yea, thou shalt lie down, and thy sleep shall
be sweet" (Proverbs III.24). Macbeth presumably knew the
meaning of this throughout most of his life; but as he is on his
way to kill Duncan, he reveals that he has suddenly all but forgotten what such peaceful sleep is like: "Now o'er the one half-
world / Nature seems dead, and wicked dreams abuse / The
curtain'd sleep (II.i.49-51). After Duncan is dead, an unidenti-
fied voice jogs his memory:

"Sleep no more!
Macbeth does murder sleep."—the innocent
sleep,
Sleep that knits up the ravell'd sleave of care,
The death of each day's life, sore labour's bath,
Balm of hurt minds, great nature's second course,
Chief nourisher in life's feast.

(II.ii.35-40)

Macbeth is counting blessings here that he has lost; for the
sleep that he has murdered is not merely Duncan's but his own,
as the voice, continuing, makes clear: "Glamis hath murder'd
sleep, and therefore Cawdor / Shall sleep no more; Macbeth
shall sleep no more" (II.ii.42-43). Macbeth continues to

threaten the sleep of others, of course. After Banquo, too, is dead and his ghost has disrupted the great banquet at Forres, Lennox recalls how Macbeth "rashly" invaded the sleep of the two grooms (III.vi.11-13), and an unnamed lord looks forward to a time that will "Give to our tables meat, sleep to our nights" (III.vi.34). Yet Macbeth fares worse than any of his victims. He observes that Duncan "After life's fitful fever . . . sleeps well"; nothing can touch him further (III.ii.23-26). He himself can only threaten that he will

> . . . let the frame of things disjoint, both
> the worlds suffer,
> Ere we will eat our meal in fear and sleep
> In the affliction of these terrible dreams
> That shake us nightly.
> (III.ii.16-19)

With his mind now "full of scorpions" (III.ii.36), he sees night as something designed primarily to provide cover for mischief (46-50); in contrast to the "Good things of day" it has only "black agents" that "to their preys do rouse" (52-53). Thus when his waking night of the banquet has in spite of wakefulness turned into a nightmare, he stands in the empty hall talking of blood until Lady Macbeth ironically observes, "You lack the season of all natures, sleep" (III.iv.141), and then goes to bed by daylight.

Along with the increasing terror of dreams Macbeth has the increasing terror of recognition. In his soliloquy before the murder of Duncan, he was confident enough to be willing to "jump the life to come." In the soliloquy that precedes his conference with the murderers of Banquo, he sings a slightly different tune:

> For Banquo's issue have I fil'd my mind;
> For them the gracious Duncan have I murder'd,
> Put rancours in the vessel of my peace
> Only for them; and mine eternal jewel

Given to the common enemy of man,
To make them kings.

(III.i.65-70)

Macbeth can now see that he has defiled his mind and that the
victim of that defilement was an innocent man, but even so, he
speaks only of "rancours in the vessel of my peace"; he cannot
repent of his deed because he still cannot see where he first went
wrong. His terror is born of the knowledge, now certain, that
he has given his "eternal jewel" to the Devil. Yet he has staked
everything upon his decision to outwit Providence, "here, upon
this bank and shoal of time," and from this course he does not
deviate: "come fate into the list," he says, "And champion me
to th' utterance" (III.i.71-72).

Macbeth's second visit to the witches is marked by the same
specious confidence. He thanks the first apparition for the
warning against Macduff. After a momentary hesitation, he
assures the second, who says that "none of woman born / Shall
harm Macbeth" (IV.i.80-81), that he will "make assurance
double sure / And make a bond of fate" (IV.i.83-84). When
the third apparition promises that "Macbeth shall never van-
quish'd be until / Great Birnam wood to high Dunsinane hill /
Shall come against him" (92-94), he laughs at the folly of such
a contingency and exults in what seems to him his own triumph
over time and mortality:

. . . never till the wood
Of Birnam rise, and our high-plac'd Macbeth
Shall live the lease of nature, pay his breath
To time and mortal custom.

(IV.i.97-100)

The "show of Eight Kings," however, which follows immediately
(upon Macbeth's own request to know more), brings forth an
unwittingly damning repudiation of devilish trumpery. "Infected be the air whereon they ride," he cries, "And damn'd all
those that trust them" (138-139). Even the information that

Macduff has fled to England does not enlighten him. He simply renews his resolution to outdo his declared adversary:

> Time, thou anticipat'st my dread exploits:
> The flighty purpose never is o'ertook
> Unless the deed go with it. From this moment
> The very firstlings of my heart shall be
> The firstlings of my hand.
>
> (IV.i.144-148)

Macbeth's determination to resort to rashness from now on is the last stage of his outrunning reason and his opposition to Providence; and, providential as that rashness itself may be, it reveals the desperateness of his situation and the utter sickness of his soul. Macbeth is indeed, as Malcolm puts it, "ripe for shaking" (IV.iii.238).

At the beginning of Act V, Shakespeare presents one of the most terrifying parodies of sleep in literature. The Doctor describes Lady Macbeth's performance there as "A great perturbation in nature, to receive at once the benefit of sleep and do the effects of watching" (V.i.10-12). Precisely what the sleepwalking scene indicates about the state of Lady Macbeth's soul is not for us to decide, but we can agree with the Doctor both when he says, "More needs she the divine than the physician" (V.i.82), and when he says, "Therein the patient / Must minister to himself" (V.ii.45-46). His words, of course, are equally applicable to Macbeth, who is now so spiritually ill that he can scarcely remember the "taste of fear." "The time has been," he says, "my senses would have cool'd / To hear a night shriek" (V.v.10-11); but now his senses are so dull that he receives the news of his Queen's death with an unfeeling "She should have died hereafter" (V.v.17). To one for whom all life has become a sleepless nightmare, mere darkness, whether of night or of death, is meaningless. Macbeth knows this, and he knows also the most that mere daylight can offer to him or to any other apostate: "To-morrow, and to-morrow, and to-morrow / Creeps in this petty pace from day to day / To the last syllable of recorded time; / And all our yesterdays have lighted fools / The way to dusty death" (19-23). He has not yet reached total despair, but he comes dangerously close to it when the messenger's report that Birnam wood has suddenly become a moving grove fulfills the seemingly impossible condition of the third apparition. His words now reveal him to be on the threshold of hopelessness: "I gin to be aweary of the sun, / And wish th' estate o' th' world were now undone" (49-50). Yet our applause for the vigorous "Blow, wind! come, wrack! / At least we'll die with harness on our back" (51-52), with which he meets the challenge, is surely premature. A lingering hope that he may still outwit the patently contradictory decrees of Providence motivates him here. What appears to be a revival of his old spirit is simply the desperate rally of a fool.

Much as he may curse the witches or "doubt the equivocation of the fiend / That lies like truth" (V.v.43-44), he still clings to the promise of the second apparition that none of woman born shall harm him. Thus he faces with equanimity both the taunts and the sword of young Siward and slays easily one more man born of women. Confronted by Macduff, however, who proclaims the proper qualification to be Macbeth's executioner, Macbeth does indeed despair and for the first time in his life declines to fight:

> Acursed be that tongue that tells me so,
> For it hath cow'd my better part of man!
> And be these juggling fiends no more believ'd
> That palter with us in a double sense,
> That keep the word of promise to our ear,
> And break it to our hope. I'll not fight with thee.

> (V.viii.17-22)

Macbeth's own easy explanation of his undoing here—if we take it as being that—is certainly not the explanation of the play. The juggling fiends usually have no power over a man who has not first tried to wear the mask of self-sufficiency, nor do Shake-

speare's fiends deceive Macbeth until he has voluntarily put on
the blindfold. What follows is a long and desperate game in
which they see while Macbeth stumbles in the dark. The end
of their game is to reveal him the fool he has elected to be and
to make him a coward.

Macduff's acceptance of Macbeth on his own terms—"Then
yield thee, coward" (V.viii.23)—marks the end of Macbeth's
playing at blind man's buff. His few words after that smack of
neither folly nor blindness:

> I will not yield,
> To kiss the ground before young Malcolm's feet
> And to be baited with the rabble's curse.
> Though Birnam wood be come to Dunsinane,
> And thou oppos'd, being of no woman born,
> Yet I will try the last. Before my body
> I throw my warlike shield. Lay on, Macduff,
> And damn'd be him that first cries, "Hold,
> enough!"
>
> (V.viii.27-34)

Here with the mask thrown aside he sees the folly of his attempt
to play God and bend Providence to his own will. All he has
left is the remnant of that great virtue with which he began.
We may call it bravery, valor, courage, or "manly readiness,"
which is Macbeth's own term (II.iii.139); and it is admirable in
its way, but it cannot save him. In spite of his apostasy he has
undoubtedly served God's providence; for we assume that God
had elected to correct Scotland in some way and prepare it for
a much greater role in history under the treble scepter of
Banquo's descendant, James VI. The choice of the way was
partly Macbeth's, and he chose foolishly.

The pathos of his action becomes apparent when we reflect
that with *both* his bravery and the recognition of his creatureliness that he was able to declare in that second scene with his
wife ("I dare do all that may become a man. / Who dares do
more is none"), Macbeth might have served Scotland well as

the Lord's anointed and ended his days heirless but with the honor, love, obedience, and troops of friends that on the day of his defeat he yearned for (V.iii.22-28). Yet having dared to do more than becomes man, he found himself qualified for only one angelic role, that of the apostate black angel. Thus he went on to play the scourge, and thus in the end he had to endure a similar scourging at the hands of another divinely appointed avenger. Macbeth's discovery at the end is really a recovery, at a terrible price, of that tiny essential bit of knowledge that he held in his hands briefly at the beginning, undervalued, and tossed aside: "Come what come may, / Time and the hour runs through the roughest day." After Macbeth is dead, Malcolm says, "The time is free" (V.viii.55); but we should not forget that briefly before the end Macbeth was finally free of his fool's dream of shackling time. Nothing in Macbeth's life became him quite like the leaving it; he died cleaner than he began, and he died with his manly readiness still about him. Undoubtedly this, too, was part of the providential plan.

Eleven

ANTONY AND CLEOPATRA

O N THE SURFACE it might seem that no story could be less
promising as material for Christian tragedy than that of Antony
and Cleopatra. As Franklin M. Dickey in his book on Shakespeare's love tragedies has shown, writers from classical times to
Shakespeare's time almost unanimously condemned the foul
and wasteful passion of the two lovers;[1] and, if Dickey is right
in his interpretation of the play, Shakespeare has preserved the
essential ingredients of this condemnatory tradition. Not all
critics, however, will agree with Dickey's reading of Shakespeare's play. Dickey himself lists a number of respectable
critics, including A. C. Bradley, R. H. Case, Mark Van Doren,
Donald Stauffer, and G. Wilson Knight, who have been inclined
to view the passion of Antony and Cleopatra in Shakespeare's
treatment of it as somehow transcending normal human limitations to become worth at least part of all the trouble it caused.[2]
One may question whether these two views of the play are
really as incompatible as they appear to be. Both are focused
on the passion as a thing in itself, over and above the characters
who participate in it; and wherever human passion is represented
as complexly and as faithfully as it is in this play, it is likely to
provoke disapproval from some and evoke praise from others.

At the risk of seeming perverse, I suggest that both of these views are allowable and even necessary in a full estimate of the play, but that the focus which has produced them is questionable. We may call *Antony and Cleopatra* a love tragedy if we like; love—or, more properly, lust—certainly provides the ground and occasion for much of the activity in it. But it is no more a play primarily about lust than *Henry V* is a play primarily about war. Lust, like war, usually turns out to be the dreary and wasteful business that moralists tell us it is; but, like most other wasteful human activities, lust can sometimes provide the occasion for a discovery of human potential that makes the waste seem worthwhile. Shakespeare's Antony may behave like a fool and his Cleopatra like a childish flirt; but they both have an extraordinary vitality that sets them apart from other people, and in the course of their action they discover a capacity for selflessness that truly distinguishes them. By stressing this aspect of the story, Shakespeare has managed to transcend the traditional moral exemplum and create a tragedy.

The unifying action of the play is suggested by a phrase which Caesar uses in the last scene when he observes that the dead Cleopatra looks "As she would catch another Antony / In her strong toil of grace" (V.ii.350-351). Regardless of what "catch an Antony" means to Caesar here, to catch an Antony—that is, to catch an image of human greatness—is precisely what Cleopatra has managed to do. And it is what all the principal characters, with varying degrees of awareness, have been trying to do since the beginning of the play. Caesar is a possible exception, because on the surface at least he seems to think greatness is already his. Thus we find him at the end coolly assuming all the glory for what has happened: "their story is / No less in pity than his glory which / Brought them to be lamented" (V.ii.364-366). Antony, however, longed for human greatness throughout his life, repeatedly snatched at it, and sometimes almost grasped it. Enobarbus, we may say, longed to share in that greatness vicariously, but came to recognize Antony's potential for it only after he had forfeited his chance to share:

O Antony,
Nobler than my revolt is infamous,
Forgive me in thine own particular;
But let the world rank me in register
A master-leaver and a fugitive.
O Antony! O Antony!

(IV.ix.18-23)

An image of human greatness is also what Cleopatra, like
Enobarbus, belatedly comes to see in the memory of her para-
mour, what she begins to find for herself only when she accepts
Antony in death, and what she articulates magnificently shortly
thereafter. "I dream'd there was an Emperor Antony. / O such
another sleep, that I might see / But such another man?" she
begins;

His face was as the heavens; and therein stuck
A sun and moon, which kept their course and
lighted
The little O, the earth. . . .
His legs bestrid the ocean; his rear'd arm
Crested the world; his voice was propertied
As all the tuned spheres, and that to friends;
But when he meant to quail and shake the orb,
He was as rattling thunder. For his bounty,
There was no winter in't; an autumn 'twas
That grew the more by reaping. His delights
Were dolphin-like; they show'd his back above
The element they liv'd in. In his livery
Walk'd crowns and crownets; realms and islands
were
As plates dropp'd from his pocket. . . .
Think you there was or might be such a man
As this I dream'd of?

(V.ii.76-94)

Dolabella, who, like most critics, has seen only Antony's element
and missed the dolphin back rising above it, answers honestly,

"Gentle madam, no." But Cleopatra, who knows what she knows, will not let his denial go unchallenged:

> You lie, up to the hearing of the gods!
> But, if there be or ever were one such,
> It's past the size of dreaming. Nature wants
>   stuff
> To vie strange forms with fancy; yet t'imagine
> An Antony were nature's piece 'gainst fancy,
> Condemning shadows quite.
>
>   (V.ii.95-100)

In this speech Cleopatra grasps the truth that makes possible the full development of *Antony and Cleopatra* as a tragedy. For in destroying Antony's opportunity to realize his potential—or, better, in frittering away her own opportunity to help him realize that potential—she has gained an image of greatness that Antony even in luckier times and circumstances might never have matched. In a way she herself perhaps does not quite realize, she has caught her Antony, the Antony that never quite was. Her vision is a glorious thing for anybody to achieve, but the unanswerable question of this or of any tragedy is, "Was the vision worth all the suffering and waste that it cost to achieve it?"

A more nearly answerable question—but one to which critics still give varying answers—has to do with the nature of the man from whom this vision was generated. Shakespeare's presentation of Antony is considerably more sympathetic than Plutarch's,[3] provided we take his whole representation of Antony and not merely the view he gives us of him in the first scene of Act I. There all we see is a general in his "dotage," whose heart has "become the bellows and the fan / To cool a gipsy's lust" (I.i.9-10). He walks across the stage, pushing messengers aside and shouting his fatuous, "Let Rome in Tiber melt, and the wide arch / Of the rang'd empire fall!" (I.i.33-34). Yet even in this scene we get a feeling that Antony is potentially greater than he seems to be: "Sir," says Philo, "sometimes, when he is not Antony, / He comes too short of that great property / Which still should go with Antony" (I.i.57-59). And even here, that great property is only just below the surface. The news of Fulvia's death in Scene ii brings him immediately to a sense of guilt at his neglect of her and his neglect of the responsibilities of his office; and from his resolution to make what amends he can, neither the cynicism of Enobarbus nor the wiles of Cleopatra can dissuade him. This is the Antony that Lepidus, whom the play judges as being of Antony's stuff though equal to him only in charity, sees and defends:

> I must not think there are
> Evils enow to darken all his goodness.
> His faults, in him, seem as the spots of heaven,
> More fiery by night's blackness; hereditary,
> Rather than purchas'd; what he cannot change,
> Than what he chooses.
>
> (I.iv.10-15)

Caesar, whom the play judges quite differently, sees only what is most convenient for him to see, and describes an Antony who "fishes, drinks, . . . wastes / The lamps of night in revel" (I.iv.4-5), and outdoes Cleopatra in effeminacy. "You shall find there," he adds, "A man who is the abstract of all faults / That all men follow" (I.iv.8-10). Caesar is too clever (honesty is not one of his virtues in this play) to pretend that Antony was never worthy of confidence. Antony is, after all, one of his "partners." Moreover, men still remember the famine that dogged Antony on his retreat from Modena, during which he drank "The stale of horses and the gilded puddle / Which beasts would cough at" and ate "strange flesh, / Which some did die to look on" (I.iv.55-68). This Antony, Caesar admits, was soldierly enough; but he hastens to recall an image of the present Antony: "Let his shames quickly / Drive him to Rome" (I.iv.72-73).

In spite of what Caesar says, Antony's behavior in the next two acts measurably increases our respect for him. In addition

to his human penchant for easy living[4] (a penchant, we should
note, that he seems to be able to leash and unleash at will), the
thing that gets Antony into trouble is his easy generosity: he
tries to observe more loyalties than the nature of things will
allow. We have already seen how his loyalty to Cleopatra, who
was at first clearly unworthy of it, caused him to neglect his wife
at Rome and the duties of his commission; yet when his responsibilities at Rome pressed themselves upon him, he responded
promptly, all the while protesting with obvious sincerity his
undiminished affection for Cleopatra: "By the fire / That quick-
ens Nilus' slime, I go from hence / Thy soldier, servant" (I.iii.
68-70). In his meeting with Caesar in Act II he handles himself
with dignity and becoming humility. He speaks respectfully
and admiringly of the dead Fulvia (II.ii.61-64) and excuses as
best he can the trouble she has made for Caesar. He freely
admits the "poisoned hours" that corrupted his judgment, yet
he does not condemn Cleopatra and he does not grovel:

> As nearly as I may,
> I'll play the penitent to you; but mine honesty
> Shall not make poor my greatness, nor my power
> Work without it.
>
> (II.ii.91-94)

His behavior here moves both Lepidus and Macenas to praise,
and it prompts Agrippa to suggest the marriage with Octavia. To
this Antony readily agrees and reaffirms his loyalty to Caesar:
"from this hour / The heart of brothers govern in our loves /
And sway our great designs!" (II.ii.149-151) He would be loyal
to Pompey too, if that were possible (II.ii.156-160); but Lepidus
persuades him that it is not. In the Roman scenes that follow,
he lives up admirably to his own statement of intention: "I have
not kept my square; but that to come / Shall all be done by th'
rule" (II.iii.6-7). He is loyal to Caesar, courteous to Pompey,
genial and gay but not undignified at the feast on board
Pompey's galley, and all understanding to the distracted Octavia
when it becomes apparent that Caesar has chosen to play false

and leave his unfortunate sister caught in the middle (III.iv. 20-38).

Plutarch's Antony gave Caesar some cause for duplicity,[5] but Shakespeare's gives him none. Antony's general, Ventidius, makes an unauthorized conquest of Parthia; but Antony knows nothing of this, nor does he make suspicious moves in the direction of Rome. He sits quietly in Athens with his new wife until the news of Caesar's double dealing, which includes also the removal of Lepidus, breaks upon him. Caesar dissembles habitually; Cleopatra dissembles naively, frivolously, and at the end disastrously; but Antony never dissembles at all. Whatever else he may be, he is as open as daylight; and this very openness, combined with his sense of loyalty, brings him to disaster and despair. Trusting Caesar, he lets the odds build up against him; trusting Cleopatra, he violates his own better judgment and that of his generals to stake his fortunes on an unreliable Egyptian fleet in the engagement at Actium. When Cleopatra and her fleet fail him, he sadly advises his attendants to take the one remaining ship of treasure and flee to Caesar. "I have fled myself," he tells them, "I follow'd that I blush to look upon; / My very hairs do mutiny" (III.xi.7-13). To Cleopatra he complains bitterly, "O, whither hast thou led me, Egypt?" (III.xi.51); but when she begs his pardon, he gives it and settles for a kiss. From this point on, his cup only grows more bitter. His appeal to Caesar brings a rebuff and a covert attempt to win Cleopatra away from him. His rash attempt to challenge Caesar to single combat brings him the contempt of Enobarbus. Finally, he comes upon Cleopatra as she is kissing the hand of Caesar's messenger and gives way completely. "O, that I were / Upon the hill of Basan," he cries after berating her as an impediment to his hopes, a liar, and a promiscuous wench, "to outroar / The horned herd. For I have savage cause; / And to proclaim it civilly were / A halter'd neck which does the hangman thank / For being yare about him" (III.xiii.126-131). But Antony is not upon the hill of Basan, at least not quite.

The allusion here is to Psalm XXII, which by almost any

criterion is one of the most striking of the so-called Messianic
Psalms. It begins with the words used by Christ on the cross,
"My God, my God, why hast thou forsaken me?"[6] and continues,
after a few verses,

But I am a worm, and no man; a reproach of men, and despised of
the people. All they that see me laugh me to scorn; they shoot out
the lip, they shake the head, saying, He trusted on the Lord that
he would deliver him: let him deliver him, seeing he delighted in him.
. . . Be not far from me; for trouble is near; for there is none to help.
Many bulls have compassed me: strong bulls of Bashan have beset
me round. They gaped upon me with their mouths, as a ravening
and a roaring lion.

(Psalm xxii.6-13)

It would be irrelevant to object here either that Antony's
allusion, taken as a reference to Christ, involves him in an
anachronism or that Shakespeare's application of it constitutes
blasphemy. To the Elizabethan audience and readers it pointed
as few other allusions could have to Antony's participation in
the common ground of humanity, seen here as the ground of
the Incarnation; but it probably never suggested to any Elizabethan that Antony is in any technical sense a figure of the
Christ. Quite obviously the speaker in Psalm xxii, surrounded
by scorners and tormentors, behaves with Christlike submissive-
ness. Just as obviously, Antony does not behave so; for he would
strike back if he could, "outroar the horned herd," and proclaim
his misfortune with anything but meek civility. But just as
Richard II's reference to his "sour cross" brought sharply to
mind both Richard's Christlike office and his un-Christlike
demeanor, so Antony's reference to the psalm brings into focus
the ironic contrast between the Antony of common repute and
that image of goodness in him which has been visible almost
from the beginning of the play. Here at the center of the play
Shakespeare underscores strikingly Antony's uniqueness and his
claim to greatness.

There have, of course, been several other suggestions of

Antony's special character before this point. Readers familiar with the Old Testament must have seen in Antony's story certain resemblances to the story of Samson, who has often been treated as a type of Christ.[7] Like Samson, Antony has his Delilah to tempt him from his destiny; but, even more important, Antony, like Samson the Nazarite, has a special destiny. Philo alludes to it in that first scene, when he speaks of "the great property / Which still should go with Antony" (I.i.58-59). Cleopatra perhaps recognizes it faintly when she calls him "The demi-Atlas of this earth, the arm / And burgonet of men" (I.v.23-24). The Egyptian soothsayer in Rome apparently knows all about it, for he advises Antony to get quickly back to Egypt and leave Caesar:

> Therefore, O Antony, stay not by his side.
> Thy demon, that thy spirit which keeps thee, is
> Noble, courageous, high, unmatchable,
> Where Caesar's is not; but, near him, thy angel
> Becomes a fear, as being o'erpower'd; therefore
> Make space between you.
>   (II.iii.18-23)

To the soothsayer as to Agrippa (who perhaps speaks better than he knows), Antony is indeed the "Arabian bird" (III.ii.12), the only one of his kind, mortal wherever he may be, but immortal only in the East, and even there only through death. Antony does not understand the soothsayer, of course; and it is doubtful whether he ever fully understands the unique role he himself plays. In his "saner" moments, he sees Egypt as the other Romans see it, speaks of "Egyptian fetters" (I.ii.120), and announces, "I must from this enchanting queen break off" (I.ii.132). Later, after the duplicity of Rome has driven him back to his enchanting queen and military disaster at Actium, he thinks that his earlier misgivings about Egypt have been amply confirmed: "my good stars that were my former guides, / Have empty left their orbs and shot their fires / Into th' abysm of hell" (III.xiii.145-147). The melting mood that follows quickly on these words and the "one other gaudy night" after that may tend to confirm our view that Antony in his saner moments was right. His "terrene moon" has been eclipsed and his destiny missed.

We should be cautious, however, about accepting too readily the Roman view of things. Antony does fulfill his destiny, which is to produce an image of greatness more striking than even his friends think possible. His refusal to take the Roman way prompts Enobarbus to contemplate for himself the Judas way (III.xiii.195-201); and the farewell supper that follows in Act IV, for all its derivation from Plutarch, continues the familiar pattern:

> Tend me tonight;
> May be it is the period of your duty:
> Haply you shall not see me more; or if,
> A mangled shadow. Perchance to-morrow
> You'll serve another master. I look on you
> As one that takes his leave. Mine honest friends,
> I turn you not away; but like a master
> Married to your good service, stay till death.
> Tend me to-night two hours, I ask no more,
> And the gods yield you for't!
>
> (IV.ii.24-33)

The suggestiveness of Antony's premonition here is intensified when we observe that the traitor Enobarbus is also at the table, cynically protesting sentimentality; yet the suggestiveness increases even more as Antony changes the tone of his remarks:

> Know, my hearts,
> I hope well of to-morrow, and will lead you
> Where rather I'll expect victorious life
> Than death and honour.
>
> (IV.ii.41-44)

Meanwhile, if we may believe the soldiers outside, Antony's god, Hercules, is forsaking him (IV.iii); and by morning Enobarbus has gone too. To compare the defeat and complete betrayal that follow to Golgotha might seem to some blasphemous and to others absurd; but Antony in the rage that Shakespeare, not Plutarch, gives him does not hesitate to draw a comparison with the death of the god he recognizes:

> The shirt of Nessus is upon me. Teach me,
> Alcides, thou mine ancestor, thy rage.
> Let me lodge Lichas on the horns o' th' moon;
> And with those hands, that grasp'd the heaviest
>   club,
> Subdue my worthiest self.
>   (IV.xii.43-47)

In this, if in nothing else that he proposes, he succeeds. He does not kill the "witch"; he does not persuade Eros to kill him; he does not even manage a decent suicide. But by all worldly standards, he does subdue his worthiest self. One might say that he confirms his own metaphor, in which he describes for Eros the evanescent shape of a cloud and then concludes, "My good knave Eros, now thy captain is / Even such a body. Here I am Antony; / Yet cannot hold this visible shape" (IV.xiv.12-14). In this very disintegration of the Antony who might have achieved greatness by Caesar's standards, however, he completes the pattern whereby the birth of a superior greatness is made possible. The death of Antony is literally the death of the "Arabian bird"—a fiery and a "shameful" death, followed by a quite unexpected kind of resurrection.

The grave of the old Antony and the womb of the new is Shakespeare's Cleopatra, the torment of several generations of critics. One critic would have us believe that she changes radically with the death of Antony; another would have it that she remains the same Cleopatra from beginning to end. Both, of course, are right; for Shakespeare's "reformations" are seldom the simple substitution of a better personality for a bad one, but the miraculous maturation of what once seemed and was defective into something incredibly rich and good. They are redemptions such as only a Christian poet can understand. Cleopatra remains Cleopatra; her "faults" after Antony's death

mature into virtues and become a claim to nobility. The cause
of this transformation in Cleopatra is not merely the death of
Antony but the vision which his death occasions and to which
she gives expression two scenes later. This vision encompasses
and goes beyond all the other intimations of a better Antony
that we have seen in the play, including Antony's hopes for
himself; it is something born of Cleopatra, a magnificent kind
of birth, we are led to believe, of which no one else in the play is
capable. Dolabella is right to doubt that there ever was or might
be such a man; for such a mere man there never could be, and
the vision itself is unique.

The generation of this vision is the love death in Act IV,
Scene xv. Cleopatra's role is the active one here; Antony's, the
passive. Antony speaks seven times in this scene: twice, his
first and last speeches, to protest that Caesar has not killed him
and to beg that only his triumphs be remembered; once to plead
for haste in the hoisting; twice to advise Cleopatra about Caesar
and those around him; and twice to utter the memorable lines,
"I am dying, Egypt, dying." To him this death is the bitterest
kind of death, providing only a fleeting opportunity to make his
final wishes known. To Cleopatra it is undoubtedly this, too;
but her words transcend the occasion and in one of the most
marvellously sustained metaphors in Shakespeare reveal what is
happening within her. For how many nights they themselves
perhaps do not know, Cleopatra and Antony have sported
together in the dark of the palace. Now Cleopatra, seeing
Antony being borne to the monument, bids the sun be dark
again: "O sun, / Burn the great sphere thou mov'st in! Darkling
stand / The varying shore of th' world" (IV.xv.9-11). This
mock night, suggesting the end of one world as prelude to
another, becomes for her the one night of all the nights to be
fruitful; and Antony's "I am dying, Egypt" in her mind turns
with one of the commonest puns in Elizabethan literature into
a lover's plea for haste as well as a dying soldier's request for
pity. Her words continue the metaphor and draw his words
into it:

> But come, come, Antony,—
> Help me, my women,—we must draw thee up.
> Assist, good friends.
>   *Ant.*   O, quick, or I am gone.
>   *Cleo.* Here's sport indeed! How heavy
>   weighs my lord!
> Our strength is all gone into heaviness,
> That makes the weight. Had I great Juno's
>   power,
> The strong-wing'd Mercury should fetch thee up
> And set thee by Jove's side. Yet come a little,—
> Wishers were ever fools,—O, come, come, come;
>   [*They heave Antony aloft to Cleopatra.*]
> And welcome, welcome! Die when thou hast
>   liv'd;
> Quicken with kissing. Had my lips that power,
> Thus would I wear them out.
>
>   (IV.xv.29-40)[8]

Within the next twenty lines Antony manages to interrupt four times and finally succeeds in delivering his brief valedictory as Cleopatra's impatience dissolves into frustration: "Noblest of men, woo't die? / Hast thou no care of me? Shall I abide / In this dull world, which in thy absence is / No better than a sty?" And then her words continue, their sexual implications stronger than ever:

> The crown o' th' earth doth melt. My lord!
> O, wither'd is the garland of the war,
> The soldier's pole is fall'n! Young boys and girls
> Are level now with men; the odds is gone,
> And there is nothing left remarkable
> Beneath the visiting moon.
>
>   (IV.xv.59-68)

The metaphor here marks the end of their last "gaudy night." It is powerful enough for all who will to see it, yet it is something best left unnoticed by those who find it distasteful or by those

who may be inclined to snicker. The honesty and power of
Antony and Cleopatra are not for readers like these. As for
Cleopatra, the habitual folly of her life has just been transformed
through her own creative poetry into the symbol for a glorious
expenditure; in losing everything she has suddenly achieved the
glory of meekness that leaves her at once pure woman and the
richest of women. Iras, who thinks (in one sense rightly) that
she is dead with Antony, addresses her as "Royal Egypt, Em-
press!" And Cleopatra replies:

> No more but e'en a woman, and commanded
> By such pure passion as the maid that milks
> And does the meanest chares. It were for me
> To throw my sceptre at the injurious gods,
> To tell them that this world did equal theirs
> Till they had stol'n our jewel.

> (IV.xv.73-78)

In Act V Shakespeare rapidly completes his portrait of Cleopatra; he takes nothing back that he has already put there, but
in his finished design he converts her blemishes into beauties.
Her first words are significant: "My desolation does begin to
make / A better life" (V.ii.1-2). And her first resolution shows
the old childish willfulness transformed into a determination of
cosmic proportions:

> 'Tis paltry to be Caesar;
> Not being Fortune, he's but Fortune's knave,
> A minister of her will: and it is great
> To do that thing that ends all other deeds;
> Which shackles accidents and bolts up change;
> Which sleeps, and never palates more the dung,
> The beggar's nurse and Caesar's.

> (V.ii.2-8)

Her reply to Proculeius, Caesar's messenger, shows no wavering,
as some have said it does, but a double-edged piece of irony,
mocking both Caesar and her old habitual vacillation:

> Pray you, tell him
> I am his fortune's vassal, and I send him
> The greatness he has got. I hourly learn
> A doctrine of obedience, and would gladly
> Look him i' th' face.
>
> (V.ii.28-32)

Her old capacity for rage is undiminished, too, as Proculeius learns when his guards seize her from behind (V.ii.49-62). But most important of all, her penchant for idle daydreaming (see especially I.v.18-26) has matured into a genuinely creative imagination, which first manifested itself when her words turned death into a victory and which now, as Dolabella enters, brings to full life the new Emperor Antony: "I dream'd there was an Emperor Antony, / O, such another sleep, that I might see / But such another man?" (V.ii.76ff). Dolabella's honesty and his frank admission that at Rome she will be led in triumph condition her encounter with Caesar. Being Cleopatra still, she follows her natural way, which is to outfox the fox, and turns the failure of a simple ruse (her attempt to withhold her treasure) into the means whereby she convinces her opponent that he is still dealing with a child. Caesar never sees, or even suspects, the existence of the Cleopatra who can say, "I am again for Cydnus / To meet Mark Antony" (V.ii.228-229); "I have nothing / Of woman in me; now from head to foot / I am marble constant; now the fleeting moon / No planet is of mine" (238-241); and finally, "Husband, I come. / Now to that name my courage prove my title! / I am fire and air; my other elements / I give to baser life" (290-292). Caesar would surely have found incomprehensible her resumption of the metaphor by which she came to know her ability to be all these things: "The stroke of death is as a lover's pinch, / Which hurts, and is desir'd" (298-299) . . . "If she [i.e., Iras] first meet the curled Antony, / He'll make demand of her, and spend that kiss / Which is my heaven to have" (304-306) . . . "Dost thou not see my baby at my breast, / That sucks the nurse asleep?" (312-313) . . . "As sweet as balm, as soft as air, as gentle,— / O Antony!" (314-315).

And when Caesar comes upon her dead, the most he can do is to play the coroner and inquire the cause of death, comment upon her "catching" ways ("she looks like sleep. / As she would catch another Antony / In her strong toil of grace"), and take all the glory for himself.

We should not be too hard upon this Caesar of Shakespeare's, for his function in the play is to stand as the sane representative of our own commonsense judgment of these events. Who of us, looking upon Antony from Caesar's seat, would not have found him one "to be chid / As we rate boys who, being mature in knowledge, / Pawn their experience to their present pleasure, / And so rebel to judgement" (I.iv.30-33)? Who, being Caesar, would not have sought to excuse his part in Antony's death as a regrettable necessity?

> O Antony!
> I have followed thee to this; but we do lance
> Diseases in our bodies. I must perforce
> Have shown to thee such a declining day,
> Or look on thine; we could not stall together
> In the whole world.
>
> (V.i.35-40)

Who, moreover, in all honesty, would not have been tempted to deal with the irresponsible Antony as Caesar dealt with him? Or would not have planned, for the good of the Empire, to make full practical use of the misfortunes of an alien queen? The bare facts of the play amply justify Caesar's attitude and his actions, provided of course that we apply to those facts Caesar's values, which are the values of the world of government, of business, and of affairs generally, wherever advantage is important and worldly success is the end in view. The actions of Antony and Cleopatra, however, have a motive which Caesar's values cannot measure—which, in fact, his values keep him from seeing.

Antony and Cleopatra insist upon their right to exist as uniquely valuable creatures in a creation that asks only to be

known and loved in its infinite variety; Caesar by contrast is
capable of seeing creation only as something imperfect, recalci-
trant, and disorderly. One might call his view puritanical, because it suggests strongly the view held by many Elizabethan
advocates of reformed religion, who not only sought to correct
their own disorderly natures but also felt obligated to bring all
nature into line and make it serviceable. In such a view as theirs
—and Caesar's—Cleopatra is an excellent example of that incorrigible part of creation which must either be exposed as
dangerous or destroyed altogether. Clearly Caesar has no intention of trying to reform Cleopatra; he will simply exhibit her
in all her disorderliness in one of his orderly triumphs at Rome.
But he does seem disposed, at least in the beginning, to give
Antony a chance to reform provided he will consent to serve
as a dignified representative of Roman authority in the domain
assigned to him. This is where the attitudes of the two men
come into open conflict. In order to be acceptable to Caesar,
Antony must cease to be true to himself. When he tries to give
the loyalty that Caesar requires, he finds that Caesar goes right
on condemning everything that has made Antony a generous
giver of loyalty in the first place. Ostensibly his rebellion against
Caesar is provoked by a discovery that Caesar cannot be trusted
(III.iv.), but it goes much deeper than that, as his remarks to
Octavia make clear: "If I lose mine honour, / I lose myself;
better I were not yours / Than yours so branchless" (22-24).
He now knows the truth of the soothsayer's warning—"near
him [Caesar], thy angel / Becomes a fear, as being o'erpower'd"
(II.iii.21-22). Thus he races back to Egypt, where in the em-
braces of the frivolous queen he sees at least some hope of
preserving his integrity.

Shakespeare does not attempt here to gloss over Antony's
extravagances or the disaster that follows; but as he presents
Antony's response to his succession of defeats and disappoint-
ments, he brings us gradually to the perception that, for Antony,
being Antony, fully and without shame, is the only thing that
really matters. Little by little he brings into focus that Antony

of godlike aspect who can stand figuratively upon the hill of
Bashan and wear the shirt of Nessus that destroyed his ancestor
Hercules. Moreover, he makes this aspect of Antony godlike
in a way that should be familiar to Christian readers; for fundamental as it is to Antony to preserve his integrity, it is equally
fundamental to his nature to give himself whole and complete
to anyone who will receive. At first, all the recipients are
unworthy: Caesar disdains the whole gift of Antony, and
Cleopatra gobbles it up as if it were a trifle. Thus Antony, being
human for all his godlike selflessness, receives their rejections
with all the savagery of which frustrated mankind is capable.
Two glories should redeem him in our eyes. The first is that
even at the end he prefers to destroy himself rather than
compromise:

> I made these wars for Egypt; and the Queen,—
> Whose heart I thought I had, for she had mine,
> Which whilst it was mine had annex'd unto 't
> A million moe, now lost,—she, Eros, has
> Pack'd cards with Caesar, and false-play'd my
> > glory
> Unto an enemy's triumph.
> Nay, weep not, gentle Eros; there is left us
> Ourselves to end ourselves.
>
> (IV.xiv.15-22)

The second and greatest glory is that, in the end, recollection
of the Antony who could not compromise effects a meta-
morphosis in the childish Cleopatra.

Antony's example does nothing for Caesar, who can see only
the Antony that would not be remade in the image of Caesar.
By his standards Antony fails miserably. But Enobarbus comes
to know better when he sees that Antony's generosity and love
will pursue him even in desertion; and Cleopatra comes to know
better when Antony's fumbling suicide makes her realize the
hollowness of her pretenses and the selflessness of a devotion that
would follow her even where "souls do couch on flowers"

(IV.xiv.51). By the manner of his dying Antony shocks Cleopatra into recognizing what integrity she herself is capable of, and in her recollection of the troubled career of her lover she discovers the pattern whereby she too may achieve greatness.

The essential character of that pattern makes complete sense only when viewed from the Christian perspective that Antony's allusion to the Messianic psalms explicitly invites. The Christian perspective in no way enables us to justify Antony's excesses *as* excesses, and it does not keep the story of the two lovers from being one of pagans who dared "rush into the secret house of death / Ere death dare come" (IV.xv.81-82). It does enable us, however, to see the main thing about them: that here were two people whose selfless expenditure of themselves enabled them to achieve an image of humanity greater than themselves and greater than the Caesar who, in a worldly sense, triumphed over them. That image embodies the distinctively Christian ideal of humanity as a collection of uniquely valuable individual human beings wholly committed to the expenditure of themselves in love—and, if need be, sacrifice—for one another. Some Christians, of course, may argue that Antony and Cleopatra never really see the parallel between their human action and that perfect action of self-sacrifice which might have saved them, but to argue in this fashion is simply to argue that Shakespeare's play is not a Christian morality. The human expenditure does not save Antony and Cleopatra any more than commonsense and morality save Caesar, but the understanding they achieve by it is more than enough to make their play a tragedy. The great irony is not that Antony and Cleopatra fail to see the full significance of the role they play, but that Caesar, who has the easily recognizable virtues of order and propriety on his side, fails to see any of the real significance of it at all.

Twelve

CYMBELINE

$\mathcal{P}$ARTLY BECAUSE of several resemblances to Beaumont and Fletcher's *Philaster* (performed in 1609) and partly because of an unusually heavy reliance upon "romantic" material, Shakespeare's *Cymbeline* is often compared with popular Jacobean tragicomedy. One must concede that the play does have certain points in common with this genre. For one thing, it has an unusually complicated plot for a Shakespeare play; for another, it has a set of characters whose behavior as the play moves along is not always predictable with reference to given motivation. Both plot and characters have something of the untransformed cliche about them; and this quality is nowhere more evident than in the evil characters, Queen, Cloten, and to some extent Iachimo, all of whom could have been taken from half a dozen popular tragicomedies that appeared during this period. Other things about *Cymbeline* are very different from Jacobean tragicomedy. *Cymbeline* abounds in examples of knotty syntax; and one point in which tragicomedy most generally pleased was the absence of inverted sentences and teasingly abnormal phrasing. Absent from *Cymbeline*, however, are the lively touches of passion with which Beaumont and Fletcher intrigued their audiences. Shakespeare's play has no setpieces, no histrionic arias; there are roles aplenty, but few "great" scenes. The most striking difference of all, however, is in the denouement. The author of a tragicomedy frequently introduced in Act V a "forgotten fact," so that instead of moving on toward a happy conclusion, the play suddenly veered toward tragedy. Total disaster was always averted, of course, thanks usually to a *deus ex machina;* but someone usually got hurt in the process, and the play had to end with a mixture of rejoicing and pathos. The denouement of *Cymbeline* is not capricious in this way. There are no forgotten facts and nothing like a *deus ex machina* to bring it off; and the play ends without the usual admixture of pathos. The living are welcomed home; the dead, such as they are, are not mourned. These differences, as I have said, are superficial ones, but they all point to a difference that is not superficial; for *Cymbeline,* like the two plays that follow it in Shakespeare's canon, is more meaningful in terms of a broad integrated view of God and human affairs than any of the plays that Shakespeare had written previously. This aspect of *The Tempest* has already been examined by critics,[1] and we shall examine *The Winter's Tale* at some length in the final chapter of this book; but *Cymbeline* presents the essential difference between Shakespeare's tragicomedy and other kinds as clearly as either of these—perhaps more clearly than they do, since it is not encumbered with a wealth of allusion and complicated detail.

Shakespeare went to several sources for his play, principal among which were Holinshed (who gave him the business about Cymbeline's opposition to Rome), a twenty-year-old anonymous play called *The Rare Triumphs of Love and Fortune* (for the banishment of Posthumus and the rustication of Imogen) and the *Decameron* (for the wager plot). Judging by the freedom with which he used the materials in these sources, he could have made *Cymbeline* into almost any kind of play he wanted to. Obviously he wanted to do several things. First, he wanted to make the quarrel with Rome Cymbeline's quarrel (it originally belonged to Guiderius); second, he arranged to have the sons lost and estranged from their father; third, he changed the wager plot into a temptation plot (Iachimo suggests the wager, not Posthumus); and fourth, he added the evil characters—Queen, Cloten, and Iachimo. The result, oddly perhaps, is more comparable to Shakespeare's own romantic tragedy *Romeo and Juliet* than to romantic tragicomedy. In *Cymbeline* as in the earlier play the relation between the two lovers has a bearing upon the relation of two larger parties, and in both the broader opposition is resolved through the lovers. The differences, of course, are equally obvious. In *Cymbeline* the two larger parties, Britain and Rome, do not bear the same relation to the lovers as the families of Capulet and Montague do to Juliet and Romeo; for in *Cymbeline* both lovers are originally from one of the conflicting parties, Britain. Moreover, in *Romeo and Juliet*, where each lover represents a separate faction, the lovers resolve the conflict by unwittingly giving themselves in a sacrifice which is immediately recognized to be pathetic. In *Cymbeline* the lovers resolve the larger conflict as well as their own by participating in the conflict itself, first on one side and then on the other; and this participation brings about not loss but gain, with the lovers reunited, the lost daughter returned, and the lost brothers found. Thus, whereas the conflict in *Romeo and Juliet* unites and purges, it wastes too. In the more optimistic *Cymbeline* nothing is wasted. Even Iachimo, whom some readers might be glad to let go, is salvaged and redeemed.

The greatest difference between these two plays, however, is the same as the difference between *Cymbeline* and the plays of Beaumont and Fletcher. It is the difference between drama that is essentially secular and drama that is essentially Christian. One does not have to be Christian to understand *Romeo and Juliet*, for all its Christian furniture; in fact, Christian interpreters are sometimes tempted to intrude serious considerations —for example, in regard to the suicides—that have to be ruled out as irrelevant. Yet one does have to accept certain Christian presuppositions in order to make sense of *Cymbeline*, which has almost no Christian furniture and few clear-cut allusions to Christian scripture, custom, or doctrine. The movement of the plot, for example, is nothing if not Christian. We have a ruler, Cymbeline, who in a series of temptations is made to lose all he has that is worth possessing, his friend, his sons, his daughter and virtuous son-in-law, and his ally. In wrongheadedly banishing his son-in-law, moreover, he exposes him also to temptation and thus indirectly exposes his daughter to temptation, so that both daughter and son-in-law become objects of public suspicion and victims of despair. His fault in causing these virtuous young people to fall is probably his most grievous one, yet this is the fault that ultimately brings about the restoration and redemption of all who are worth saving and the purgation of the evil that has been causing trouble. Thus in Shakespeare's story we have nothing more or less than a version of the Christian paradox of the fortunate fall, which, in the familiar words of St. Paul (I Corinthians 1.18), "is to them that perish foolishness; but unto us which are saved it is the power of God." One might say, as Posthumus says of his dream in Act V:

> 'Tis still a dream, or else such stuff as madmen
> Tongue and brain not; either both or nothing;
> Or senseless speaking, or a speaking such
> As sense cannot untie. Be what it is,
> The action of my life is like it, which
> I'll keep, if but for sympathy.
>
> (V.iv.146-151)

In short, the action of this play, senseless or not, is like the mysterious Christian pattern of redemption; and it places squarely in the hands of the Almighty the disposition of men's affairs and the election of those who are to be redeemed from and through the sin in which all participate. Iachimo, Posthumus, Imogen, and Cymbeline, all come clean in the end because they recognize fully who and what they are and accept their salvation (if I may use the term as a metaphor here) as something operating miraculously from without.

The focus of the play, quite obviously, is on only two of these characters, Posthumus and Imogen, and of these two, primarily

on Posthumus. We see this partly in what Shakespeare has each
of them do and partly in the way he has arranged the scenes.
Acts I and II keep the focus pretty consistently on Posthumus:
he leaves Britain, goes to Italy, falls in with Iachimo, is tempted
to wager, is deceived, and is disillusioned:

> Is there no way for men to be, but women
> Must be half-workers? We are all bastards;
> And that most venerable man which I
> Did call my father, was I know not where
> When I was stamp'd. Some coiner with his tools
> Made me a counterfeit; yet my mother seem'd
> The Dian of that time. So doth my wife
> The nonpareil of this. O vengeance, vengeance!

> (II.v.1-8)

After this we see nothing more of Posthumus for two whole
acts (III and IV); for these are given over to setting forth a
similar fate for Imogen, who having learned of Posthumus'
distrust of her and wish to kill her, condemns her husband,
abandons both Britain and her sex, sickens, and, after taking the
"cordial" that Pisanio has given her, apparently dies (IV.ii).
After this point in her two acts, however, Imogen goes beyond
Posthumus. Recovering from the effects of the sleeping potion,
she wakes to find the headless body of Cloten beside her and
mistakenly thinks it the body of the banished Posthumus;
thereupon she begins to know her own frailty and to comprehend
something of the abiding affection she has always had for her
husband even while she was condemning him most bitterly.
Imogen's two acts, in short, establish a parallel with Posthumus'
misfortunes and point toward a happy resolution of them. This
resolution begins immediately with Act V, when Posthumus on
receiving the bloody token mistakenly thinks Imogen dead and
undergoes a genuine repentance. Three scenes later, in prison,
he begs the Almighty to take his life, worthless as it is, for the
life presumably lost:

For Imogen's dear life take mine; and though
'Tis not so dear, yet 'tis a life; you coin'd it.
'Tween man and man they weigh not every
                                        stamp;
Though light, take pieces for the figure's sake;
You rather mine, being yours; and so, great
                                        powers,
If you will take this audit, take this life,
And cancel these cold bonds.

(V.iv.22-28)

At this point, and not before, Posthumus is ready to receive the truth, about himself and about all the others of true blood and election in the play. He gets it, of course, from that crucial and much criticized Vision of Jupiter, which Shakespeare, if he did not write it himself (and there is really no sound reason for believing he did not), at least sanctioned and accepted.

Looking back over the play from the vantage point of Act V we see that this matter of blood and true nobility has been a leading theme of the play from the beginning. The first gentleman in Act I, Scene i, may be exaggerating when he describes Posthumus as

                    . . . a creature such
As, to seek through the regions of the earth
For one his like, there would be something
                                        failing
In him that should compare. I do not think
So fair an outward and such stuff within
Endows a man but he.

(I.i.19-24)

But Posthumus has the "election" of Imogen, in which, the first gentleman continues, "may be truly read / What kind of man he is," and he is acknowledged superior by almost everyone else in the play except possibly Cloten, who pretty obviously stands to him as a puttock to an eagle and hence is hardly capable of judging. Even Iachimo, who makes pretensions to nobility of blood, recognizes the nobility of Posthumus when Posthumus is still disguised as a simple countryman. "If that thy gentry, Britain," he says, "go before / This lout as he exceeds our lords, the odds / Is that we scarce are men and you are gods" (V.ii.8-10).

But this play does not stop with the assertion that Posthumus' natural nobility is recognizable; it asserts that all men of natural nobility are recognizable in some way. Shakespeare's device for getting this across is his representation of Belarius and the two princes. Belarius, alias Morgan, after much discussion of the superiority of rude Nature to a corrupt court, tells us out of the princes' hearing in Act III:

> How hard it is to hide the sparks of nature!
> These boys know little they are sons to th' King,
> Nor Cymbeline dreams that they are alive.
> They think they're mine; and, though train'd
>   up thus meanly
> I' th' cave wherein they bow, their thoughts
>   do hit
> The roofs of palaces, and nature prompts them
> In simple and low things to prince it much
> Beyond the trick of others.
>   (III.iii.79-86)

In Act IV the young princes show such a princely impatience to be about the business of war that Belarius is compelled to say: "their blood thinks scorn / Till it fly out and show them princes born" (IV.iv.53-54). And in Act V the British soldiers, who think the trio indeed peasants, confirm Belarius' somewhat prejudiced view: "'Tis thought," say they, "the old man and his sons were angels" (V.iii.85).

The play also recognizes that rank, even when not accompanied by natural nobility, deserves respect. The example of that in this play is Cloten, who is demonstrably ignoble in behavior yet whose headless trunk at Belarius' insistence gets proper burial:

Though mean and mighty, rotting
Together, have one dust, yet reverence,
That angel of the world, doth make distinction
Of place 'tween high and low. Our foe was
                                                    princely;
And though you took his life, as being our foe,
Yet bury him as a prince.

                                    (IV.ii.246-251)

We are expected to take Belarius' way as the way of safety, I
suppose; but we sympathize with Guiderius, who preferred not
to say anything at all the funeral. As the princes' song in Act IV
("Fear no more the heat o' th' sun") reminds us, at the center
of Shakespeare's *Cymbeline* is the good Christian axiom that
dust is dust. Even true nobility must recognize that; and where
such recognition falters, dust blinds the eyes. Cloten and his
mother, of course, have the blindness of death about them
from the beginning; they are completely ignoble, and no amount
of rank can save them. Dust also temporarily blinds those of
genuine nobility in the play, Cymbeline first and then Posthumus
and Imogen; but these, being of the elect, have the grace to see
their errors and repent. Iachimo, however, is the best example
of this; for, though a very bad man indeed, he has in him enough
of true nobility to recognize his misdoing and try to make
amends. His wickedness is of a wholly different order from that
of Cloten and the Queen, and Posthumus sees that fact clearly.
"Kneel not to me," he says modestly; "The power that I have
on you is to spare you, / The malice towards you to forgive you.
Live, / And deal with others better" (V.v.417-420). To this the
King echoes appropriately, "Nobly doom'd! / We'll learn our
freeness of a son-in-law; / Pardon's the word to all."

Posthumus and Imogen seem to be pretty well matched in
the order and degree of nobility within them. He is, in her
phrase, "a holy witch / That . . . enchants societies unto him"
(I.vi.166-167), and she, in his description, "more fair, virtuous,
wise, chaste, constant, qualified, and less attemptable than any
the rarest of . . . ladies in France" (I.iv.64-66). Moreover, as

each by virtue of virtue in himself recognizes virtue in the other,
so each recognizes the blindness of his own error. Imogen says,
"Our very eyes / Are sometimes like our judgements, blind" (IV.
ii.301-302); and Posthumus, after he has regained his senses,
"there are none want eyes to direct them the way I am going,
but such as wink and will not use them" (V.iv.192-194). Both
have winked and both have ceased to wink; yet in the end it is
Posthumus who receives the full epiphany. He receives it, as
has already been said, in the famous masquelike scene called
the Vision of Jupiter, which constitutes a revelation given
directly by God under the aspect of Jupiter in justification of his
ways. It should be stressed that there is no question of a pagan
Jupiter here. Jupiter is the One God, called Jupiter in this play
simply because the setting happens to be pre-Christian Britain.
Furthermore, he is no *deus ex machina*: he does not intervene,
he changes nothing, he adds nothing, he cuts no knots. He
merely reveals what might have been inferred anyhow—that
his Providence has been controlling things from the beginning.
The significant thing that he does is to emphasize and give
divine sanction to the paradox contained in Lucius' enlightened
remark to the grieving Imogen, "Some falls are means the
happier to arise" (IV.ii.403).

A bare statement of this is about all that Imogen gets before
the final accounting at the end of Act V—that and the
observation, also from Lucius, that the name Fidele "well fits"
her faith (IV.ii.381). For Imogen is distinguished primarily
by her faith; she is like those saints mentioned in Hebrews
xi.38-39 "of whom the world was not worthy": "they wandered
in deserts and in mountains, and in dens and caves of the earth.
And these all, having obtained a good report through faith,
received not the promise." The "promise" is for Posthumus;
and it comes to him properly, in the form of the Vision, upon
his profession of complete surrender, "Take this life, / And
cancel these cold bonds" (V.iv.27-28). The Vision falls into
two parts. The first is the appeal of Posthumus' family (all
ghosts, of course); and the second, Jupiter's reply. Of the

details of the appeal the following should be noted here. First, Sicilius Leonatus, father to Posthumus, raises the question of "undeserved" human suffering—"Hath my poor boy done aught but well?" He also observes that the "mould" or form of Posthumus (note where the virtue lies) has been pronounced good by the world. The First Brother notes that Posthumus alone of all the Britons has found favor with Imogen. Posthumus' mother wants to know why, once her son was elevated in such a marriage, he deserved to be "mocked" with exile. And Sicilius comes in again to demand why, further, he should be tempted by the wicked Iachimo with "needless" jealousy. Finally, all point out Posthumus' positive claims, lately proved in valorous deeds, to Jupiter's favor. The effect of all this is to raise the more general question of Jupiter's goodness and justice; but it should be noted that these questionings merely pick up, emphasize, and summarize the main threads of movement as they have been developing in the play from the beginning. *Cymbeline* as a whole has all along been inching toward the overwhelming question, "Is God good?" And now that Jupiter speaks in reply, he does so in terms that are as simple and as conventionally Christian as the prototype for them in Hebrews:

And ye have forgotten the exhortation which speaketh unto you as unto children, My son, despise not thou the chastening of the Lord, nor faint when thou are rebuked of him: For whom the Lord loveth he chasteneth, and scourgeth every son whom he receiveth. If ye endure chastening, God dealeth with you as with sons; for what son is he whom the father chasteneth not? But if ye be without chastisement, whereof all are partakers, then are ye bastards, and not sons.

(Hebrews xii.5-8)

The tenor of Jupiter's remarks to the suppliant ghosts is that his Providence accounts for everything, that he has chosen whom he will love, and that he will punish whom he has chosen:

Whom best I love I cross; to make my gift,
The more delay'd, delighted. Be content;

> Your low-laid son our godhead will uplift.
>   His comforts thrive, his trials well are spent.
> Our jovial star reign'd at his birth, and in
>   Our temple was he married. Rise, and fade.
> He shall be lord of Lady Imogen.
>   And happier much by his affliction made.
>
> (V.iv.101-108)

After this there can be no fear of bastardy for Posthumus, such as he once entertained (II.v.2), nor doubt of his election. The dream has been his revelation:

> Sleep, thou hast been a grandsire and begot
> A father to me, and thou hast created
> A mother and two brothers; but, O scorn!
> Gone! they went hence so soon as they were born.
> And so I am awake. Poor wretches that depend
> On greatness' favour dream as I have done,
> Wake and find nothing. But, alas, I swerve.
> Many dream not to find, neither deserve,
> And yet are steep'd in favours; so am I,
> That have this golden chance and know not why.
> What fairies haunt this ground?
>
> (V.iv.123-133)

The riddling prophecy which comes to him now (138-145), with its fresh mixture of Biblical echoes—the stately cedar suggesting the great tree of Ezekiel xxxi.3 and the metaphor of grafting from Romans xi.15-25—is the promise by which not only Posthumus, but all those of virtue may be saved. The good fortunes of Posthumus, Imogen, Cymbeline, and the two sons are all implicit in it; Posthumus, who possesses the promise but does not understand it, is nevertheless made happy by it. "The action of my life is like it, which / I'll keep, if but for sympathy," he says to himself (V.iv.150-151); then to the bewildered Gaoler, "I am merrier to die than thou art to live" (V.iv.176).

The long concluding scene of Act V is a series of discoveries and regenerative experiences for the characters who are entitled to them. Cymbeline's regenerative experience comes first, as he acknowledges Posthumus' virtue without really knowing who Posthumus is, grants dignities to the brothers and old Belarius without knowing who they are, and admits his own folly in submitting to the influence of the wicked Queen. Next he recognizes the virtue in young Fidele, without seeing of course that Fidele is really Imogen; and the result of this additional recognition of virtue in disguise is the repentance of Iachimo, which brings about the rediscovery of Posthumus, which in turn reunites the two lovers. An interesting development occurs shortly before the lovers are reunited when Posthumus, overcome with the realization that there was no justice at all in his order to have Imogen killed, strikes down the disguised Imogen as she protests his excessive grief. Cymbeline's startled exclamations here, as Pisanio reveals that it is Imogen and not some obscure servant who has been struck, help us see what is happening: "Does the world go round?" and "the gods do mean to strike me / To death with mortal joy." The Christian paradox which gives the whole play its meaning, "Whom the Lord loveth, he chasteneth, and scourgeth every son whom he receiveth," here gets perfect and clear realization at the historical level of the play. Posthumus in his last moment of blindness, inadvertently and not wantonly, does what God in the fullness of knowledge and perfect wisdom continually does: he chastens the one whom he loves. As a human being he errs, and as human being he is mercifully forgiven; the result, however, is wholly good. Imogen, come again to life, embraces him as the soul the body or fruit the tree, and Cymbeline pronounces benediction upon them both: "My tears that fall / Prove holy water on thee" (V.v.268-269).

In the remaining portion of this scene other necessary business takes place: Belarius and the brothers are properly identified, the family is made whole again, and Iachimo, unwitting agent of a good deal of the divine chastening, is forgiven. The most interesting business, however, has to do with the yet unexplained prophecies. The first of these, we recall, is the one given to Posthumus; and this, with the possible exception of that detail about "tender air," virtually explains itself. Lucius' soothsayer makes the obvious explanation official. The other is that prophecy, first mentioned in Act IV, Scene ii, just before Lucius discovers Imogen-Fidele prostrate on Cloten's headless body. As delivered and explained by the Soothsayer at that point in the play, it goes as follows:

> Last night the very gods show'd me a vision—
> I fast and pray'd for their intelligence—thus:
> I saw Jove's bird, the Roman eagle, wing'd
> From the spongy south to this part of the west,
> There vanish'd in the sunbeams; which portends—
> Unless my sins abuse my divination—
> Success to the Roman host.
>   (IV.ii.346-352)

The point should be made, however, that the Soothsayer's explanation is not quite accurate. It is the British host, not the Roman, thanks largely to Posthumus, Belarius, Guiderius, and Arviragus, that has succeeded on the battlefield; and because the battle *has* been won by these four—principally with the aid of Posthumus—the victory for Britain can be a victory for Rome too. Lucius can thank Posthumus for a regenerated Cymbeline, for whom victory involves—something that would be utter madness in any context except a Christian one—paying tribute to the vanquished and forgoing all special prerogatives due to an earthly victor. Thus the Soothsayer can say, without referring to his previous error, that the dream "foreshow'd our princely eagle, / Th' imperial Caesar, should again unite / His favour with the radiant Cymbeline, / Which shines here in the west." In our own day it is fashionable to say that no one ever really wins a war; here no one loses. The conflict ends with victory and happiness for both sides, praise to the gods, and ratification of the peace in the temple of Jupiter.

Tragicomedy also usually ends with peace and kisses all round;

but Cymbeline, though related to tragicomedy by both materials and convention and therefore clearly a member of that family, has, as we have seen, a very different spiritual lineage. Because it participates in a Christian point of view, *Cymbeline* is related also to the Corpus Christi plays, to the English moralities, and to the Shakespearean tragedies; but it differs from these spiritual predecessors much as Pauline Christianity ("unto the Jews a stumblingblock, and unto the Greeks foolishness") differs from some of the other early formulations of the faith. Having accommodated itself to the morality and the more classical modes of drama, Christianity here adapts itself to a mode so fantastic that to many minds the new mode can only be an impediment to understanding. There is still current a Hebraic kind of puritanism that demands drama like the morality, and a Hellenic kind that demands something of which Aristotle conceivably might have approved; moralists and philosophers alike decline to take seriously the pleasant capriciousness of tragicomedy, which many sophisticated Jacobeans applauded. What Shakespeare has done, however, is to discover in the very capriciousness of this ephemeral art form a symbol of something that neither the morality nor the classical modes of drama had adequately accounted for—the mystery of a gracious Providence and its inscrutable workings among mankind. Shakespeare's *Cymbeline* moves in the same spirit as Paul's words to the Romans:

And we know that all things work together for good to them that love God, to them who are the called according to his purpose. For whom he did foreknow, he also did predestinate to be conformed to the image of his Son, that he might be the firstborn among many brethren. Moreover whom he did predestinate, them he also called: and whom he called, them he also justified: and whom he justified, them he also glorified.

(Romans viii.28-30)

Here is the context for Posthumus, for Imogen, for Cymbeline, Belarius, Arviragus, Guiderius, and wily Iachimo. It is not the

context for the characters of *Philaster*, *A King and No King*, and
The Maid's Tragedy. T. S. Eliot once compared the tragicomedies of Beaumont and Fletcher to flowers stuck in sand.[2]
Shakespeare's tragicomedies, if we should really call them that,
are plants of the same species, but they have roots in damp, rich,
ancient soil; and they are legitimately gaudy.

Thirteen

THE WINTER'S TALE

J n *The Winter's Tale* Shakespeare continued his transformation of tragicomedy. We sometimes hear it said that this play, like *Cymbeline*, is simply a kind of tragicomedy, more or less after the manner of Beaumont and Fletcher and very likely designed for performance at Blackfriars. It is certainly true that many things about *The Winter's Tale* remind us of those tragicomedies which were becoming popular with Jacobean audiences, and it is reasonable to suppose that the Jacobeans themselves, in retrospect at least, thought of Shakespeare's play as another specimen of that form. Nevertheless, Shakespeare's startling restoration of Hermione in the last scene, together with his relegation of the reunion of Perdita and Leontes to a narration by three gentlemen, marks a shift of emphasis in the development of his plot that probably disturbed some members of the original Jacobean audience almost as much as it has worried modern scholars. We normally expect to find a large element of surprise in the denouement of a tragicomic plot; and we are prepared to receive surprises that will make us doubt, right up to the very end, whether the play can possibly end happily. What we do not expect is that the plot will move, as that of *The Winter's Tale* does, toward what promises to be a perfectly satisfactory denouement, bypass that lightly, and then proceed to a completely gratuitous miracle so arresting that it overshadows everything that has gone before.

A look at Shakespeare's source for the play, Robert Greene's popular *Pandosto*, suggests no explanation at all for this seeming caprice in plotting. In Greene's novel the character who corresponds to Shakespeare's Hermione actually dies, and the narrative moves on without impediment to a climactic meeting between father and daughter. Greene, of course, represented this meeting as something considerably less than happy, having the aging but lustful king, ignorant of the girl's identity, first woo his daughter with unbecoming ardor and then kill himself out of remorse. Shakespeare's efforts toward removing such unpleasant features as these from his own version of the story are understandable, and we can be grateful to him for making them. For that matter, we can be grateful to him for deciding to spare the lovely thing he himself made of Hermione; but our gratitude need not blind us to the fact that nothing in the plot required him to spare her. And nothing in Greene's narrative provides any real answer to the tantalizing question: Why did Shakespeare go out of his way to let Hermione return after being presumed dead for sixteen years?

The only halfway satisfactory answer that has been advanced so far is that Shakespeare somehow meant his play to be taken as a parable of sin and redemption with Hermione serving as a sort of vague symbol for divine grace. There is much in the play to support this thesis—for example, Hermione's identification of her acceptance of Leontes' suit with grace in Act I, Scene ii:

> My last good deed was to entreat his
>   [Polixenes'] stay;
> What was my first? It has an elder sister,
> Or I mistake you. O, would her name were Grace!
> But once before I spoke to th' purpose; when?
> Nay, let me have't; I long.
>   *Leon.*   Why, that was when

Three crabbed months had sour'd themselves to
death,
Ere I could make thee open thy white hand
And clap thyself my love, then didst thou utter,
"I am yours for ever."
     Her.   'Tis grace indeed.
                  (I.ii.97-105)

Admittedly, Hermione is being playful here, but there is at
least as much justice as playfulness in her remark. For if it was
as grace that she came to Leontes in his innocent youth and so
remained with him until he, blinded by his own willful error,
cast her off, it was certainly as divine grace that she returned
at last to take him up again when his hope of justification had
completely melted away. At any rate, Leontes himself is prepared to call her that when in the last act he looks at what he
thinks is a statue:

Chide me, dear stone, that I may say indeed
Thou art Hermione; or rather, thou art she
In thy not chiding, for she was as tender
As infancy and grace.
                  (V.iii.24-27)

Grace, then, is the theme of the play, according to this thesis;
and Shakespeare's last scene is necessary to complete the exploration of that theme. Thus we have an interpretation that even
the most conservative of us can accept. We may suppose either
that Shakespeare began with his theme and shaped Greene's
tragicomic fable to fit it, or perhaps that he simply set out to
dramatize Greene's fable and somewhere along the way found
that he had drawing unconsciously upon a doctrinal pattern so
inextricably woven into the contemporary fabric of belief that
even the barest hint of it in the material he was working on
could make it operative. In any case, we can be confident that
only a very devious dialectician would ever attempt to disprove
the connection between Hermione and that Christian grace

which comes not so much as the result of man's deserving it as of man's contrition and willingness to receive.

The unfortunate thing about this conservative approach to *The Winter's Tale* is not that it heads in the wrong direction (the direction seems to be right), but that it betrays a timidity unworthy of its object, to say nothing of a willingness to stop short just as the exploration begins to get really interesting and profitable. There is something far more interesting in this play than a correspondence between Hermione and divine grace, and that something is her correspondence to the incarnation of divine grace, Jesus Christ. This does not mean that Hermione stands for Christ or serves as an allegory for Christ in the sense that a pelican in an emblem may, but rather that she has the status of a lesser incarnation. That is, the manifestation of grace in her is so discernible as an imperfect realization of that quality which is perfectly manifested in the Son of God that we are led to see in her simple acts of forgiveness the pale but unmistakable reflection of His mercy and redeeming love. We see this, moreover, not merely because true forgiveness is always Christlike, but because the whole world of the play in which Hermione appears is involved with her in this lesser incarnation: all the principal characters and events with which she is associated share her recognizable status and correspond analogically, though imperfectly, to characters, institutions, and events associated historically with the perfect Incarnation.

When an interpretation of a play is to turn upon an analogy of this kind, the best place to begin is at some passage in which the analogy tends to become explicit. There are several such passages in *The Winter's Tale*, but the most interesting is probably that in Act III, Scene ii, in which Hermione, replying to Leontes' invitation to "feel our justice," delivers this speech (the italics are, of course, my own):

> Sir, spare your threats.
> *The bug which you would fright me with I seek;*
> To me can life be no commodity.

The crown and comfort of my life, your favour,
I do give lost; for I do feel it gone,
But know not how it went. *My second joy*
And first-fruits of my body, from his presence
I am barr'd, like one infectious. *My third*
                                        comfort,
Starr'd most unluckily, is from my breast,
The innocent milk in it most innocent mouth,
Hal'd out to murder; myself on every post
Proclaim'd a strumpet; with immodest hatred
The child-bed privilege deni'd, which longs
To women of all fashion; lastly, *hurried*
Here to this place, i' th' open air, before
I have got strength of limit. Now, my liege,
Tell me what blessings I have here alive,
That I should fear to die? Therefore proceed.
But yet hear this: mistake me not; no life,
I prize it not a straw; but for mine honour,
Which I would free,—*if I shall be condemn'd*
Upon surmises, all proofs sleeping else
But what your jealousies awake, I tell you
'Tis rigour and not law. Your honours all,
I do refer me to the oracle:
Apollo be my judge!

                    (III.ii.92-97)

Reading these lines with special attention to those in italics makes it hard to avoid the notion that Shakespeare himself, either while working with the passage or on looking back at it afterward, saw emerging from it the central analogy of the play. Hermione, refusing to fear the death that is offered her as a form of justice, proclaimed a strumpet on every post, and hurried into a place in the open air before she has her strength—all this should suggest readily enough, even to a modern reader, the familiar career of Jesus from Gethsemane to Golgotha. But what of the other details? What of Leontes, the crown and comfort of her life; Mamillus, the firstfruits of her body, from whom she is barred; and Perdita, her third comfort, innocent

yet haled out to murder? If these cannot be linked to Hermione
as part of the central analogy, there is not much point in pur-
suing our inquiry further. Merely to find a Christlike character,
however interesting, in a play or story is not to find in it the
kind of analogy we are dealing with here; for that kind of
analogy requires that the fable as a whole, or at least the
essential parts of it, participate with the Christlike character
in the same general analogy. But Leontes, Mamillus, and
Perdita, to say nothing of the others, do participate in Hermione's action in this way; and they do so recognizably for us,
once we have accustomed our eyes to the light which can help
us see how they do.

There is some light available to that end in the ninth, tenth,
and eleventh chapters of St. Paul's Epistle to the Romans, which
deals with the historical realization of that course of redemption
which parallels the action of this play. If we are willing to grant
that Hermione the redeemer is like St. Paul's Christ who saves
by grace (Romans xi.5-6), we shall have little difficulty in seeing
that the appropriate analogy for Leontes is the Jew, whom St.
Paul declared it was his heart's desire to see saved (x.1). It was
Leontes, remember, who first paid court to grace and first on
earth received it; and it was he who learned through the bitter
process of stumbling, jealous fury, and alienation the meaning
of that paragon he had previously taken for granted as his legal
right. This is precisely the course that Paul predicted for the
disinherited Jew: "And David saith, Let their table be made a
snare, and a trap, and a stumblingblock, and a recompence unto
them: Let their eyes be darkened, that they may not see, and
bow down their back alway. I say then, Have they stumbled
that they should fall? God forbid: but rather through their fall
salvation is come unto the Gentiles, for to provoke them to
jealousy" (xi.9-11). Following this line of interpretation we
arrive naturally at the following analogies for Mamillus and
Perdita. Mamillus, who dies, suggests the Jewish church, beloved
of Christ but ultimately denied to him; for, from the Christian
point of view, that church died upon the cross. And Perdita,

who is consistently referred to as the *heir* in the play, suggests the true Church, rejected, "hal'd out to murder" even in infancy, yet destined to survive, be grafted on to alien stock, and provide the occasion of that general reconciliation which precedes the general outpouring of grace at the end.

It is important to use the word "suggests" here. The kind of absolute correspondence, traceable point by point through every line of a poem, that is sometimes used as a criterion by academic allegory hunters is not a characteristic of this play—or, for that matter, of any really respectable literary work. A play, after all, is a literary symbol, not a mathematical equation; and such correspondences as may appear in the finished piece are at first discovered rather than wrought—by the author as well as by the reader. In fact, a reader may discover, quite properly, a good many things in a work that the author himself has never seen. The correspondences noted here, however, between the Pauline outline of the course of redemption and the general pattern of *The Winter's Tale*, were surely part of Shakespeare's own comprehension of the play. It is even conceivable that his recognition began with that rough suggestion of Calvary in Hermione's speech in Act III, and that it was his exploration of the implications in that climactic speech that led him ultimately to see the whole application—to see even in the initial situation in Act I a neat parallel to the situation of mankind at the time of Christ, when in a world divided into Jew and Gentile the promised Messiah, having come to the Jew first, made invitation to his brother also.

Be that as it may, in Act I the parallel comes pretty close to being explicit; and with the help of the insight that enables us to see Hermione as a type of Christ we grasp it almost as soon as the principals make their entrance in Scene ii. Here Polixenes' polite refusal of his hostess' entreaty to stay and Hermione's reply, playing upon that "verily" with its Biblical associations, tap at our recollection until the door is ajar (I.ii.46-56). Then Polixenes delivers the following startling description of himself and Leontes in their youth:

We were as twinn'd lambs that did frisk i' th'
                                            sun,
And bleat the one at th' other. What we chang'd
Was innocence for innocence; we knew not
The doctrine of ill-doing, no, nor dream'd
That any did. Had we pursu'd that life,
And our weak spirits ne'er been higher rear'd
With stronger blood, we should have answer'd
                                          Heaven
Boldly, "Not guilty"; the imposition clear'd
Hereditary ours.

                                    (I.ii.67-75)

Now the way is clear for the flood of recognition to begin. We proceed to Polixenes' description of their "fall," Hermione's identification of herself with grace, her successful persuasion of Polixenes to stay in Bohemia, and finally her pronouncement upon her own acceptance of Leontes' suit, "'Tis grace indeed." Such hints as these must have enabled at least some members of Shakespeare's audience to grasp, at the start, the nature of the informing action of the play and to watch the progressive realization of that action unperturbed by one detail that frequently plagues a modern reader or auditor.

Honesty compels a good many critics who otherwise praise *The Winter's Tale* to admit a tendency to boggle at the suddenness with which Shakespeare has Leontes fly into a jealous rage. An early grasp of the action of the play precludes such a tendency. From the first appearance of Leontes' jealousy in Act I to that point in Act II (i.36-37) where it settles into the undisguised pharisaical pride of "How blest am I / In my just censure, in my true opinion," it is understandable by analogy with Paul's observation, "salvation is come unto the Gentiles, for to provoke them [that is, the Jews] to jealousy" (Romans xi.11). From this point on, Leontes becomes so obsessed with the legality of his unwarranted censure that we tend to think of it as his own special guilty stain. A perfect example of this perverted legality is the address he makes to Hermione in Act II,

Scene i. His formal, point-by-point indictment of her is so patently false that refutation of it is impossible; and Hermione can only deny with dignity the charges he makes. Yet by the time she bids him farewell with the significant observation, "this action I now go on / Is for my better grace" (II.i.121-122), her innocence is so manifest that old Antigonus is moved to say, "Be certain what you do, sir, lest your justice / Prove violence; in the which three great ones suffer, / Yourself, your queen, your son" (127-129). The legal business of the trial scene is, of course, natural and appropriate and does not call attention to itself; but Hermione's remark at the end of her long speech there pinpoints the essential conflict of the play:

> . . . if I shall be condemn'd
> Upon surmises, all proofs sleeping else
> But what your jealousies awake, I tell you
> 'Tis rigour and not law.
> (III.ii.112-115)

The trouble with Leontes is not that he does not love justice but that in his rigorous legalism he cannot possibly know what justice is. Again St. Paul's text happily provides a perfect gloss: "For I bear them record that they have a zeal of God, but not according to knowledge. For they being ignorant of God's righteousness, and going about to establish their own righteousness, have not submitted themselves unto the righteousness of God. For Christ is the end of the law for righteousness to every one that believeth" (Romans x.2-4). This of the zealous Jews. But it fits equally well the ignorant zeal of Leontes, and it points to the nature of his salvation as well as that of Israel.

Before Leontes can be saved he must come to know the meaning of the oracle, which declares Hermione chaste, Polixenes blameless, Leontes a jealous tyrant, and the babe truly begotten, and concludes, "the King shall live without an heir, if that which is lost be not found" (III.ii.133-137). That is, he must see his errors for what they are (and this means also

recognizing Hermione for what she is) and learn to nourish a
faith that Heaven may mercifully restore what he himself can
never bring back. Fortunately, Leontes has a St. Paul to help
him to that point of understanding; for this is precisely the function of Shakespeare's Paulina, who has no counterpart in
Greene's narrative. As early as Act II, before the trial scene,
it is she who undertakes the task of his conversion:

> If she dares trust me with her little babe,
> I'll show't the King and undertake to be
> Her advocate to th' loud'st. We do not know
> How he may soften at the sight o' th' child.
> The silence often of pure innocence
> Persuades when speaking fails.
>
> (II.ii.37-42)

After this attempt has failed and Leontes has gone on to make
himself "scandalous to the world," Paulina slips quietly into the
role of comforter, confessor, and guide and does her work there
with more success. When we next see them, sixteen years later,
Leontes is painfully penitent and completely prepared to accept
Paulina's judgment on Hermione:

> If, one by one, you wedded all the world,
> Or, from the all that are, you took something
>   good
> To make a perfect woman, she you kill'd
> Would be unparallel'd.
>
> (V.i.13-16)

He is also quite willing to reject the advice of his official
counselors, who would have him marry and get another heir,
and take instead that of Paulina, who reminds him:

> There is none worthy,
> Respecting her that's gone. Besides the gods
> Will have fulfill'd their secret purposes;

For has not the divine Apollo said,
Is't not the tenour of his oracle,
That King Leontes shall not have an heir
Till his lost child be found?

.   .   .   .   .

. . . Care not for issue
The crown will find an heir.

(V.i.34ff)

He must not marry again, she tells him, till his "first queen's again in breath"—a remarkable condition in view of the apparent circumstances and one which imposes upon him a sturdy exercise of faith. Yet faith is always the condition essential to salvation. Even as she prepares to bid the statue step down, she reminds him, "It is required / You do awake your faith" (V.iii.94-95). And then she adds, with an oblique reference to the state of mind that brought about his downfall, "those that think it is unlawful business / I am about, let them depart." This is intended for Leontes, of course, as is her remark a few lines later: "Start not; her actions shall be holy as / You hear my spell is lawful." But Leontes is no longer a zealot for legality, rigorous or otherwise. "If this be magic," he exclaims, "let it be an art / Lawful as eating."

Thus Leontes' twofold reconciliation, first with Perdita and then with Hermione, may be viewed as a literal fable with an analogical center in regenerated Jewry's expected reconciliation to the body of true believers and subsequent reception into Heaven at the Second Coming. The objection that the center of this play (which includes also Jesus' rejection and crucifixion by the Jews) thus belongs in part to the province of eschatology need not prevent a Christian's treating it as history. From the Christian point of view, the Second Coming is as much a part of history as the Creation or the Crucifixion. The outline given here of events leading up to it has, as we have seen, the authority of St. Paul's admonition to the Jews in Romans. Furthermore, there is good evidence in Act IV to show that

Shakespeare not only saw the analogy but also made direct use
of Paul's epistle.

The long period of penance and instruction that follows
Leontes' rejection of grace suggests only half of what happens
between Calvary and Judgment. Shakespeare's play gives more
prominence to the preservation and fostering of the heir, or
true Church, in Gentile Christendom, all of which is reflected
in Perdita's preservation in a foreign land and her betrothal to
a foreign prince. From the beginning there is more to Perdita
than meets the eye. We note that her part of the action begins
properly in Act III with Antigonus' account of the dream in
which the "ghost" of Hermione (who, of course, is very much
alive) has given "fate" the responsibility for the child's casting
away, hinted that the child is only "counted" lost forever,
named the child Perdita, and accurately prophesied Antigonus'
own death (III.iii.27-36). The shepherd who finds her discovers
also the gold that Antigonus has left, but gold is scarcely
enough to account for his growing "from very nothing, and
beyond the imagination of his neighbours, . . . into an unspeak-
able estate" (IV.ii.44-46). "If young Dorides / Do light upon
her," he tells the disguised Polixenes, "she shall bring him that
which he dreams not of" (IV.iv.178-180). Perdita, in short, is
herself the "fairy gold" that transforms all who come within her
range—not only the shepherd and Florizel but also Leontes and
eventually the stubborn Polixenes, who even at the outset is
moved to admit, "Nothing she does or seems / But smacks of
something greater than herself, / Too noble for this place"
(IV.iv.157-159). She is, moreover, the seeker as well as the
sought. Florizel's wooing of her and his constancy in standing
by her do him great credit; but Perdita, knowing perfectly well
who he is and the disparity of their stations, also woos, first with
flowers and then with words. She would strew him with gar-
lands, she says for all to hear, "like a bank for to lie and play
on; / Not like a corse; or if, not to be buried, / But quick and
in mine arms. Come, take your flowers" (IV.iv.130-132). When
Florizel before witnesses declares that without her love he is

nothing (380-388), she modestly declines to try to match his language yet manages a declaration of her own that is as forthright as it is simple:

> I cannot speak
> So well, nothing so well; no, nor mean better.
> By th' pattern of mine own thoughts I cut out
> The purity of his.
>
> (IV.iv.390-393)

Polixenes' royal tantrum that follows shortly after this tempts her to press her initiative even further and declare to the King's face the truism of Matthew v.45 ("for he maketh his sun to rise on the evil and on the good"):

> I was not much afeard; for once or twice
> I was about to speak, and tell him plainly
> The self-same sun that shines upon his court
> Hides not his visage from our cottage, but
> Looks on alike.
>
> (IV.iv.452-456)

Yet Perdita forbears here because the initiative is no longer rightfully hers. She has done all she can. It remains for Florizel to prove his love for her by renouncing everything for her sake, and this he does promptly and beautifully with, "Lift up thy looks. / From my succession wipe me, father; I / Am heir to my affection" (IV.iv.489-491).

Shakespeare's execution is so deft and charming here in Act IV that we can perhaps excuse critics for protesting his shift of focus away from Perdita to Hermione in Act V, but the shift was necessary if Shakespeare was to make of his play something more than routine tragicomedy. At least it was necessary if his play was to continue to bear scrutiny as a partial realization of that divine action which is described explicitly in Paul's prophetic account of the remnant in his Epistle to the Romans. The primary function of Act IV is to fulfill the prophecy and make possible the return of Hermione, which, as we have seen, suggests the return of the Messiah to a Jewry that had previously rejected him. Thus it is not surprising to find Shakespeare choosing as his central metaphor for the relationship between Perdita and Florizel the same metaphor of grafting that Paul used to refer to the union of the Gentile and Christ's representative on earth, the Church. Paul was speaking sharply to Gentiles here, warning them against writing off the Jew entirely. The eleven verses in which he developed his figure need to be quoted in full:

For if the casting away of them be the reconciling of the world, what shall the receiving of them be, but life from the dead? For if the firstfruit be holy, the lump is also holy: and if the root be holy, so are the branches. And if some of the branches be broken off, and thou, being a wild olive tree, wert graffed in among them, and with them partakest of the root and fatness of the olive tree; Boast not against the branches. But if thou boast, thou bearest not the root, but the root thee. Thou wilt say then, The branches were broken off, that I might be graffed in. Well; because of unbelief they were broken off, and thou standest by faith. Be not high-minded, but fear: For if God spared not the natural branches, take heed lest he also spare not thee. Behold therefore the goodness and severity of God: on them which fell, severity; but toward thee, goodness, if thou continue in his goodness: otherwise thou also shalt be cut off. And they also, if they abide not still in unbelief, shall be graffed in: for God is able to graff them in again. For if thou wert cut out of the olive tree which is wild by nature, and wert graffed contrary to nature into a good olive tree: how much more shall these, which be the natural branches, be graffed into their own olive tree? For I would not, brethren, that ye should be ignorant of this mystery, lest ye should be wise in your own conceits; that blindness in part is happened to Israel, until the fulness of the Gentiles be come in.

(Romans XI.15-25)

It takes very little imagination to see the action of Shakespeare's play paralleled here in St. Paul's metaphor of the wild olive branches grafted into the stock of a good olive from which some of the original branches have been temporarily cut off: the firstfruit suggests Mamillus (as in III.ii.98); the root and tree of good olive suggest Hermione and Perdita; the branches broken off, Leontes; and the wild branches grafted in, Florizel and Polixenes. The parallel would be striking enough even if Shakespeare had not used the same metaphor. But he did use it, of course, and he gave it appropriately to Polixenes, the "highminded" Gentile of the play.

Perdita has just been explaining that her garden contains no gillyflowers, because they are hybrids, "Nature's bastards": "For I have heard it said / There is an art which in their piedness shares / With great creating Nature." To this Polixenes replies:

> Say there be;
> Yet Nature is made better by no mean
> But Nature makes that mean; so, over that art
> Which you say adds to Nature, is an art
> That Nature makes. You see, sweet maid, we
> marry
> A gentler scion to the wildest stock,
> And make conceive a bark of baser kind
> By bud of nobler race. This is an art
> Which does mend Nature, change it rather, but
> The art itself is Nature.
>
> (IV.iv.88-97)

Polixenes, to be sure, uses the figure here with unconscious irony, thinking of his son Florizel as the "bud of nobler race" and Perdita as "bark of baser kind." But we the audience, with our better vision, have already identified Perdita as the good olive tree in this grove and Florizel as the sprig of wild olive. We excuse Polixenes' ignorance and perhaps pardon his pride; but we see his attitude (which is precisely that described by St. Paul) as something of which he must be purged, "lest he continue wise in his own conceit" and be himself cut off. Even so, we acknowledge that the blindness of Polixenes is necessary;

for without that blindness there can be no return of the heir, no reconciliation of estranged friends in human brotherhood, and no final outpouring of grace for anyone. As St. Paul sums it up in verse 12 of that same chapter in Romans, "God hath concluded them all in unbelief that he might have mercy upon all." Blindness is for Polixenes, as for Leontes and for all of us, the prerequisite for mercy, and mercy crowns the end.

Thus three of the plays that we have considered in this study —*The Merchant of Venice, Measure for Measure,* and finally *The Winter's Tale*—each representing a different period in Shakespeare's development, have rung into the sphere of a fictitious story something of the Christian view of the historical redemption of the human race. Of these three, *The Winter's Tale* with its suggestion of analogies for Jew, Gentile, Christ, Paul, and the Christian church comes closest to incorporating the whole view. *The Merchant of Venice* gives us a more suggestive examination of man's redeemer; and *Measure for Measure* provides a more searching study of the conflict between law and grace and the reconciliation of the two at the Last Judgment. But in *The Winter's Tale* Shakespeare included something of all these matters and in addition courageously undertook to suggest the miraculous aspect of divine mercy that has always made Christian teaching about the subject seem "foolishness to the Greeks." Here, when he brought Hermione back after sixteen years from what everyone thought was her grave, he ran the risk, even in an age of romances and tragi-comedy, of having his denouement "hooted at / Like an old tale" (V.iii.116-117) by sophisticated audiences. We have seen that nothing in his source suggested that he end his play in this way. The idea for doing so seems to have been purely his own. Consequently many readers have regarded the play as a whimsical though lovely fairytale with serious overtones here and there. From the Christian point of view, however, *The Winter's Tale* makes the hardest possible sense, though with no diminution of loveliness, as having ended in the only possible way for a play designed to suggest not only man's utter folly and helplessness but also his only hope of salvation. Here in the end those who survive are "precious winners all," as Paulina calls them (V.iii. 131); and they are that because the dead has miraculously come to life and they have been granted grace to see the resurrection. *The Winter's Tale* makes no demands upon us beyond this— that we, too, see the miracle of resurrection. It does not preach; it offers no moral, no lesson, no paradigm for truth. Like St. Paul's prophetic discourse, it is in itself a realization, a legitimate object of knowledge; and to come to know it is to share some of the happiness of discovery that Shakespeare must have felt on seeing a meaningful shape emerge from the cloudy surface of Greene's tale. All that we really need to be able to share Shakespeare's vision, here in *The Winter's Tale* and in the other plays, is that "whole heart and free mind" which Mark Van Doren once wisely asked his readers to bring to their study of Shakespeare[1]—that and the ancient habit of seeing which once caused St. Augustine to pronounce the whole world "a fair field, fresh with the odor of Christ's name."

THIS STUDY ends with *The Winter's Tale*, but it might have gone on to include chapters on *The Tempest*, where the demonstration of Shakespeare's habit of thinking analogically would have been fairly easy, and *Henry VIII*, where the habit is still discernible though perhaps less pervasive in its influence. It might also have included examinations of such plays as *Twelfth Night*, *All's Well*, *Lear*, and *Coriolanus*, all of which bear the marks of that same habit of thinking—it might be better to say habit of seeing—which was referred to earlier in this study as "Hippolyta's view." Yet those plays which we have considered, from *Richard II* to *The Winter's Tale*, illustrate fairly well the range and variety of the operation of this habit in Shakespeare's plays, where almost invariably it does its work within a demonstrably Christian context. In each play Shakespeare's transfiguration of a tale, whether historical or not, has produced a "dream" that is more real than the source from which it was derived; and in each the transfiguration has included some aspect of the Christian faith, which was for Shakespeare's audience, and for his early readers at least, man's closest approach to ultimate truth.

That habit of seeing is never entirely extinct, but nowadays it seems to be relatively rare. Apparently the unlettered audiences of our earliest vernacular plays, the fourteenth-century cycles, had some experience of it. We may be sure that they did not concern themselves with the various twofold, threefold, and fourfold explanations of *multiplex intelligentia*. But they did know that the New Testament was written large in the Old and that future glory was manifest in the Incarnation of the Gospels. In short, they understood that in the text "I am the way, and the truth, and the light," is all that man on earth can know and needs to know. The secularization of the cycles, which, in their Old Testament plays at least, had employed allegorical interpretation of Scripture, provided an inadvertent but positive step in the direction of secular application of the schema. For here were popular plays, standing almost at the beginning of one of the greatest dramatic literatures the world has seen, asking to be looked upon as history, allegory, trope, and anagoge, all in one. It was inevitable, then, that with the increasing secularization of literature in the Renaissance some writers and readers should bring to a more realistic fiction, if not the formal schema of fourfold interpretation, at least the presuppositions upon which that schema rested. That is, it was inevitable that some poets should still be able to look at a story from Greek or Roman myth or a story of Italian domestic life or an incident from history as potentially having significance, though perhaps not authority, analogous to the fables of Scripture—as being in some sense an incarnation of truth rather than an exposition of it.

One must be careful here to say *some* writers, *some* poets, and *some* readers. Admittedly, almost any Christian in any age will be willing to acknowledge that to some extent the events and objects of this world provide analogies with, or imperfect incarnations of, divine actions; yet it can hardly be said that writers generally even in sixteenth-century England went around looking for such things in the subjects of their poems, tales, and plays. The evidence that Shakespeare did, however, appears throughout his work, clearly in *Richard II* and with increasing clarity and frequency thereafter. G. Wilson Knight has gone so far as to say that in Shakespearean tragedy the "unique act of the Christ sacrifice can . . . be felt as central" and that "Shakespeare's final plays celebrate the victory and glory, the resurrection and renewal, that in the Christian story and in its reflection in the Christian ritual succeed the sacrifice."[2] This is closer to the truth than a good many modern scholars are willing to acknowledge. Profitable as it is to consider Shakespeare's plays as studies in human relations or as reflections of the Elizabethan world picture, we are lingering on the periphery when we limit our attention to such matters. Whatever else they may be, Shakespeare's plays are fundamentally developments of the great archetypal myths of the human race, whereby his dramatic fables, whether drawn from English history, Roman history, Italian novella, or English fabliau, are revealed as participating by analogy in an action which, from the poet's point of view, is Christian, divine, and eternal.

Notes

Chapter One

[1] A notable exception is Howard Nemerov's brilliant essay, "The Marriage of Theseus and Hippolyta," *Kenyon Review*, XVIII (1956), 633-641, which also interprets the Theseus-Hippolyta relationship as a parable about poetry, but in a somewhat different way. Nemerov sees the two characters as representative of two kinds of poetry, both necessary, and concludes, "Their wedded life, with its vicious quarrels and long intervals of separation (not extending as yet to final divorce) is the history of poetry in the English language."

[2] Edwyn Bevan, *Symbolism and Belief* (New York, 1938), 256-257.

[3] *Dante's "Convivio,"* trans. William Walrond Jackson (Oxford, 1909), 73.

[4] See Richard Hamilton Green, "Dante's 'Allegory of Poets' and the Mediaeval Theory of Poetic Fiction," *Comparative Literature*, IX (1957), 118-128, and Charles S. Singleton's corrective rejoinder, "The Irreducible Dove," *ibid.*, 129-135.

[5] Singleton, 130. See also Singleton's *Dante Studies I* (Cambridge, Mass., 1953), 13-16, 29.

[6] *Letter XI*, trans. Charles Sterrett Latham in *A Translation of Dante's Eleven Letters*, ed. George Rice Carpenter (Boston, 1891), 193.

[7] *Summa Theologica*, trans. Fathers of the English Dominican Province (22 vols., London, 1920-1925), Pars I, Q. 1, Art. 10.

[8] Any reasonably complete survey of the subject will show this. See, for example, Frederic W. Farrar, *History of Interpretation* (New York, 1886), 135-152.

[9] Origen, who used a threefold system of exegesis, had a tendency to use his meanings in this way; see his *De Principiis*, IV.ii.4, trans. G. W. Butterworth (London, 1936), 275-276. See also R. P. C. Hanson, *Allegory and Event* (London, 1959), 245-246. The most influential example of this tendency is, of course, the work of Dionysius the Pseudo-Areopagite; see especially "On the Heavenly Hierarchy" in *The Works of Dionysius the Areopagite*, trans. John Parker (2 vols., London, 1897-1899), II.

[10] This was especially true of Hugh of St. Victor and his successors, who insisted upon the importance of the literal sense but consistently taught the superiority of the spiritual senses; see Beryl Smalley, *The Study of the Bible in the Middle Ages* (Oxford, 1952), 87-106, 242-263.

[11] Ruth Wallerstein, *Studies in Seventeenth-Century Poetic* (Madison, 1950), 27-58.

[12] *City of God*, xvi.37.

[13] See particularly the conclusion to *The Dry Salvages*.

[14] Arnold Williams, *The Common Expositor: An Account of the Renaissance Commentaries on Genesis, 1527-1633* (Chapel Hill, 1948), 20-21.

[15] For an account of the place of typology in the history of Christian exegesis see Jean Daniélou, *Sacramentum Futuri* (Paris, 1950). See also Rosemond Tuve's *A Study of George Herbert* (Chicago and London, 1952) for much useful material about the prevalence of typology in English devotional literature and iconography.

[16] Erich Auerbach, *Mimesis: The Representation of Reality in Western Literature*, trans. Willard R. Trask (Princeton, 1953), 74.

[17] Bartholomew Chamberlaine, *The Passion of Christ, and the benefits thereby* (London, 1595), sig. B7^r-B7^v.

[18] John Foxe, *A Sermon preached at the Christening of a certaine Iew, at London* . . . *Containing an exposition of the xi. Chapter of S. Paul to the Romanes*, trans. James Bell (London, 1578), sig. D8^v-E1^r.

[19] *The Wedding Garment*, in *The Works of Henry Smith*, ed. Thomas Smith (2 vols., Edinburgh, 1866-1867), I.

[20] Henry Ainsworth, *Annotations Vpon the Five Bookes of Moses, and the Psalmes* (London, 1622).

[21] William Whitaker, *A Disputation on Holy Scripture, Against the Papists, especially Bellarmine and Stapleton*, ed. trans. William Fitzgerald (Cambridge, 1849), 405.

[22] Whitaker, 407-408.

[23] *Essays in Divinity*, ed. Evelyn M. Simpson (Oxford, 1952), 20.

[24] *A Lecture or Exposition upon a part of the v. Chapter of the Epistle to the Hebrues* (1572), from *Maister Derings Works* (Middleburg [?], 1590), sig. C4^r-C4^v.

[25] See Richmond Noble, *Shakespeare's Biblical Knowledge and Use of the Book of Common Prayer* (London, 1935).

[26] Helen Gardner, *The Limits of Literary Criticism: Reflections on the Interpretation of Poetry and Scripture*, University of Durham Riddell Memorial Lectures, Twenty-eighth Series (London, 1956), 46-55.

[27] Gardner, 55.

[28] But one should not overlook the valuable comments by S. L. Bethell,

Shakespeare and the Popular Dramatic Tradition (Durham, N. C., 1944), 119-128.

Chapter Two

[1] E. M. W. Tillyard, *Shakespeare's History Plays* (New York, 1946), 245-259.

[2] J. Dover Wilson, ed., *Richard II* (Cambridge, Eng., 1939), xiii.

[3] F. M. Cornford, *The Origin of Attic Comedy* (London, 1914), 53 ff.

[4] "An Exhortation to Obedience," in *Certain Sermons or Homilies Appointed to Be Read in Churches in the time of Queen Elizabeth of Famous Memory* (2 vols., London, 1846), I, 119.

[5] See J. Mitchell Morse, "Cain, Abel, and Joyce," ELH, XXII (1955), 51-54.

Chapter Three

[1] Sir Israel Gollancz, *Allegory and Mysticism in Shakespeare. A Medievalist on "The Merchant of Venice"* (London, 1931).

[2] See Hope Traver, "Four Daughters of God," *PMLA*, XL (1925), 44-92, and J. D. Rea, "Shylock and the *Processus Belial*," *Philological Quarterly*, VII (1929), 311-313.

[3] Benjamin N. Nelson, *The Idea of Usury* (Princeton, 1949), 144 n.

[4] Nevill Coghill, "The Governing Idea. Essays in Stage Interpretation of Shakespeare," *Shakespeare Quarterly* (Vienna), I (1947), 12.

[5] For a convenient account of the provenance and dissemination of this work see Sidney J. H. Herrtage's introduction to *The Early English Versions of the Gesta Romanorum*, Early English Text Society, Extra Series, XXXIII (1879).

[6] *Gesta Romanorum*, ed. Herrtage, 155.

[7] Quoted by John R. Brown, ed., *The Merchant of Venice*, New Arden Series (London, 1955), 174.

[8] *Il Pecorone*, trans. Geoffrey Bullough, in *Narrative and Dramatic Sources of Shakespeare*, I (New York, 1957), 463-476.

[9] Antonio repeats his condition to the gaoler (III.iii.35-36): "pray God Bassanio come / To see me pay his debt, and then I care not."

[10] *The Works of Iohn Boys, Doctor in Diuinitie and Deane of Canterburie* (London, 1622), 803. *An Exposition of the Proper Psalmes Vsed in Ovr English Litvrgie* was published separately in 1616.

[11] Boys, 804.

[12] Brown, ed., *The Merchant of Venice*, lvii-lviii.

[13] Coghill, 16.

[14] E. E. Stoll, *Shakespeare Studies: Historical and Comparative in Method* (New York, 1927), 255-256.

[15] See page 12.

[16] *A Sermon preached at the Christening of a certaine Iew*, sig. D8ᵛ-E1ʳ.

[17] The suggestion, supported by Gollancz, that her name is that of Milcah, daughter of Haran (Genesis xii.29), spelled as *Iscah* in some early Bibles and glossed as "she that looketh out," is hardly credible.

[18] See I Corinthians vii.14.

Chapter Four

[1] J. Dover Wilson, *The Fortunes of Falstaff* (Cambridge, 1943), 20.

Chapter Five

[1] Kenneth Muir, "Troilus and Cressida," *Shakespeare Survey*, VIII (1955), 38.

[2] Noble, *Shakespeare's Biblical Knowledge and Use of the Book of Common Prayer*, 214.

[3] See Richard Chenevix Trench, *Notes on the Parables of Our Lord*, 12th ed. (New York, 1870), 111-114.

[4] See H. C. Goddard, *The Meaning of Shakespeare* (Chicago, 1951), 398-400.

[5] Noble, 214.

Chapter Six

[1] R. W. Chambers, "*Measure for Measure*," in *Man's Unconquerable Mind: Studies of English Writers from Bede to A. E. Housman and W. P. Ker* (London, 1949), 227-310; Roy W. Battenhouse, "*Measure for Measure* and the Christian Doctrine of Atonement," *PMLA*, LXI (1946), 1029-1059; Elizabeth M. Pope, "The Renaissance Background of *Measure for Measure*," *Shakespeare Survey*, II (1949), 66-82; Nevill Coghill, "Comic Form in *Measure for Measure*," *Shakespeare Survey*, VIII (1955), 14-27.

[2] Gardner, *The Limits of Literary Criticism*, 60.

[3] G. Wilson Knight, *The Wheel of Fire: Interpretations of Shakespearian Tragedy with Three New Essays*, 4th ed. rev. (London, 1949), 83.

[4] Chambers, 304.

[5] Battenhouse, 1053.

[6] Coghill, 19-26.

[7] Wilson Knight, 2.

[8] Coghill, 22-25.

[9] Battenhouse, 1038, n. 29.

[10] John Hooper, Bishop of Worcester and Gloucester, "A Godly and most necessary Annotations in the xiii Chapyter too the Romans," in *Later Writings of Bishop Hooper, together with His Letters and Other Pieces,* ed. Charles Nevinson, Parker Society Publications, Vol. XXI (Cambridge, 1852), 99.

[11] Gardner, 60.

[12] M. C. Bradbrook, "Authority, Truth, and Justice in *Measure for Measure,*" *Review of English Studies,* XVII (1941), 385-399. See also L. C. Knights, "The Ambiguity of *Measure for Measure,*" *Scrutiny,* X (1942), 222; and F. R. Leavis, "The Greatness of *Measure for Measure,*" *Scrutiny,* X (1942), 241.

Chapter Seven

[1] Sylvan Barnet, "Some Limitations of a Christian Approach to Shakespeare," *ELH,* XXII (1955), 85-86.

[2] Sir Philip Sidney, *The Defense of Poesy,* ed. Albert S. Cook (Boston, 1890), 8-9.

Chapter Eight

[1] E. M. W. Tillyard, *Shakespeare's Problem Plays* (Toronto, 1949), 34.

[2] I. J. Semper, *Hamlet without Tears* (Dubuque, 1946), 14-20.

[3] G. R. Elliott, *Scourge and Minister: A Study of "Hamlet"* (Durham, 1951).

[4] Fredson Bowers, "Hamlet as Minister and Scourge," *PMLA,* LXX (1955), 740-749.

[5] Francis Fergusson, *The Idea of a Theater: The Art of Drama in Changing Perspective* (Princeton, 1949), 98-142.

[6] Fergusson, 141.

[7] J. Dover Wilson, *What Happens in Hamlet,* 3rd ed. (Cambridge, Eng., 1951), 55 ff.; Roy W. Battenhouse, "The Ghost in *Hamlet:* A Catholic 'Linchpin'?" *Studies in Philology,* XLVIII (1951), 161-192; Robert H. West, "King Hamlet's Ambiguous Ghost," *PMLA,* LXX

(1955), 1107-1117. See also I. J. Semper's reply to Battenhouse, "The Ghost in *Hamlet*: Pagan or Christian," *The Month*, CXCV (1953), 222-234.

[8] West, 1115.

[9] West, 1107n.

[10] Semper has perceived something of the importance of this; see *Hamlet without Tears*, 19.

[11] Semper, *Hamlet without Tears*, 19 ff.

[12] *Summa Theologica*, trans. Fathers of the English Dominican Province, II-II, Q. 108, Art. 1.

[13] Bowers, 747n.

[14] Bowers, 746.

[15] See Louis Ginzberg, *The Legends of the Jews* (7 vols., Philadelphia, 1909-1938), I, 116-118; and also Angelo S. Rappoport, *Myth and Legend of Ancient Israel* (3 vols., London, 1928), I, 198.

[16] *Patrologiae Latinae*, ed. Jacques Paul Migne (221 vols., Paris, 1844-1864), CLVIII, 39-44.

[17] The incident is treated as an episode of the Noah play in the Hegge cycle or *Ludus Coventriae*, ed. K. S. Block, Early English Text Society (London, 1922). Miss Block believes that the source of this episode is the *Historia Scholastica* (pp. lii-liii); but Hardin Craig has noted the wide dissemination of the story and suggested that there may have been other sources for the play, *English Religious Drama of the Middle Ages* (Oxford, 1955), 257-258.

[18] For a discussion of her allusions here to Hamlet, Hamlet's father, Polonius, and perhaps also Claudius, see Roy Walker, *The Time Is out of Joint: A Study of "Hamlet"* (London, 1948), 124-128.

Chapter Nine

[1] The source of the story is Novel VII of the Third Decade of Giraldi Cinthio's *Hecatommithi* (Monreale, 1565).

[2] See especially Paul N. Siegel, *Shakespearean Tragedy and the Elizabethan Compromise* (New York, 1957), 119 ff., and Roy W. Battenhouse, "Shakespearean Tragedy: A Christian Interpretation," in *The Tragic Vision and the Christian Faith*, ed. Nathan A. Scott, Jr. (New York, 1957), 87-89.

[3] *City of God*, xvi.1-2.

[4] Williams, *The Common Expositor*, 117-118.

[5] See R. H. Charles, ed., *The Apocrypha and Pseudepigrapha of the Old Testament in English*, II (Oxford, 1913), 134-137.

[6] Launcelot Andrews, *The Wonderfull Combate (for Gods glorie and Mans saluation) betweene Christ and Satan. Opened in seuen most excelent learned and zealous Sermons, vpon the Temptations of Christ, in the wildernes, &c.* (London, 1592), sig. 32ᵛ.

[7] C. J. Sisson, *New Readings in Shakespeare* (2 vols., Cambridge, Eng., 1956), II, 246-247.

[8] Sisson, II, 251.

Chapter Ten

[1] Noble, *Shakespeare's Biblical Knowledge and Use of the Book of Common Prayer*, 232-236.

[2] Jane H. Jack, "*Macbeth*, King James, and the Bible," *ELH*, XXII (1955), 173-193. As her title suggests, Miss Jack stresses as a link between Shakespeare and the Bible several works by James I, notably *Daemonologie, Basilikon Doron,* and a 1603 edition of his sermon on Revelation xx.

[3] W. C. Curry, *Shakespeare's Philosophical Patterns* (Baton Rouge, 1937), 97-137.

[4] Roy Walker, *The Time Is Free* (London, 1949), 72.

[5] Jack, 180. See also G. R. Elliott, *Dramatic Providence in "Macbeth": A Study of Shakespeare's Tragic Theme of Humanity and Grace* (Princeton, 1958), 7-8.

[6] Francis Fergusson, "*Macbeth* as the Imitation of an Action," in *The Human Image in Dramatic Literature* (New York, 1957), 115-125.

[7] Fergusson, "*Macbeth* as the Imitation of an Action," 118.

[8] Walker, *The Time Is Free,* 8.

[9] Elliott, *Dramatic Providence in "Macbeth,"* 16 ff. Among the "blackeners" that he cites are Walker and Curry, whose works have already been referred to, Henri Fluchère, *Shakespeare* (Toulouse, 1948), and M. D. H. Parker, *The Slave of Life* (London, 1955).

[10] For example, John Meredith, *The Sinne of Blasphemie Against the Holy Ghost Scholastically examined* (London, 1622), and Sebastian Benefield, *The Sinne Against the Holy Ghost Discovered and other Christian doctrines delivered: in twelve Sermons vpon part of the tenth Chapter of the Epistle to the Hebrewes* (Oxford, 1615).

[11] John Dennison, *Fowre Sermons* (London, 1620), 103-104.

[12] Dennison, 146.

[13] See *Catholic Encyclopedia*, s.v., "Apostasy."

[14] "Of Repentance and true Reconciliation unto God," in *Certain Sermons or Homilies Appointed to Be Read in Churches in the Time of Queen Elizabeth of Famous Memory*, II, 568.

Chapter Eleven

[1] Franklin M. Dickey, *Not Wisely but too Well: Shakespeare's Love Tragedies* (San Marino, 1957), 144-176.

[2] Dickey, 177.

[3] M. R. Ridley's New Arden edition of *Antony and Cleopatra* (Cambridge, Mass., 1954) contains a convenient reprinting of the pertinent section from the 1579 edition of North's *Plutarch* (pp. 258 ff.).

[4] See J. Leeds Barrol's analysis of this as sloth, "Antony and Pleasure," *Journal of English and Germanic Philology*, LVII (1958), 708-720.

[5] See Ridley, 269-270.

[6] See Matthew xxvii.46 and Mark xv.34.

[7] For a full treatment of this piece of typology see F. Michael Krouse, *Milton's Samson and the Christian Tradition* (Princeton, 1949).

[8] Contrary to the practice of many modern editors, I have retained Folio's *when* in line 38 and rejected Pope's *where*. C. J. Sisson, defending the substitution of *where* in his *New Readings in Shakespeare*, II, 273, argues that *when* "seems a tasteless conceit and out of key." Whether it is tasteless or not depends upon one's point of view, but it is certainly not out of key. *Where*, however, fits almost equally well with the interpretation I have given.

Chapter Twelve

[1] See Colin Still, *Shakespeare's Mystery Play: A Study of "The Tempest"* (London, 1921), and Nevill Coghill, "The Basis of Shakespearian Comedy: A Study in Medieval Affinities," *Essays and Studies*, III (1950), 23-28.

[2] T. S. Eliot, "Ben Jonson," *The Sacred Wood. Essays on Poetry and Criticism*, 6th ed. (London, 1948), 116.

Chapter Thirteen

[1] Mark Van Doren, *Shakespeare*, 2nd printing (New York, 1954), xii. First published in 1939.

[2] G. Wilson Knight, *Principles of Shakespearian Production* (London, 1936), 234.

Index

J. A. BRYANT, JR., the author of this book, has been awarded the Ph.D. degree by Yale University and the M.A. by Vanderbilt University. He now teaches courses in Shakespeare and Elizabethan drama at Duke University, and has contributed articles on Medieval and Renaissance poetry and drama to various scholarly periodicals.

HIPPOLYTA'S VIEW was composed and printed by the Division of Printing of the University of Kentucky. It is set in Linotype Electra, with initials and other display in Klingspor Kumlein. The book is printed on Warren's Olde Style antique paper and bound by the C. J. Krehbiel Company in Holliston's Roxite vellum cloth.